ANGLICANIS

CW00507844

In a world in which reaction frequently overwhelms reflection, and information trumps wisdom, Martyn Percy's perceptive reflections provide fresh and challenging ways in which to consider the life and mission of the church.
Frank Griswold, former Presiding Bishop and Primate of the Episcopal Church, USA

This is one of the best books I have ever read on Anglican identity and mission. It is a wonderfully inclusive book that is a challenge to all sections of the church.
George Carey, Lord Carey of Clifton, Archbishop of Canterbury, 1991–2002

This focused concentration and celebration of Anglican life could not be more timely. Debates on sexuality and gender (including women bishops), whether or not the church has a Covenant, or can be a Communion, and how it is ultimately led, are issues that have dominated the ecclesial horizon for several decades. No book on Anglicanism can ever claim to have all the answers to all the questions. However, Martyn Percy's work does offer significant new insights and illumination – highlighting just how rich and reflexive the Anglican tradition can be in living and proclaiming the gospel of Christ.

These chapters provide some sharply-focused snapshots of contemporary Anglicanism, and cover many of the crucial issues affecting Anglicans today, such as the nature of mission and ministry, theological training and formation, and ecclesial identity and leadership. Church culture is often prey to contemporary fads and fashion. Percy's work calls Anglicanism to deeper discipleship; to attend to its roots, identity and shape; and to inhabit the world with a faith rooted in commitment, confidence and Christ.

Ashgate Contemporary Ecclesiology

The field of ecclesiology has grown remarkably in the last decade, and most especially in relation to the study of the contemporary church. Recently, theological attention has turned once more to the nature of the church, its practices and proclivities, and to interpretative readings and understandings on its role, function and ethos in contemporary society.

This new series draws from a range of disciplines and established scholars to further the study of contemporary ecclesiology and publish an important cluster of landmark titles in this field. The Series Editors represent a range of Christian traditions and disciplines, and this reflects the breadth and depth of books developing in the Series. This Ashgate series presents a clear focus on the contemporary situation of churches worldwide, offering an invaluable resource for students, researchers, ministers and other interested readers around the world working or interested in the diverse areas of contemporary ecclesiology and the important changing shape of the church worldwide.

Anglicanism
Confidence, Commitment and Communion

MARTYN PERCY
Ripon College Cuddesdon, UK

ASHGATE

Published by
Ashgate Publishing Limited
Wey Court East
Union Road
Farnham
Surrey, GU9 7PT
England

Ashgate Publishing Company
110 Cherry Street
Suite 3-1
Burlington, VT 05401-3818
USA

www.ashgate.com

British Library Cataloguing in Publication Data
Percy, Martyn.
  Anglicanism : confidence, commitment and communion. –
  (Ashgate contemporary ecclesiology)
  1. Anglican Communion–Doctrines.
  I. Title II. Series
  230.3-dc23

The Library of Congress has cataloged the printed edition as follows:
Percy, Martyn.
  Anglicanism : confidence, commitment and communion / By Martyn Percy.
      pages cm. – (Ashgate contemporary ecclesiology)
  Includes index.
  ISBN 978-1-4094-7035-9 (hardcover) – ISBN 978-1-4094-7036-6 (pbk.) – ISBN 978-1-4094-7037-3 (epub) 1. Anglican Communion. I. Title.
  BX5005.P47 2013
  283–dc23

                                                                    2012049670

ISBN   9781409470359 (hbk)
ISBN   9781409470366 (pbk)
ISBN   9781409470373 (ebk-PDF)
ISBN   9781409470380 (ebk-ePUB)

Printed and bound in Great Britain
by MPG PRINTGROUP

For Students and Staff at Cuddesdon

Contents

Chapter Sources

We wish to thank and acknowledge the following people and publications for their contribution to this volume:

Chapter 1 was an inaugural address to alumni and students of Cuddesdon in 2004, and parts of this lecture recently appeared in an essay in *A Point of Balance* (edited by Rob Slocum and Martyn Percy, Church House Publishing New York, 2012).

Chapter 2 originally appeared in the 2008 Lambeth Conference edition of the *Anglican Theological Review* (volume 90, issue 2).

Chapter 3 was first published in *Re-Shaping Rural Ministry* (edited by James Bell, Jill Hopkinson and Trevor Wilmott, SCM Canterbury Press, 2009).

Chapter 4 originally appeared in *The Art of Tentmaking: Making Space for Worship* (edited by Stephen Burns, SCM-Canterbury Press, 2012).

Chapter 5 first appeared in *The Future of the Parish System* (edited by Steven Croft, Church House Publishing, 2006).

Chapter 6 is drawn from Paul Avis' edited *Public Faith: The State of Religious Belief and Practice in Britain* (SPCK, 2003).

Chapter 7 draws on a recent chapter which appeared in *The Established Church* (edited by Mark Chapman, Continuum, 2011).

Chapter 8 initially appeared as a chapter in *Evaluating Fresh Expressions* (edited by Louise Nelstrop and Martyn Percy, SCM-Canterbury, 2008).

Chapter 9 draws on material first published in *Managing the Church* (edited by Martyn Percy, Sheffield Academic Press, 2000).

Chapter 10 was originally published in *Intercultural Theology* (edited by Mark Cartledge and David Cheetham, SCM Press, 2011).

Chapter 11 draws on a chapter in *The Hope of Things to Come* (edited by Mark Chapman, Continuum, 2010).

Chapter 12 develops an exploratory chapter which first appeared in *Creative Church Leadership* (edited by John Adair and John Nelson, SCM-Canterbury Press, 2004).

Acknowledgements

This book is dedicated to friends and colleagues at Cuddesdon. I particularly want to thank them for all that they contribute towards the shaping of an environment of wisdom, nourishment and support here on the 'Holy Hill'. Special thanks are also due to all those in training in Ludlow and Gloucester with the West of England Ministerial Training Course (WEMTC), and at Cuddesdon with the Oxford Ministry Course (OMC), as well as the Oxford Local Ministry Programme (LMP), and the Ordained Pioneer Ministry Scheme – a partnership with the Church Missionary Society. As part of the Cuddesdon family, these programmes, and all who train on them, provide fruitful and rich environments that have prompted a number of the reflections in this volume. I am deeply grateful to the students who train for ordained and Reader ministry in this way, alongside all those in full-time formation at Ripon College.

Dawn Ingram was extremely helpful in the preparation of this text, and I am deeply grateful to her for all her advice and assistance. And I would like to pay special tribute to Sarah Lloyd, who has encouraged this project at Ashgate Publishing. Her insight and oversight has, as ever, been a source of great sustenance.

All of these chapters initially began life as lectures, and have then been worked into subsequent shorter and longer published articles. A significant number are drawn out of the more recent concerns to have occupied the Anglican Communion and Church of England: mission, polity, praxis and unity. Initiatives such as the Covenant (derived from the Windsor Report) weave their way through several of the chapters. In the first part, however, we begin at the beginning. Chapter one, fittingly, was an inaugural address to Cuddesdon alumni in 2004, and parts of that lecture have since been incorporated into a number of volumes, most recently in *A Point of Balance* (edited by Rob Slocum and Martyn Percy, and published by Church House Publishing New York, 2012). Chapter two originally appeared in the 2008 Lambeth Conference edition of the *Anglican Theological Review*. Chapter three originally began life as a set of talks to clergy in primarily rural dioceses, and was first published in *Re-Shaping Rural Ministry* (edited by James Bell, Jill Hopkinson and Trevor Wilmott, SCM Canterbury Press, 2009). An earlier version of chapter four originally appeared in *The Art of Tentmaking: Making Space for Worship* (edited by Stephen Burns, SCM-Canterbury Press, 2012).

In the second part of the book, chapter five owes its origins to on-going work on the nature of the parish church, and some initial reflections first appeared in *The Future of the Parish System* (edited by Steven Croft, Church House Publishing 2006). Chapter six is drawn from Paul Avis' fine edited volume, *Public Faith: The State of Religious Belief and Practice in Britain* (SPCK, 2003). Chapter seven draws on a substantial interest in the nuances of establishment and national church identity, and first kindled when New Labour came to power in 1997, which led to the meetings of the 'Sheffield Colloquium' and a range of more public debates. An earlier version of this chapter recently appeared in *The Established Church* (edited by Mark Chapman, Continuum, 2011). The eighth chapter owes its origins to a substantial funded research project conducted by Cuddesdon through our renowned Oxford Centre for Ecclesiology and Practical Theology (OxCEPT), and one of several subsequent publications, including the seminal *Evaluating Fresh Expressions* (edited by Louise Nelstrop and Martyn Percy, SCM-Canterbury, 2008).

In the third part of the book, chapter nine has originated out of a series of conversations, colloquia and lectures that can be traced back to *Managing the Church* (edited by Martyn Percy, Sheffield Academic Press, 2000), and which were originally prompted by the proposed managerial reform of the Church of England introduced by George Carey when Archbishop of Canterbury (1991–2002). Chapter ten was recently published in *Intercultural Theology* (edited by Mark Cartledge and David Cheetham, SCM Press, 2011). Chapter eleven draws on a lecture given several years ago at a Windsor Consultation (St George's House), and subsequently published in *The Hope of Things to Come* (edited by Mark Chapman, Continuum, 2010). Finally, chapter twelve – and indeed much of the third part of the book – draws on a variety of lectures and papers, including an exploratory essay in *Creative Church Leadership* (edited by John Adair and John Nelson, SCM-Canterbury Press, 2004).

I remain, as ever, deeply indebted for the forbearance of my wife Emma, and for her patience in the crafting of this volume. Most especially as she was completing her own doctoral thesis during the gestation of this book. Her love and support, and that of my sons, Ben and Joe, are beyond price.

MWP

Introduction

Contexts, Challenges and the Church

Since no-one is an island, as the Anglican poet John Donne observed, so no book about Anglicanism can ever be separated from the context in which it is written. And this one – a collection of essays about Anglicanism that mark a decade at Cuddesdon – is profoundly shaped by the challenges and contexts that the church finds itself facing in the early years of the twenty-first century. Some of these are specific to the Church of England. Others are related to the wider Anglican Communion. And I suspect that all of them are, in one way or another, common to other churches and denominations too, and their contexts. So although we are paying close attention to Anglicanism and the Church of England in this volume, it is clearly a work of contemporary ecclesiology that has much wider application. And we should perhaps begin by being clear about the issues we face in mission and ministry today, and the challenges posed by contemporary culture particularly. A colleague and friend of mine, the (late) sociologist of religion Peter Clarke, recently recounted the following tale. He had come to Cuddesdon for lunch, and he was recalling an overheard conversation between two female postgraduates shortly before he began to lecture. One turned to the other, and said,

> 'You know, I think you really should try Roman Catholicism.'
> 'Really? Why? I mean, why do you say that?'
> 'I don't know, really. I mean, I just think it's so totally *you*. I think you might find something in that, I guess. I think it would add something to your life – enhance it, maybe?'
> 'Gosh, really? I had never thought of it that way. It can't do any harm to try it, right? You know, I might just give it a go…'

This is zeitgeist; and in a single exchange between two women before a lecture begins. Neither of them was especially religious, I suppose. But both saw religion as something that might add a dimension to their lives: an enhancer; an accessory. Religion here is a commodity: a resource that can add value and meaning in much the way that other consumable gifts might. And here, the exhortation is 'try before you buy'.

We already know, I think, that secularisation – whatever that contestable process actually is – does not produce secularity. Rather, it squeezes and compacts religion into new margins and zones. Faith still flourishes, but increasingly as private and personal spirituality. Religion moves from the mainstream to the orbit of leisure time. Consumerism enables individuals to choose their faith, and once chosen, to choose the terms on which they consume it. The customer is king (or queen). Even for those who adopt conservative Christian values and belong to more fundamentalistically orientated churches, there is plenty of evidence to show that the terms of believing and belonging are now defined more by the members than by the managers and owners.

But lest this sound too complacent, it is important to remember that there is *something* in secularisation. True, whatever that process is supposed to describe, it can probably never do justice to the intrinsically inchoate nature of religious belief that characterised the Western European landscape and its peoples long before the Enlightenment, let alone the industrial revolution of the nineteenth century and the cultural revolutions of the twentieth century. 'Standard' secularisation theories are weak and unconvincing because they tend to depend on exaggerating the extent and depth of Christendom. They assume a previous world of monochrome religious allegiance, which is now (of course) in tatters. But in truth, the religious world was much more plural and contested before the twentieth century ever dawned. The twenty-first century has already proven to be just as challenging.

So what, exactly, has changed? As Woodhead and Catto have shown in their recent book – and despite an understandable reticence to cede too much ground to proponents of secularisation theses – it can still be readily acknowledged that the post-war period in Britain has been one of the most seminal and challenging periods for the churches and other faiths in all of time.[1] Leaving aside its own struggles with pluralism, post-colonialism, modernity, postmodernity and wave after wave of cultural change and challenge, the biggest issue the churches

---

[1]   Woodhead and Catto, *Religion and Change in Modern Britain*.

have had to face up to is, ironically, a simple one: choice. Increased mobility, globalisation and consumerism have infected and affected the churches, just as they have touched every other aspect of social life. Duty is dead: the customer is king. It is no surprise, therefore, to discover churches adopting a consumerist mentality, and competing with one another for souls, members or entering the marketplace, and trying to convert tired consumers into revitalised Christians.

Thus, fewer regular or frequent church-goers now attend church twice on a Sunday, which was once normal practice. For most, once is enough. Many who do attend on a regular basis now attend less frequently. Even allowing for holidays and other absences, even the most dedicated church-goer may only be present in church for 70 per cent of the Sundays in any given year. Many clergy now remark on the decline in attendance at Days of Obligation (e.g., saints' days or Ascension-tide). The committed, it seems, are also the busy. The response to this from amongst the more liturgical churches has been to adapt their practice subtly and quietly, whilst preserving the core tradition. For example, the celebration of Epiphany may now take place on the Sunday nearest to 6 January, and not on the day itself. A number of Roman Catholic churches now offer Sunday Mass on Saturday evenings, in order for Sunday to be left as a family day, or for whatever other commitments or consumerist choices that might now fall on the once hallowed day of rest.

Added to this, we also note the rising number of 'new' spiritualities, their range and volume having increased significantly in the post-war era. Again, choice (rather than upbringing, location, etc.) is now a major factor in determining the spiritual allegiances that individuals may develop. Moreover, it is not easy to discern where the boundaries now lie between leisure, exercise and spirituality. As the consumerist-individual asserts their autonomy and right-to-choose, clear divisions between religion and spirituality, sacred and secular, and church and society are more problematic to define. Thus, consumerism and choice simultaneously threaten but also nourish religion and spirituality. Spiritual self-help books and other products, various kinds of yoga and meditative therapies, plus an ample range of courses and vacations, all suggest that religious affections and allegiances are being transformed in contemporary society rather than being eroded. 'Secular' society seems to be powerless in the face of a curiously stubborn (and growing) social appetite for inchoate religion and nascent spirituality, in all its various forms.

Whilst it is true that many in Western Europe are turning from being religious assumers to religious consumers, and are moving from a culture of religious assumption to religious consumption, in which choice and competition in the spiritual marketplace thrive, there may be little cause for alarm. Faith is just as vibrant in the twenty-first century as it was for the Victorians. It is just that today, in Britain, the landscape of belief really has changed, and that is what the editors so skilfully narrate. Statistics for English church attendance, if still read crudely, retell one of the great lies of the modern age, namely that secularisation is 'real'. It is, rather, an older sociological and interpretative construct that is placed upon select data, and continually reapplied. Thus, secularisation theories tend not to take 'implicit' or 'folk' religion that seriously; and neither do the proponents of the 'classic' theory pay much attention to the rising interest in spirituality. Similarly, the appeal of fundamentalism and new religious movements in the West, to say nothing of the explosive growth in Christianity and Islam in the developing world, are also dismissed. But as Woodhead and Catto have recently explained, and as earlier scholars such as David Martin and Grace Davie confirm, such phenomena cannot be ignored. Religion and faith are diversifying, not dying. This presents new challenges to faith groups. But it indicates a slightly out of control liveliness, not an imminent death.

Ultimately, crude readings of church attendance or plotting declining membership figures for faith groups say very little about the faith of a nation; believing and belonging should not be confused. In contemporary Western society, very few people choose not to relate at all to the church, or to mainstream religion. In any secular age, there is space and demand for religion, faith and spirituality. This is important, for it reminds us that religion provides enchantment within modernity, and that in Britain, at least, churches are still often the only bodies that provide public and open places within a community for tears, grief, remembrance, laughter and celebration. Religion in England – Christian and otherwise – is alive and well. But some of the challenges faced in England by the established church, other denominations and faith groups actually are quite new, and will require some tenacious and imaginative engagement for the mission and ministry of Christian denominations.

Yet whilst I would not want to understate the significance of the challenges the Church of England faces, and the equally demanding contexts in which Anglicanism today seeks to minister faithfully and globally, this is primarily a book of essays that is confident in tone, albeit tempered with realism and critical reflection. The book itself is a collection of essays and lectures that have been published, more or less over the last 10 years at Cuddesdon, and whilst as Principal of Ripon College. The context is significant – one of rich and deep ministerial formation for ordained ministry – in the company of women and men, young and old, part-time and full-time, all training to become clergy to serve God, and the people and places Christ lays before them. It is a privilege to be amongst them, and to share in this work with a rich variety of skilled and talented staff, who do so much to shape the formational ethos, community spirit and curriculum. It is this starting point – a community that is rich in wisdom, confident, open-minded, prayerful, generous of heart and hospitable – that forms the context for this book. For the buoyancy and belief I encounter here, on a daily basis, nourish the mind and spirit, and reinforce the sense of there being profound hope for the future of the church.

One reason to bring these essays, lectures and articles on Anglicanism together in one volume was, therefore, to have a focused concentration and celebration of the church. The intention is to have one volume of essays that was consciously rooted in the history and legacy of Cuddesdon itself. The seminary nestles atop 'God's Holy Hill', and is, at its best, something of a quintessential distillation of the Anglican Spirit. It is a unique theological college, being a few miles outside Oxford, embedded in a small rural village of less than 500 people. Sometimes (in jest) known as 'Holy Hogwarts' (a quizzical reference to the buildings, I think, and their passing resemblance to the world of Harry Potter), the college has come to embody something of the soul of Anglican identity. I do not mean this in an exclusive or privileged way, of course. By making this claim for Cuddesdon, I do no more than point to its breadth and depth in formation, and to the remarkable way in which the community continues to cherish all that is good in our polity, and yet combines this with a tenacious and skilful engagement with our current contexts. Mission and ministry, when they are studied (through education and training) are always rooted in the richness of the tradition, as much as they are shaped and adapted to the needs of the present and future. And it is precisely because of that hope – combined with realism – that difficult issues and challenging contexts cannot be evaded or avoided. The way of the cross is a road that runs through the real world with all its pain and darkness; it does not bypass it.

Although these essays have appeared before in other volumes, this is the first time that they have been drawn together in a book that is explicitly concerned with Anglicanism and the Church of England. The impetus for a focused concentration and celebration of Anglican life seems to be especially important at present. Debates on sexuality and gender (women bishops), whether the church has a Covenant, or can be a Communion, how it is ultimately led, are issues that have dominated the ecclesial horizon for several decades now. Of course, this volume cannot claim to have all the answers to all the questions. But these 'Cuddesdon Essays' are an attempt to offer insight and illumination, and highlight how rich and reflexive the Anglican tradition can be in preaching and proclaiming Christ.

The three parts of the volume naturally reflect Anglican concerns, though they have much wider ecumenical bearing. The first part explores formational issues for ministry, examining not only theological education, but also the contexts for parish ministry today, with some reflection on how to interpret churches and sacred space. The second part examines the more public dimensions to mission and ministry, with attention given to youth ministry, the emerging church movement, establishment and parochial identity. The third part examines leadership in the church, with reflections on mediation and conflict resolution, the nature of the church and the dynamics of leading an institution.

I am well aware that the essays move in something of a North Atlantic current. In terms of readership, however, that does not exclude issues raised in the text concerning wider Anglican Communion, including Africa, Asia, the Far East and Australasia. Correspondingly, chapters do touch on ministries and mission in Hong Kong and Macau, as well as Ulster, North America and Great Britain. And although the North Atlantic current of the essays dominates, and there is a great deal more to be said about Anglicanism in Africa and other parts of the developing world, to be sure, there is equally a sense in which the volume as a whole pleads for a theological leadership in the church today that is not only able to surf waves, but can also read the cultural tides that buffet our age.

To continue with the metaphor, this is therefore also a book that actually seeks to turn some tides – those that may be of fad and fashion – which sometimes appear to overshadow ecclesial ecologies, and cause them to suffer and wilt. I hold, for example, for the need to correct (or at least check) the current and unquestioned trend and trajectory of managerially led missiology always governing and shaping ecclesiology. Good ecclesiology leads to good missiology; but the reverse, alas, is not always true. So, some of the chapters here clearly reject the trend towards mission-shaped church, whilst affirming church-shaped mission.

One reason why these essays are secured in and emerge out of a decade of theological education at Cuddesdon is that the context itself is formational for a particular kind of theology. All seminaries are, of course. But we perhaps underestimate the extent to which they shape the wider church both now and in the generations to come. And this is why what is practised at seminaries and theological colleges is perhaps so critical for subsequent ecclesial formation. The concept of practice has recently received significant interest in organisational circles through the work of Etienne Wenger. Wenger assessed workplace habits, and then attempted to develop a social theory of learning. It is this that gave birth to the concept of communities of practice, which Wenger defines as 'groups of people who share a concern or a passion for something they do and learn how to do it better as they interact regularly'.[2] Even if participants in such communities are innocent of their membership and unaware of their practices – which they often are in churches – the very idea of a concept of practice includes:

> both the explicit and tacit. It includes what is said and what is left unsaid: but is represented and what is assumed. It includes the language, tools, documents, images, symbols, well-defined roles, specified criteria, codified procedures, regulations, and contracts that various practices make explicit for a variety of purposes. But it also includes all the implicit relations, tacit conventions, subtle cues, untold rules of thumb, recognizable institutions, specific perceptions, well-tuned sensitivities, embodied understandings, underlying assumptions, and shared worldviews. Most of these may never be articulated, yet their unmistakable signs of membership in communities of practice are crucial to the success of the enterprises.[3]

---

[2] Wenger, *Communities of Practice*, p. 139.
[3] Ibid., p. 47.

Wenger sees one of the primary functions of communities of practice as the formation of identity. And identity, according to Wenger, is negotiated through the shared membership of social communities, and 'practice defines a community through three dimensions: mutual engagement, a joint enterprise, and a shared repertoire'.[4] His approach remains realistic throughout – identity is not something we construct in our heads intellectually or in our imagination, but rather something that is constructed by our day-to-day practices. Seminaries and theological colleges are primary examples of this: they shape identity.

So perhaps more than anything else, this book owes its origins to the extraordinary community that is Cuddesdon. It is the people and the place, together with the college, courses and community that have come to shape my thinking on Anglicanism over the years. It is in the regular cycle of the daily office; the simple practice of generous orthodoxy; the humanity touched by divinity; the gentle humour and the utter seriousness. These are the disciplines and practices that are formational. And they enable a character of confidence, commitment and communion, held with humility and grace, to take root. Theological colleges really only do three things: eating, worshipping and learning together. How that is done is what ultimately gives birth to our ecclesiology – open, hospitable, humble – yet also sagacious, rich and generative.

Finally, then, it is important to say a word about the shaping of this kind of approach to contemporary ecclesiology. Rather like the work of David Martin, Robin Gill, Grace Davie and one or two of the other interlocutors who occur with some frequency in these chapters, I am shaped by two intellectual genealogies. One is broadly a fusion of sociology and anthropology. The legacy of Clifford Geertz, for example, is constantly in the background. The other is theological, and shaped by writers such as James Hopewell, Jim Nieman, Denham Grierson and Nicholas Healy. In other words, these are contextual theologians of varying hue and colour. And these two intellectual genealogies produce a kind of 'binocular' approach to the study of the church, with all that this metaphor implies. Some things, in the distance, come in to view; only a few things are focused upon, but in order to extrapolate a larger picture.

So, as someone working with a framework of sociology and anthropology, I am naturally wary (some might say suspicious) of the ways in which structures

---

[4]   Ibid., p. 152.

and practices are legitimised by appeals to fundaments – be they biblical or drawn from the 'tradition'. And one must be equally wary of the idea that the development of structures and practices can be further legitimised by appeals to the work of the Holy Spirit. That said, the theological element to the 'binocular' is receptive to revelation, and to ways in which the body of Christ grows and develops in local contexts – denominations, places and times, and amongst people genuinely and truly seeking to live authentic and faithful Christian lives that correspond to God's revealed will for the world. It has been my practice, in studying and writing on contemporary ecclesiology, fundamentalism and revivalism, and Christianity and contemporary culture, to deploy this 'binocular' approach. I regard it as complementary, not competitive.

This approach becomes helpful when considering something as simple as the apparent sluggishness of the church. Why does it take so long to reach decisions in an ecclesial body? When the truth, or clarity, seems so obvious and within our grasp, what is the value in pausing, waiting and in continuing discussions? To outsiders, this looks like vacillation and dithering. But to scholars and observers, the waiting has theological and socio-anthropological purpose. Christianity is a faith – indeed history – of resolving differences through conversations and meetings. From Councils of Jerusalem, Nicea, Chalcedon, to the Diet of Worms, right through to Vatican II and the Lambeth Conferences, Christian denominations meet, deliberate and share their faith – often over sharp differences and contested convictions. They are socially and sacramentally bound together in a meeting and meal – the Eucharist – that bids them make peace and break bread together, even though they may not see eye to eye. Where two or three are gathered, Christians are promised, Christ dwells in their midst. We find God and truth not alone, but together: in meeting, and in the breaking of bread and the shared study of the word. We meet.

I suppose that part of the problem the church faces today – perhaps especially Anglicanism (but surely not exclusively) – may lie in the lengthy institutional intermissions that develop in its life, largely due to its spiritually laudable emphasis on internal mutual forbearance and consensus. But in its own way, that is a very Anglican sentiment. As a church, we tend to cook issues slowly. We savour and discern the varying flavours of the issues that unite and divide us. We believe that to become church takes time; that unity is not uniformity; and that some of the sharpest and seemingly bitterest things we chew on are best taken slowly. Sometimes, that frustrates and infuriates. But it is also what we celebrate too. Church, like prayer itself, is a banquet to savour, even if not everything at table is to our liking. Perhaps above all else, this really should not be hurried. Church, like prayer, is for growing into; we break bread apart so we can share in Christ's body corporately. So we always break it together; and this necessarily takes time – which is what the church ultimately is; rich time, shared with each other, feasting on the bread of life.

PART I
Confidence in Formation

Chapter 1

A Flight of Starlings: Cuddesdon and the Forming of Anglicanism

Here's an old joke about Anglican polity. One day, the queues of people to get into heaven are so long and thick that the Angels guarding the Pearly Gates begin to panic. They fly off to see Jesus and ask for advice. Jesus suggests that potential entrants are graded. He will ask a question of everyone seeking entry, and depending on how they answer, they will either be placed in the slow track, or granted immediate entry. The question Jesus proposes to use is the same question he once put to the disciples: 'Who do you say that I am?' The first person Jesus encounters at the gates is a Methodist minister. Jesus asks her, 'who do you say that I am?' The minister hesitates, and then answers 'well, at Conference last year …'. But Jesus interrupts her immediately. 'I am sorry', he says, 'but I asked you for your opinion, and not for your denominational line. Would you mind going to the back of the queue? Thank you.' The next person to step forward is a Roman Catholic monk. Jesus poses the same question, to which the monk replies, 'well, our Pope says…'. But Jesus again interrupts, and points out that he wanted the monk's opinion, not the Pope's. Third, a Baptist minister approaches. His response to Jesus' question is emphatic: 'the Bible says …'. But Jesus again interrupts, and reminds the minister that he wanted his opinion, not his knowledge. Finally, an Anglican priest approaches. Jesus regards the minister somewhat quizzically and with suspicion, but puts the question to him nonetheless. The Anglican replies categorically: 'You are the Christ – the Son of the living God.' Jesus is slightly taken aback by such an ardent response from an Episcopalian, and is about to let the Anglican priest in, when the minister adds, 'but then again, on the other hand…'.

Some years ago my two sons encountered the joys of a *Thesaurus* for the first time, and delighted in discovering new and familiar words, and their alternative meanings. The first modern *Thesaurus* was published by Dr Peter Mark Roget in

1852. 'Thesaurus' means 'treasury' or 'storehouse'; but what words, I wonder, would Roget have linked to 'Anglican'? It is a potentially awkward question, since the answer will almost certainly depend on the virtues or vices that the enquirer has already attributed. For some, it will be: indecisive, vacillating or compromised. For others: solid, reliable and predictable. Still for others: conservative – or liberal; historic – or innovative; Protestant – or Catholic.

Interestingly, Roget did include 'Anglican' in his original *Thesaurus*, and attributed only one comparable word to the term: Protestantism. But then beneath this entry, under 'Anglicism' (not Anglicanism, note – but a near neighbour, so to speak), he suggests 'dialect' – a particularly distinctive mode of speech. It is a matter of debate as to whether Anglicanism is a distinctive mode of English Protestantism. It is; and then again it isn't; it is more than that. But Roget's range of allusion set us an intriguing question: what does the word 'Anglican' mean today?

There is complex history to the term. It is a seventeenth-century 'nickname' that did not acquire common usage until quite late in the nineteenth century – and only then to describe a church that had always known what it was in itself, but had never really needed to offer an explicit articulation of that self to others. But whatever the word might have meant theologically or liturgically, it is its ecclesiological use that is the most elastic. So much so, in fact, that the term 'Anglican' has become a cipher for linking a series of opposites or polarities, that in turn express its diversity. So, if one is to return to *Roget's Thesaurus* for a moment, what words might Anglicans add from their own treasury to the label? Solid, yet flexible; strong, yet yielding; open, yet composed; inclusive, yet identifiable. The list could go on. But I suppose that in pointing out the connection of opposites, I am appealing for having some confidence in our un-decidability and elasticity, in the very midst of our concreteness. Anglican identity only begins to make proper sense when it is related to its mirror image or opposite number. No one wing or facet of the church can begin to be true without relation to its contrary expression.

We need both, of course. And at a time when we are being sorely pressed to decide and define instead of living together in patience, we need to have the courage to be, above all, *Anglican*. And this is especially suggestive for the way in which the church might be led at present. Holding together polarities is no easy business, especially when competing convictions can themselves be held with passion and zeal that will not only refuse to compromise, but perhaps even to dialogue. Are there systems that can enable the Anglican Communion or Church of England to negotiate intense disagreements, or navigate through complex arguments? Is it possible to find consensus in the midst of heated debates and a distancing in relations? Unsurprisingly, I don't have the answers to these questions, but here are three modest pointers as to how the polity might be held together, as it attempts to negotiate its own future within a context of increasing diversity and difference.

First, Anglicanism is generally easier to identify through persons rather than systems: examples of faith and polity matter rather than theories of it. In this respect, heroes or exemplars of the faith turn out to be those characters, individuals or communities that exhibit the gifts and fruits of the Holy Spirit. Although Anglicanism has articles of faith (39 of them), it is rare to appeal to these when pointing to striking and inspiring exemplars of Anglican ecclesial polity. Our heroes, therefore, are Herbert and Hooker, or Tutu and Temple – to name but a few.

Second, those charged with the ministry of oversight may need to come to some understanding of how those under them learn. Often, this is not done through the simple or mechanistic transferral of principles, rules and propositions. It is, rather, through a deeper formational wisdom rooted in tactical suavity, emotional intelligence, reflexivity and responsiveness. Often, we learn from those in oversight who are able to display character and virtue, not just skill; enormous reserves of resilience, patience and energy. In which insight and courage are fused to gentle but firm will.

Third, the realisation that exemplars matter to the shaping of our polity has profound implications for the practice of the church. Much of this is tacit. Clergy, for example, when they gather and share, often discuss the most testing funerals or occasional offices they have presided over of late. Generally, this is not boastful behaviour. It actually points to something deeper in ordained life here; namely that the church reflects on experiences, and draws from that principles, ideas and conclusions about how it is incarnate in particular times and places. In other words, it elaborates and reflects upon how it is being Christ for others, and bread for the world. This is theological reflection.

Starlings and Anglican Identity

With these comments in mind, let me say something about Anglican distinctiveness in the midst of our current cultural diversity. It would be quite possible here to talk at length about our explicit theological identity. But I prefer instead to address a few aspects of what I take to be our anthropological identity, which in turn suggests a nascent value-based implicit theological shape. It is said that Henry Scott Holland once stood on the hill at Garsington shortly before his death, and gazed over the valley to Cuddesdon College and parish church, where he had asked to be buried. He noticed a flock of starlings flying past, and remarked how like the Anglican Church they were. Nothing, it seemed, kept the flock together – and yet the birds moved as one, even though they were all apart and retained their individual identity. In an increasingly diverse and cosmopolitan world, of which the Anglican Communion is a part, birds of a feather still need to flock together, even though each creature is individual.

Holland's observation allows us to develop another analogy here, centred on the identity of the species. The Anglicanism of the twenty-first century is recognisably different from that of the end of the nineteenth century. The flock, if you like, is no longer one type of bird. Evolution – through cultural and theological diversity – has meant that many Anglican provinces have evolved to 'fit' their contexts, and the ultimate diversity of the species clearly threatens its unity. But to extend the analogy just a little further, is it possible to still speak of a connecting DNA – some of the deep, core but hidden constituents of our identity which relate us, even though they may not be immediately apparent?

The Church of England, on the whole, has a somewhat understated ecclesiology: its self-understanding, a bit like DNA, is often a matter of deeply coded and implicit language, not explicit statements. As one commentator has recently noted, can it really be any accident that cricket is the preferred game of the clergy in the Church of England? An individual, yet collaborative game; full of manners, codes of conduct – 'sporting' sport; strenuous and restful by turns, combining subtlety and strength (speed is rarely valued); where all may have different gifts and functions, yet be equally valued; and where the side about to lose can gain an honourable or even heroic draw, either due to rain or bad light. Results really don't matter; it's how you play. The other game that clergy play a lot of is chess (with their own magazine, *Chess Minister*). It's all about plots, pace and plans; a kind of surrogate for the Parochial Church Council (PCC). So there is perhaps no need to speculate on the significance of clergy and model railway clubs – you can probably begin to work that out for yourselves; it's all to do with things running to order, and on time – quite unlike normal ministry.

It was Jeremy Paxman who once quipped that the Church of England is the kind of body that believes that there was no issue that could not be eventually solved over a cup of tea in the Vicar's study. This waspish compliment directed towards Anglican polity serves to remind us that many regard its ecclesial praxis as being quintessentially peaceable and polite, in which matters never really get too out of hand. For similar reasons, Robert Runcie once described Anglican polity as a matter of 'passionate coolness'. In the past, and in my own reflections on Anglican polity, these are sentiments with which I have tended to concur:

> In some of my conversations with Anglican theologians … I have been struck by how much of the coherence of Anglicanism depends on good manners. This sounds, at face value, like an extraordinarily elitist statement. It is clearly not meant to be that. What I mean by manners is learning to speak well, behave well, and be able to conduct yourself with integrity in the midst of an argument … It is often the case that in Anglicans' disputes about doctrine, order or faith, it is actually the means that matter more than the ends … politeness, integrity, restraint, diplomacy, patience, a willingness to listen, and above all, not to be ill-mannered – these are the things that enable the Anglican Communion to cohere.[1]

In macro-theological disputes, such as those over the ordination of women, part of the strategy that enables unity can be centred on containing some of the more passionate voices in the debate. Extreme feelings, when voiced, can lead to extreme reactions. And extreme reactions, when allowed full vent, can make situations unstable. Nations or federations fall apart; Communions can fracture; families may divide. Things said briefly in the heat of a moment can cause wounds that may take years to heal. What is uttered is not easily retracted.

Good manners, then, is not a bad analogy for 'ideal' Anglican polity. In a church that sets out to accommodate many different peoples of every theological

---

[1]   Percy, 'On Sacrificing Purity?', pp. 118–19.

hue, there has to be a foundation – no matter how implicit – that enables the Communion to cohere across party lines, tribal borders and doctrinal differences. And just as this is true for macro-theological disputes, so is it also true for micro-ecclesial squabbles. Often, congregational unity in the midst of disputes can only be secured by finding a middle open way, in which the voices of moderation and tolerance occupy the central ground and enable a church to move forwards.

This is something that the *Windsor Report*[2] understands, and it is interesting to note how much attention the Report gives to the virtues of patience and restraint, whilst also acknowledging the place of passions and emotions in the sexuality debate. Clearly, there is a tension between these polarities (the polite–passionate axis), which is partly why the cultivation of 'mannered-ness' in ecclesial polity can be seen to be as essential as it is beguiling.

This means, of course, continually listening to the experiences that lead to anger, and seeing them as far as possible from the perspective of those with less power. It means humility on the part of those who hold power, and an acknowledgement of the fear of losing power and control. It means a new way of looking at power relationships that takes the gospel seriously in their equalising and levelling. I am aware that this is one of the most demanding aspects of oversight, namely having the emotional intelligence, patience and empathy to hold feelings, anger, disappointment and frustration – other people's, as well as your own. Oversight, it seems to me, is less about strategy and more about (deeply learnt) poise, especially in holding together competing convictions and trying to resolve deep conflicts.

But before conflicts can be resolved, they must first of all be *held*. And here we find another of the most demanding aspects of oversight within the context of considerable theological and cultural diversity. Because one of the tasks of the church is to soak up sharp and contested issues, in such a way as to limit and blunt the possibility of deep intra- and inter-personal damage being caused, as well as further dislocation in people's sense of faithful identity. Retaining composure, and somehow holding people together who would otherwise divide (due to the nature of their intense and competing convictions), is a stretching vocation.

Anyone exercising a ministry of oversight will understand the costly nature of this vocation – a kind of servant leadership – that understands that much of Anglican polity is 'open' in its texture; and although it has a shape, is nonetheless

---

2   Lambeth Commission on Communion, *Windsor Report*.

unresolved and incomplete. Therefore, issues that cannot be determined often require being held; a deliberate postponement of resolution. Put another way, there is a tension between being an identifiable community with creeds and fundaments; and yet also being a body that recognises that some issues are essentially un-decidable in the church. Indeed, 'Anglican un-decidability' (a phrase coined by Stephen Pickard), may turn out to be one of the chief counter-cultural Anglican virtues; it is very far from being a problem, as some appear to believe.

The desire and need to sometimes reach settlements that do not achieve closure, is itself part of the deep 'habit of wisdom' that has helped to form Anglican polity down the centuries. It is embodied liturgically in the Book of Common Prayer, but can also be traced in pastoral, parish and synodical resolutions that cover a significant range of issues. Essentially, this 'calling' is about inhabiting the gap between vocation, ideals, praxis and action. No neutral or universally affirmed final settlements can be reached on a considerable number of issues within the church. But provisional settlements have to be reached that allow for the possibility of continuing openness, adjustment and innovation. Inevitably, therefore, any consensus is a slow and painful *moment* to arrive at, and even when achieved, will usually involve a degree of provisionality and more open-endedness. This is, of course, a typical Anglican habit, embodying a necessary humility and holiness in relation to matters of truth, but without losing sight of the fact that difficult *decisions* still need to be made.

Allied to this, of course, is an appreciation that one of the chief virtues of living within a Communion is learning to be patient. Churches, each with their distinctive own intra-denominational familial identity, all have to learn how to negotiate the differences they find within themselves. For some churches in recent history, the discovery of such differences – perhaps on matters of authority, praxis or interpretation – has been too much to bear: lines have been drawn in the sand, with the sand itself serving only as a metaphor for the subsequent atomisation. Yet where some new churches, faced with internal disagreement, have quickly experienced fragmentation, most historic denominations have been reflexive enough to experience little more than a process of elastication: they have been stretched, but they have not broken. This is perhaps inevitable, when one considers the global nature of most mainstream historic denominations. Their very expanse will have involved a process of stretching (missiological, moral, conversational, hermeneutical, etc.), and this in turn has led directly to their (often inchoate) sense of accommodation. However, this process itself has led to two very different versions of the Communion and its future, and these polarities need sketching briefly.

The first sees Anglicanism in concrete terms. Here, the polity will be governed by law, and scripture will be its ultimate arbiter. Here, Anglicanism will become a tightly defined denomination in which intra-dependence is carefully policed. Diversity of belief, behaviour and practice will continue, but they will be subject to scrutiny and challenge. The second sees Anglicanism as a more reflexive polity; one that has a shape, but is able to stretch and accommodate considerable diversity. Here the polity will be governed by grace, not law, and the Communion itself will continue to operate as both a sign and instrument of unity. Anglicanism will continue to be a defined form of ecclesial polity, but one that tolerates and respects the differences it finds within itself.

Personally, I pray and hope for option two. But I also pray that I will not be divided from my sisters and brothers who favour the first option. I pray that in the midst of our common and diverse struggles, we will discover ourselves afresh in the learning church, within that community of peace we still know as the Anglican Communion. I believe that this may well stretch the Communion to its limits, and test its viability vigorously. But I believe the stretch will ultimately be worth it. For in reaching out just beyond ourselves, and moving outside our normal boundaries and comfort zones, God's own hand is already waiting to clasp at our feeble groping.

But to concretise these reflections just a little more, let me offer three further brief remarks to help us in our thinking. First, Anglicanism is something that is formed by worship, praying the scriptures and through an ecclesial practice that is, at one, local and catholic. A Communion is a complex body immersed in the complexity of the world, in which all seek to participate in God's purposes for a wide range of reasons. Anglicanism is, then, a kind of practical and mystical idea that embodies how people might be together. It is not a confessional church in which membership is conditional upon precise agreement with articles or statements. In spite of the internal difficulties that global Anglicanism encounters, its strength may still lie in its apparent weaknesses: its unity in its diversity; its coherence in its difference; its shape in its diffusiveness; its hope in a degree of faithful doubt; its energy in passionate coolness. It embodies 'feint conviction';

it practises 'truthful duplicity'; it is Protestant and Catholic; it is synodical and Episcopal; it allows for 'troubled commitment'; or, as one commentator notes (Urban Holmes), it can hardly ever resist the pairing of two three letter words: 'Yes, but …'.

Second, maintaining unity in the midst of considerable cultural diversity will lie in developing our poise and capacity to hold together intensely held competing convictions. In the past, this rhetoric of 'holding' has been treated with jocularity or even cynicism by the church and the public (including the media); it has been a kind of code for saying that no decisions can or will be made (or the bishop doesn't like to make decisions, and prefers to sit on the fence). But increasingly, I think, the language and business of 'holding' will need to come to the fore, and this work and vocation is very far from being vapid or neutral. 'Holding' together intensely held competing convictions is, to my mind, one of the most demanding and costly tasks in episcopacy; a ministry of oversight that presides over conflicts of belief and interests. Under such conditions, the demand for a serious emotional and organisational intelligence (or wisdom) in dealing with passionately held beliefs is becoming increasingly vital.

Third, we may need to learn to celebrate the gift of our 'un-decidability' a little more. In being able to sustain a community of intense difference and competing convictions, we are actually offering a form of witness rather than a lack of unity. As the American theologian Urban Holmes notes,

> I have never known two Episcopalians agree totally … [but] the fact that we can admit our disagreements is indicative of our Anglican freedom to acknowledge the polymorphous nature of all human knowing – something that not every Christian body is comfortable admitting.[3]

Holmes realises that Anglicanism, although a system of a kind, is more identifiable through persons than articles of faith. It models itself through *examples* of faith. It is a mode of making sense of the experience of God – a particular approach to the social and sacred construction of reality, and to the building of the world. Anglicans occasionally write great theology; but they are better known for poetry, hymnody, liturgy, music and spirituality. When we do get round to theology, we

---

[3]   Holmes, *What Is Anglicanism?*, p. 48.

remain absorbed, interestingly, with the incarnation, ethics and ecclesiology: all of these being person-centred and systematic attempts to concretise our witness within the world.

We can say that it is partly for this reason that our deep desire for Anglican comprehensiveness is so manifest. It is not the case, I think, that Anglican consciousness is essentially accommodating – especially in its more vapid forms. It is, rather, that comprehensiveness prioritises conversation and quest over precision and absolute resolutions; at its best, Anglicanism is a community of being, love, thought and worship, rather than being a definitive body that has achieved mutually agreeable confessional closure. In other words, we remain open because we see ourselves as incomplete; we are constantly caught between innovation and stability; the possibility of new patterns of being, and faithfulness to what has been revealed; between loyalty to what has gone before and still is, and what might or shall be.

Furthermore, the embodiment of this accommodation is, strangely, a person-centred ecclesial polity rather than being system-driven. This is hardly surprising when one considers the historic Anglican affection for the doctrine of the incarnation: salvation comes through embodiment, example, sacrifice and inclusiveness. Anglicans know – through their deep tacit knowledge and instinct, I think – that systems or formulae do not redeem us. Nor do they make our church. We're called, held and saved by a person, and our polity seems to know that our being together (even with our differences) is primarily human and relational. This is why being together in some kind of 'centre', where we can face one another with our different perspectives, and be in a place of conversation, is so vital for our future polity.

And this now means, of course, that the centre ground is becoming the *radical* ground: ironic and oxymoronic, I know – but holding to some kind of centre is, to a large extent, evolving into a task and role which makes the hardest demands upon those charged with oversight. All the more so, because as those who work and study in the field of international conflict resolution remind us, the most difficult and demanding battles are those which involve our own allies or close relationships: what one scholar rather tamely terms 'cooperative disputes'. It was Bill Vanstone, I think, who once remarked that the Church of England is like a swimming pool – all the noise comes from the shallow end. It's true, isn't it? On issues of major gravity, all the noise tends to come from the shrill reactionary voices that grab the headlines. The voices from the deep centre are seldom heard: the real words we need to hear are drowned out by the splashing and the shouting.

So, our future life together as Anglicans is probably dependent on appreciating those deep implicit 'centralist' charisms and virtues that have shaped us for so long, and beginning to make them more explicit. Of having confidence in our un-decidability and elasticity. And in holding the church together, and keeping it open, remembering that we are first and foremost, held by God in his open hands, who knows our weaknesses and differences only too well; but will still cling to us, and not let us go. As we try to hold our people and ourselves together, so shall we be held. Urban Holmes ends his meditation on Anglican polity, written 25 years ago, with these words:

> [our] course leads to living in the world as God sees the world. We can debate the trivial points, but the vision is largely clear. To love God is to relieve the burden of all who suffer. The rest is a question of tactics.[4]

Conclusion: Cuddesdon in the Future of Anglicanism

Speaking of tactics, naturally, we turn, finally, to Cuddesdon and our life together here. You will know that Ripon College seeks to prepare men and women for God's mission in a changing world through the imaginative pursuit of academic excellence, spiritual depth and pastoral engagement within the rhythm of daily life together. The College seeks to prepare ordained ministers who are disciplined in the life of prayer, competent and creative leaders of worship, and aware of their own needs and motivations; who are critical and constructive theologians, who can draw on and interpret the riches of the Christian tradition in the light of contemporary problems and needs; who are able to understand the nature and purpose of Christian community through the experience of living together and are equipped to be leaders in its renewal in this and future generations; and who are able to interpret the world to the church in order to demonstrate the love of God for all people.

---

[4]   Ibid., p. 181.

This requires not only faith, but also innovation and excellence in theological thinking: reflexive theology for a fast-changing world in which the church needs to both adapt and maintain itself. Such a theology, which together with worship and spiritual life forms the heart of the College, should change the way we look at the world. And the art of developing this lies in provoking curiosity in equal measure with illumination. In other words, our tradition is not material to be 'banked'; it is, rather, to be discovered anew. And such discoveries spring from informed and humble encounters that are more wont to pose questions than offer ready answers. The Caribbean theologian Kortright Davis expresses this moment of epiphany simply enough:

> Western theologians are [now] attempting to educate themselves about the new theological surges emanating from the Third World. They have finally realized that there is no universal theology; that theological norms arise out of the context in which one is called to live out one's faith; that theology is therefore not culture free; that the foundations on which theological structures are built are actually not transferable from one context to another. Thus, although the Gospel remains the same from place to place, the means by which the Gospel is understood and articulated will differ considerably through circumstances no less valid and no less authentic.[5]

Within this economy, we return to the *Thesaurus* mentioned earlier – the treasury or storehouse of terms that attempts to capture something of our unity and diversity through ciphers that frame polarities of meanings, and yet at the same time, connect opposites. The College motto, intriguingly, asks us to 'Guard the deposit' or 'Guard the treasure', and I hope that I have managed to indicate that this deposit or treasure is, strangely, a rather mixed bag of offerings. It is a delicate combination of opposites, which suggests to me, at least, that our treasure lies in our very breadth of expression, and our refusal to become tribal or too closely identified with any single party; that the College is at its best when it is serving the church by being faithful to its middle, open way, which welcomes and affirms diversity as much as it promotes unity.

---

[5]   Davis, *Emancipation Still Comin'*, p. 70.

Granted, there will be distinctive flavours and accents that mark the College out from time to time; but intriguingly, and at the moment, the College may offer most to the church by offering training and formation that prepares people for ministry in what I have already termed 'the radical centre'. The place that mediates between polarities, stretches to accommodate, continues to discern and still dares to believe that breadth may in fact be our mission, and not some artefact that condemns the church to some kind of slow implosion. Indeed, I take note of the William Ferguson tune, set to a version of the Gloria penned by Christopher Idle, which goes by the name of 'Cuddesdon'. Ferguson suggests the tune is sung in 'unison'. The breadth of Cuddesdon is rooted in a generous orthodoxy: a union of mission and ministry.

In all of this, the mission of the College remains resolutely focused on formation and training for parish ministry, seeking to offer clergy who are broad in their outlook; widely deployable yet deeply distinctive; and genuinely hospitable and inclusive in their ecclesiology and spirituality. At the same time, the catholic ethos continues to be preserved and developed in worship and ecclesiology, whilst the commitment to be evangelical in mission and ministry is continually augmented and progressive. We are trying, if you like, to turn out intelligent and theologically curious learners; not ministers who think that they are now 'the taught'; spiritually aware and creative practitioners whose lives reflect the example of Christ; and who are deeply pastoral – experienced through engagement, reflection and challenge. In all of this, we seek to balance realism and idealism, humour and seriousness, mellowness and urgency.

To be sure, this is an interesting and challenging time to be within theological education, and within the wider Church of England. And of course, we continue to ask for your prayers and support as we try to address the needs of the church and the world which we seek to serve. In the midst of this, I also invite you to reflect on how the College itself – I mean in its buildings and situation – speaks of the tasks and opportunities that lie ahead. Sometimes when I am showing potential ordinands around the College, I am struck by the relationship between the architectural and theological ethos. The College buildings, like our theology and ecclesiology, are continually in need of renewal and adjustment. The College offers a place of nurture and nourishment that is contained and sustained. And yet it looks out, all the time, gazing upon other horizons. There is a real sense in which the buildings reflect a state of mind, and a spirituality: a place that both looks out, yet nourishes within.

I am reminded of how one writer expresses some similar sentiments (with a description of a great Gothic cathedral):

> One walks through such a building conscious of continually unfolding vistas. It is a whole, yet it cannot be seen as a whole. Nor, though it is handed down to us by the past, it is never completely finished. New spaces expressing new needs, new altars representing a multiplicity of concerns and commitments, new decorative details celebrating new ideas and discoveries, can go on being added. It is also constantly decaying and constantly being rebuilt. It can represent both diversity, and the imperfection of incompleteness, without compromising its unity or confusing its purpose. A cathedral points beyond itself. It is not definable like a city, but open to all. Its verticality is a reminder that it is not just about human beings and human relationships. It provides a complex space which can bring home to us where, as transitory, contradictory, sinful and yet ultimately hopeful and receptive human beings, we really stand before God.[6]

These words from John Milbank, offer a positive metaphorical framework which encapsulates much of what we aspire to. Milbank is reminding us that the church of Christ is a complex and reflexive *space* in a complex and ever-changing world, and one through which we move throughout our lives. This, I think, is not just a true image of faith, but also one of pilgrimage. It invites us to imagine that our incompleteness is part of the glory of being together in church; it is partly this that keeps us open. And in belonging to that complex but perpetually incomplete space, we discover that there is now also room to be surprised and engaged by Christ afresh. This is the Christ, who in his wisdom calls us but never compels us; loves us yet frees us; and who sends us out into the world, not only to help save it, but also to meet the very same God who is already out there, 'reconciling all things in Christ'. It is for this kind of vision that our predecessors tarried; to offer a space where the starlings may both flock and be in flight. To be broad, yet distinct; united, yet different; formed, yet open.

---

6   Milbank, *The Word Made Strange*, p. 284.

So may God give us grace to hold this treasure, and to treasure what we share; for his church, and for his world, and for all our futures.

Chapter 2

Sacred Sagacity: Formation and Training for Ministry

I suppose that the first and most obvious thing to say about the purpose of ordination training – formation and education for ministry – is that it isn't immediately obvious. What, after all, is one being prepared for? As Urban Holmes III presciently observed more than 30 years ago, the roles and tasks of the clergy are not nearly as palpable in the late twentieth century as they might have been 100 years earlier.[1] It almost goes without saying that if the professional status of clergy is somewhat ambivalent, then the training and formation that seminarians (or ordinands) receive is also likely to reflect this.[2] Yet this is not quite so. Students preparing for ordained ministry – in whatever institution they are being trained, formed and educated in – can point to a curriculum (usually with a multiplicity of options, but also a 'core'); some kind of disciplined approach to prayer and worship; an ecclesial tradition that (at least) adds some kind of accent to the ethos of the institution; some practical assignments that continue to test the depth and trajectory of a vocation; and a continuous process of theological reflection that links the personal, social, intellectual and transcendent dynamics of formation.

Yet such a sketchy and skeletal outline of the priorities for theological education affords considerable licence to any ecclesial tradition and its training institutions. What then, if anything, can be said about Anglican theological education? Is there anything that might be said to unite the diversity of institutions one encounters within the global Communion? Beyond the superficial obviousness of differences – in terms of resources, history and ecclesial emphasis – is there some kind of trace

---

[1]   Holmes, *The Future Shape of Ministry*; Percy, *Clergy*.
[2]   See Towler and Coxon, *The Fate of the Anglican Clergy*; Russell, *The Clerical Profession*; Schillebeeckx, *Ministry*; Foster, Dahill, Golemon and Tolentino, *Educating Clergy*.

or sense of a common 'genetic code' that might be said to be distinctive, especially in relation to the rather nebulous concept of 'formation'? Several observations can be made. But before that, it is necessary to make a few more general remarks relating to theological education, and the bearing this has on the kind of preparation for ministry that institutions are inherently responsible for.

For example, and over the past three decades, the Church of England has witnessed a number of quite significant sea-changes in the profile and delivery of formation and training for ordained ministry. In the mid-1970s, almost three-quarters of ordinands were under the age of 30. Today, that figure has dropped to a little over 10 per cent of the total numbers in training – almost the same as those in training over the age of 60. The average age of ordination is now around 40. Correspondingly, there has been a significant shift in the expectations provided through training. Ordinands enter colleges and courses with significantly more life experience and maturity. They are also likely to be of similar age to the teaching staff, which has inevitably led to the development of more consensual and negotiated patterns of training, in place of programmes that might have once been (simply) imposed. Here at Cuddesdon, the average age of ordinands in residential training was 38 in 2006, and those in non-residential training 49. (In 2012, the average age for residential training had fallen to 31; and for non-residential training it has also dropped by several years to 42.) The male–female ratio is around 50:50, but with more women in part-time training than men; and vice-versa for residential training – a normal feature of the training context in England. The numbers in non-residential training covering the Oxford Ministry Course and the West of England Ministry Course – which are part of Cuddesdon – comprise around 80; those in residential training comprise around 70.

To complement this development, the Church of England has also witnessed a significant change in the range of contexts for formation and training. Thirty years ago, more than two-thirds of ordinands trained in residential colleges, with part-time training in non-residential courses a relative novelty. The tables are almost entirely turned at the beginning of the twenty-first century, with the majority of ordinands now being formed on a variety of non-residential courses. So although six of the 11 residential colleges are broadly evangelical (reflecting the popularity of that wing of the church), there are over two dozen regional training schemes and ordained local ministry courses. The latter are ecclesiologically and theologically broad, continuing to reflect the historic strength of and English spiritual proclivity for openness: articulate, conversational and inclusive breadth that serves the whole needs of the parish, rather than a particular confessional stance.

At the core of training and formation – and this will be true for almost all Anglican training institutions – is a commitment to interweaving theology with experience, and usually in some kind of dynamic reflective practice. Often this is done through the exercise of ministry: observing, participating, leading and then reflecting. In such a context, the experiences of ordinands can often be quite turbulent before they become fulfilling. They may undergo a process of 'dis-membership' before 're-membering', as they encounter a range of experiences and practices that can comfort and disturb in equal measure. The teaching underpinning this activity will most likely be constructive and edifying. Yet the very act of education (from *educare* – to literally 'draw out') can be costly – but an essential prerequisite to the process of trans-formation that ministerial formation is concerned with.

So the very nature of contemporary parochial ministry in England can place a demanding onus on institutions preparing individuals for the ministry of the church.[3] This might include, for example, instilling some sort of recognition that the (somewhat dubious) distinction between mission and maintenance is often a false dichotomy in the majority of parochial contexts, where the historic religious resonance of the church building will have a widespread (if sometimes unclear) spiritual significance. Thus, good maintenance of a building ('sermons in stone') is likely to be, *de facto*, good mission in any parochial context. The building may involve and affirm the neighbourhood in myriad ways (beyond the merely functional operation of providing a place for meeting), thereby nourishing social and spiritual capital. The relationship between a church and its people in many parishes is essentially perichoretic – the 'mutual indwelling' of various cultural and religious currents that blend and inter-penetrate, producing new spiritual meanings, whilst also maintaining distinctive sodalities. (Although my comments mostly relate to preparation for parish ministry, the church increasingly recognises that many engaged in training spend the majority of their ministry

---

[3]   See Torry, *The Parish*; Markham and Percy, *Why Liberal Churches Are Growing*; Percy, *Engaging with Contemporary Culture*.

in a variety of sector ministries, or possibly new and innovative missiological initiatives that are non-parochial.)

These remarks are perhaps especially suggestive for parochial ministry, but also for formation and theological education more generally, whether in residential or non-residential contexts. Quality may need to be valued more than quantity; pace, solidarity and connectedness more than haste, energy and apparent achievement. It may be important to encourage ordinands to see that the worth of affirming the resonance of the past may have a higher spiritual value than the apparent obviousness of the need for relevance and progress. Presence and deep relational engagement may have a greater missiological impact than overt evangelistic schema and initiatives. And clearly, the ministerial 'blend' of being and doing (i.e., the clergyperson as both contemplative and activist) may need to be adjusted in any transition from urban or suburban contexts to rural ministry. Context may have a direct bearing on theological output. In other words, theology can be a rather 'slow' discipline; it takes time to accrue wisdom for the journey. Part of the process of formation is to comprehend the vision for theological reflection, which is attending patiently and deliberately to all kinds of material. This means helping ordinands to 'loiter with intention' in issues and encounters; to consciously and purposefully dawdle in their deliberations, so that clarity and wisdom come to fruition. Theology is not a discipline for hurrying.

Some Characteristics of Formation

That said, what might some of the common denominators in formation within Anglican theological education be? Here I want to confine my observations to residential and non-residential education and training within the context of an Anglican seminary in England, and make some remarks about the shape of formation as it particularly relates to such institutions, rather than to elucidate the principles of theological reflection more generally.[4] I suspect that these observations will resonate with other parts of the Anglican Communion, and theologies of ministry in most mainline Protestant denominations. Here then, are several suggestions; a list that must be, clearly, far from exhaustive, and is

---

4   See for example Volf and Bass, *Practicing Theology*.

perhaps quite personal. I have listed several characteristics that I would venture are relatively common to flourishing institutions, although they are clearly rooted in my own experiences and expectations.

First, the individual and the institution are set apart for deep and rich composition. There must be some understanding that the person in training, as a character formed within the Christian story and the demands of the gospel, has responded to a vocational call, and has in some sense now been set apart. Ordination is the process and event whereby this calling is recognised, and then established in office. Correspondingly, one of the primary tasks of education and formation for ministry is to integrate the individual character with the catholicity of the office. One of my predecessors at Cuddesdon articulated some of the dynamics within this process, in his inimitable manner:

> (A priest) will not depend on status, nor upon his own abilities, nor upon a system, but upon God. (The primary quality) required is a man's sincerity in prayer and faith and compassion. These may yet be hardly developed, but the relevant signs will consist in obstacles overcome, work voluntarily undertaken and thoroughly performed, and a general attitude of responsibility as a Christian man rather than an interest in the social and ornamental aspects of the priesthood. Then they (the selectors) will look for something which can be described as a love of God's world and his people. Affectation and pretence are danger signs, and the sociability required of a priest consists in a spontaneity of interest in a world and a society of which he feels himself instinctively and naturally a part.[5]

Correspondingly, some understanding of the place or institution set apart for formation and training is also necessary, preferably with some evidence of the capacity to read the dense encryption of the distinctive ethos of the institution they are in, which is usually born out of an alloy of alliances. For example, Cuddesdon College was founded by Bishop Wilberforce in 1854 as a mainstream Anglican college, 'free from party and sectarian disputes'. That said, one should note the opposition to the founding of Anglican theological colleges in nineteenth-century England. Unlike the colonies, none existed in England before the early nineteenth century. There was initial suspicion and hostility directed towards the burgeoning

---

5   Runcie, *Church Observer*, p. 11.

number of new institutions that were founded, with fears expressed that education and formation for ministry taking place outside the control of the major universities could lead to elitism and sectarianism on the part of the church. As late as in 1921, Arthur Headlam, the then Regius Professor of Divinity of Oxford and a somewhat ambiguous conservative Churchman, wrote that:

> there is a great danger of theological teaching being given in theological colleges ... the students are trained exclusively according to one particular point of view. Their minds, instead of being accustomed to examining and weighing the merits of different opinions, become stereotyped ... The tendency of a theological college will be to give a man a set of opinions and to teach him to pass by and ignore those who differ from him. The tendency of a University is to make a man compare different points of view, to form his opinions after weighing alternatives, and therefore to hold the system which commends itself to him with due respect for the opinions of those who differ from him.[6]

Ripon Hall was first established at Ripon in 1898 by the diocesan bishop, William Boyd Carpenter, as a hostel for theological students. His vision for theological training was that 'ordinands had to take on board the new needs of society', and embrace the lessons that were to be found in life and learning outside the control of the church. The two institutions were merged in 1975, and their distinctive and combined ethos remains detectable. A third institution was added in 2006, with the incorporation of the Oxford Ministry Course, a non-party and non-residential training institution, which could legitimately claim to be faithful to the vision of both Wilberforce and Carpenter – broad and non-party in its ecclesiology, and open-minded in its theological outlook. Cuddesdon currently has more than 120 students training for ordained ministry in the Church of England: 65 per cent are residential, and 55 per cent are non-residential. This breadth, of course, is not without complications. Granted, theological programmes are aligned with the spiritual ethos (i.e., open, enquiring, etc.). But disagreement can be the price we pay for diversity and depth – as in any rich and cosmopolitan institution. But this is arguably preferable to the comforts of narrow confessional conformity, which can

---

[6]   Headlam, *Theological Education at the Universities*, p. 22.

breed its own tensions. So for ordinands, some understanding of the composition of the institution they are in will have a direct bearing on their own formation.

Second, formation is a progressive and subtle journey. Whatever a theological college is, it is not an ecclesiastical boot camp. There is no 39-buttoned-cassock drill sergeant to rouse the students to prayer. Yet most institutions, whether residential or non-residential, will speak quite naturally of 'the discipline of prayer' as foundational. But it will invariably be something that is instilled rather than imposed. Similarly, despite all the assignments and other tasks to complete, institutions will require their students to pay attention to the condition of the heart as much as the head. In that sense, the process of formation requires students to adopt a sense of perspective and pace; to borrow a phrase from Roosevelt, 'make haste slowly' (i.e., the Latin motto, *festina lente*). Discipleship is a marathon, not a sprint. Correspondingly, there has to be some trust in the continuing process of discernment, and less concern about the outcome: Christ is Lord of the Journey.

It therefore follows that ordinands should be encouraged to immerse themselves in the flow of what is happening; how they are becoming; and what they will be. Institutions invest much time and energy in trying to develop and cultivate a certain sagacity, shrewdness and wisdom for the journey ahead, to say nothing of emotional and ecclesial intelligence. But in pedagogical terms, this is more of an art than a science; a world for the reflective practitioner rather than the pure theorist. One writer (John Paul Lederach) invites us to engage and trust in a process that is sometimes led by the heart as much as the head. His advice provides a good fit for any 'recipe' in the field of theological education, reflection and formation:

> ...the more I wanted to intentionally produce a result, the more elusive it seemed to be; the more I let go and discovered the unexpected openings along the way, at the side of the journey, the more progress was made ... [The] greatest contributions to peace building did not seem to be those that emerged from accumulated skill or intentional purpose. They were those that happened unexpectedly. At a certain time, I came to call this divine naivety ... the practitioners' dilemma of learning more from mistakes than successes. But the reality was that they were not mistakes in the proper sense of the word; they were important things I learnt along the way that were not planned. I needed a

combination of [the] divine and naïve. [The] divine pointed to the transcendent and unexpected – but that led towards insight and better understanding. To see that which is not readily planned or apparent, however, requires a peripheral type of vision, the willingness to move sideways – and even backward – in order to move forward ... an innocence of expectation that watches carefully for the potential of building change in good and in difficult times ... foster[ing] the art of the possible ... the key is to [learn how] to build from the unexpected ... to connect [the apparently] accidental with sagacity ...[7]

Third, the type of knowledge acquired in formation is also at issue. Those charged with the ministry of oversight – in both sacred and secular spheres – often speak of *intuition* rather than extended calculation or analysis when dealing with 'unique situations to which they must respond under conditions of stress and limited time'.[8] This 'knack' or 'wisdom' depends on 'tacit knowing', where over-seers seldom turn to theories or methods in managing situations, but instead realise that their own effectiveness depends on having learnt (and continuing to learn) through the 'long and varied practice in the analysis of ... problems, which builds up a generic, essentially un-analyzable capacity for problem-solving'.[9] In other words, ordinands learn by experience in the field. Moreover it is probably the case that Anglicanism is often easier to identify through persons rather than systems: *examples* of faith and polity rather than theories of it. Here, the management of a congregation within the context of the challenges of contemporary culture is much more like a 'knack' than a skill; organising or shaping the church is about learned habits of wisdom more than it is about rules and theories.

Acknowledging the place of tacit and intuitive knowledge has important implications for teaching those engaged in the task of Christian leadership. It is in sharing – sometimes quite deeply, I think, and at quite a personal level – how issues are addressed and resolved, and how individuals and organisations fare in this, and what reflections or analysis one may have, that 'tacit knowledge' is built up – within relationships based on trust, such that the organisation may then experience both stability and a degree of transcendence. There is a valuable

---

7   Lederach, *The Moral Imagination*, p. 115 adapted.
8   Schon, *The Reflective Practitioner*, p. 239.
9   Ibid., p. 241.

repository of spiritual treasure in (dense, and occasionally tense) collegiality, and in the storied communion of shared wisdom. This is why the *character* of the theological college or non-residential course, as a community of fellow learners on the viaticum, is so important in formation and training. Thus, how we teach ordinands to 'hold' complex issues; the character that teachers and mentors exhibit under pressure; and how individuals continue to embody being the very best kinds of 'reflective practitioner' – these are the skills that often make their deep mark in the formational process.

Fourth, openness and vulnerability have a role in learning. Thinking and practising needs to be continually returned to the heart of the vocation, which is, of course, a mystery of risk. Unpacking it takes time and energy, but it also invites seminarians and ordinands to journey deeper into wisdom and wholeness. There is, therefore, a vested interest in encouraging students to engage with and encounter some of the things they might actually fear (e.g., issues, ideas, scenarios, etc.). This goes hand in hand with sounding the depths of the complexities of all kinds of encounters, and developing the habit of deep listening, of imagining beyond what is seen, and what presents on the surface. Risking vulnerability is part of the price we pay for love; and this kind of openness belongs to the economy of vocations. In this sense, every truly self-conscious theological college will know, somewhere, that all the members of its community are beginners.

To complement this, there must be the possibility of failure. However, it is also recognised that institutions are often best judged not by how many stellar scholars they produce, but by how they care for and mentor the weak and the vulnerable. Mistakes happen, and I think the best thing those charged with teaching and mentoring can try to do is encourage seminarians to learn from these things when they happen. Failure is not the worst thing; letting it utterly defeat you is. It takes a special kind of wisdom and courage to face failure and defeat, and then to try and move on from this. But this kind of maturity should perhaps especially be cultivated, in order to help cope with the reality of life's miscibility.[10]

Fifth, the relationships between embodiment, power and wisdom need continual exploration. There is arguably something to be said for a formational process that probes and loosens any relationships with power and privilege. It is perhaps good to be reminded that the gospel is about eternal rewards, not the temporal baubles of

---

[10]   Freire, *Pedagogy of the Heart*.

the church. Our eyes are to be fixed on Jesus, not on achievement. God is interested in: 'much more than a set of competencies. No accumulation of skills impresses God. God is interested in the heart of the priest, more than how impressive his or her curriculum vitae appears to be.'[11]

Yet there is no substitute for the cultivation of holy wisdom. All of us, I think, encounter projects and persons in ministry that either fail to turn out to be all that we hoped, or can even become arenas of defeat. It is reminiscent of what Graham Greene has to say in *The Power and the Glory*, namely that hatred is the failure of the imagination. Holy wisdom, then, is something related to but 'other' than conventional wisdom. It is an embodied form of spiritual intelligence that is more than mere shrewdness. It is interpretative, lived and transformative; and those who encounter it will more often speak of an epiphany than mere insight.

An Analogical Coda

In summary, there may be something to be said for theological institutions – of whatever tradition, and whether residential or non-residential – placing a stress on the great Benedictine virtues of hospitality, service and listening. Each of these is vital to the flourishing of the community of learning and the individual in formation. Being open to God, paying attention to others and deep listening – these are the profound spiritual exercises that allow individuals and communities (whether gathered or dispersed) to attend to the cadence, timbre and rhythm of what they are about. So how can we understand the dynamics that take place during ministerial training and formation? Mere description, I think, does not do justice to the depth and richness of the process that takes place. The language we need to capture the journey often comes to fruition by being framed in paradox. Paradoxical images include 'wise fool', 'servant-leader', 'wounded healer' and 'intimate stranger'. These images help frame the pastoral nature of ordained ministry, alongside the classic biblical models ('shepherd') and those drawn from contemporary life (e.g., coach, or manager, etc.).[12] And this is where the analogical imagination can be helpful. Thus, one aspect of what takes place in formation is

---

[11]   Pritchard, *The Life and Work of a Priest*, p. 4.
[12]   See Dykstra, *Images of Pastoral Care*.

that seminarians learn to find ourselves in what one writer describes as 'God's orchestra'. John Pritchard puts it like this:

> Christian leaders are like conductors of God's local orchestra. Our task is multi-layered. We have to interpret the music of the gospel to bring out all its richness and textures and glorious melodies. We have ourselves to be students of the music, always learning, and sharing, with the orchestra what both we and they have learned about this beautiful music. We have to help members of the orchestra to hear each other, and to be aware of each other as they play their 'instrument' or use their gift. Without that sensitivity to each other both an orchestra and a church descend into a cacophony of conflicting noises.[13]

To continue with this analogy, and to apply it more directly to theological institutions, three key observations seem to be particularly pertinent. First, whatever part one plays in the orchestra, institutions have to try and pay attention to the bass-line, and not to get overly distracted by the melody. The bass-line is all about patience, depth and pace. It may also contain the givens of theological discourse. It is about developing sustainable rhythms for the entire symphony – not just the short movements in which one part of the orchestra might mainly feature.

Second, teachers and mentors have the task of coaching and conducting. There may be some new scores to teach as well; and the performance of these helps to form the necessary skills in theological and pastoral discernment. In turn, this enables ordinands to develop intuition in relation to knowledge; to become reflexive, yet also sure-footed. Thus, institutions carry the responsibility for developing the natural and given talents, rather than simply replacing them with new instructions. Education is both input and drawing out, to enable spiritual, pastoral and intellectual flourishing.

Third, just as scripture is symphonic in character – many different sounds making a single, complex, but beautiful melody – so it is with God's church, and the institutions that equip ministers for the communities in which they serve. The task of the teacher and mentor is, then, not just to help students understand and critique the scores they read and perform, but also to try and help each seminarian

---

[13]   Pritchard, *The Life and Work of a Priest*, p. 109ff.

play beautifully and function faithfully – and all within the context of the diversity of the many different sounds and notes that God gives an institution to make.

Chapter 3

Yeast and Salt: Ministerial Formation for Rural Contexts

Not so long ago, the village of Elmdon could justly claim to be one of the most studied rural communities in England. Two anthropologists – Marilyn Strathern and Jean Robin – published their ground-breaking studies that explored the changing face of village life in rural Essex, and how these communities were evolving.[1] Robin's study charted continuity and change in village identity from the mid-nineteenth century through to the 1960s. Covering the ownership of land, labour, farming, marriage and social mobility, it is one of the first analyses that points to the present context of a typical rural village today. Namely, profound shifts in the composition of such communities; yet at the same time a sense of continuity with the past that seemed to be remarkably resilient.

Similarly, Strathern was able to map the underlying value-systems that seemed to shape community identity. This included the persistent notion of a 'Real Elmdon' (used to distinguish it from anything apparently alien or new), which she maintained was held through tightly formed patterns of kinship. Indeed, Strathern argued that the concept of kinship provided a vital key to understanding the delicate way in which the community was arranged. Kinship cuts across employment, class, gender and other apparent divisions, and identifies who 'really belongs' and who has yet to be integrated. To 'outsiders', the question as to who is a 'real' villager may seem unnecessarily parochial and quirky. Strathern showed, however, that kinship played a vital role in identifying Elmdon.

Both Robin and Strathern were able to foresee something of what the future might hold for villages such as Elmdon towards the end of the twentieth century

---

[1]   Robin, *Elmdon*; Strathern, *Kinship at the Core*.

and the beginning of the twenty-first. Factors included increasing numbers of commuters, who would slowly turn the community into a predominantly dormitory village. Less work would be available for local people, as rural industries changed or disappeared. Rising house prices would force some settled and established forms of kinship to become more attenuated, as the economic pressures caused greater degrees of familial dispersal. The effect of this, ironically, is often to intensify a sense of community identity. Resilience is manifested in both resistance and accommodation. (Indeed, this kind of outlook can powerfully influence the whole approach to rural ministry, especially in the occasional offices.[2])

Yet despite the depth of their ethnography and anthropological analysis, Robin and Strathern devoted little time to the church itself. This omission is comprehensible, in some sense. The blindness to the presence of the church arises directly out of a collation of social sciences that colluded with the classic secularisation theses from the 1960s. These tended to stress the increasing impotency of 'established' religion, and assumed that its residual power lay merely in rituals that affirmed kinship, ties to the land, the capacity to engage folk religion and the rites of passage that marked generational continuity and change. The authors therefore might be surprised to see that many rural churches are surviving in the twenty-first century or even flourishing, occupying a pivotal position in their respective communities. In some cases, the church will be the sole public community building remaining; not only a spiritual amenity, but also a place for the whole village to gather. In other cases, the church will have a key role in supporting or hosting a Post Office or small shop, and acting as a conduit for a range of voluntary and care services.

As David Martin has noted, churches are markers and anchors in many rural communities; the primary or sole repository of all-embracing meanings pointing beyond the immediate to the ultimate.[3] Rural churches are institutions that deal in tears and concern themselves with the breaking points of human existence. They provide frames of reference, narratives and signs to live by. And they continue to offer persistent points of reference that are beyond consumerism, fashion or other forms of transitory existence. This is why burial places can be so important – the availability of a public space that still enables a real relationship between the living

---

[2]   For further discussion, see Clark, *Between Pulpit and Pew.*
[3]   Martin, *On Secularization.*

and the dead to be appropriately maintained. Moreover, this is not mere maintenance. Rather, it is mission – providing the space in which people can live and move and have their being, within a context of bereavement and its attendant ministry.

Contemporary English church-going habits correlate with the two main religious economies that can be observed in Europe. The first is a 'market model', which assumes voluntary membership will soon become the norm. The second model is 'utility', where membership is ascribed rather than chosen. In the first model, individuals opt in to become 'members'. In the second model, all in some sense are deemed to 'belong', unless they opt out. The two models are in partial tension, and arguably depend upon each other. One may further characterise these differences as 'intensive' and 'extensive' forms of ecclesial polity. Some sociologists of religion think the extensive will not be able to survive without the intensive. Some ecclesiologists think that the intensive is fundamentally dependent upon the extensive.

The dominant paradigm for rural ministry in England is essentially 'utility-extensive'. Indeed, many forms of 'market-intensive' ecclesial polity have been evaporating from English villages in the post-war era – often leaving Anglican churches and ministers to cater for residual non-conformist congregations. Correspondingly, appropriate initial and continuing ministerial training may need to pay careful attention to a variety of relationships (e.g., land and people; economy and ecosystems; tradition and values; continuity and innovation; constructions of 'local' identity; politics and culture; collaboration and rivalry; etc.), and work within contexts that are simultaneously delicate and robust, as well as reticulate, subtle and discrete.

The nature of contemporary rural life places some interesting demands and challenges upon the ministry of the church. These include the recognition that the (somewhat dubious) distinction between mission and maintenance – so easily assumed in urban and suburban contexts – is a false dichotomy in the majority of rural contexts. Good maintenance is likely to be, *de facto*, good mission. It involves and affirms the wider community, thereby nourishing social and spiritual capital. The relationship between a church and its people in many rural village contexts is essentially perichoretic – the 'mutual indwelling' of various cultural and religious currents that blend and inter-penetrate, yet also maintain their distinctive identities.

Formation for Ministry

This is especially suggestive for ministerial formation and education. Quality may need to be valued more than quantity. Affirming the resonance of the past may have a higher spiritual value than the apparent obviousness of the need for relevance and progress. Presence and deep relational engagement may have a greater missiological impact than overt evangelistic schema and initiatives. The ministerial 'blend' of being and doing (i.e., the clergyperson as both contemplative and activist) may need to be adjusted in any transition from urban or suburban contexts to rural ministry. Because rural ministry may only have one 'professional' clergyperson for several parishes, she or he will normally fare better as a generalist than as a specialist; as a person of breadth and accommodation rather than being overly particular in theological outlook; of accepting the prioritisation of extensity (partly brought about by there being less choice) instead of the comfort of distinctive intensity.

Lest this sound too romantic – and the reality of rural ministry is that it often suffers from being misconstrued as some kind of idyll-type activity – there can be no question that recent political, economic and cultural challenges have transformed the landscape of perception. Whilst every generation that has ever lived has faced its own modernity, the rural ministry of today is clearly different from that which was known by George Herbert, Parson Woodforde and other classic exemplars from previous centuries. Rural ministry is now, arguably, at the 'cutting edge' of the church (i.e., the most obvious and identifiable model of 'utility-extensive' ecclesial polity, and therefore of 'classic' English Anglicanism); is therefore sustainable, as well as under threat; and is arguably one of the more challenging and rewarding contexts for ministry at present.

But what kind of preparation is needed for this ministry? The most obvious thing to say about the purpose of ordination training – formation and education for ordained ministry – is that it isn't immediately obvious. What, after all, is one being prepared for? Indeed, what is ministry *like*? It is like nothing else, I think – in that sense that it is hard to establish any kind of professional boundary between practitioner and client in the way, perhaps, that a doctor, dentist, lawyer, teacher or other professional might. Clergy are available to their people – and mostly anytime, in any place and anywhere. Clergy cannot easily seal themselves off from those for whom they have a care for, or the cure of souls. 'Off duty' is a noble sentiment, but for many or most clergy, ultimately inimical to the depth of their vocation. So the formation and training that clergy have is, for the most part, a schooling in the deepening of virtue and character, in which the overt curriculum serves a deeper, more hidden purpose: training for righteousness and spiritual resilience.

Yet this is not quite so. Students preparing for ordained ministry – in whatever institution they are being trained, formed and educated – can point to a curriculum (usually with a multiplicity of options, but also a 'core'); some kind of disciplined approach to prayer and worship; an ecclesial tradition that (at least) adds some kind of accent to the ethos of the institution; some practical assignments that continue to test the depth and trajectory of a vocation; and a continuous process of theological reflection that links the personal, social, intellectual and transcendent dynamics of formation. It is purposeful, too – as this rather light-hearted (but affectionate) description suggests:

> Our ordinands are only allowed to graze on the richest, most fertile theology. We don't use artificial preservatives, cut corners or mass-produce to grow our students. We simply combine centuries of tradition and know-how with wisdom and new insights. This natural diet is complemented by a fresh, open, organic approach to formation, which together with our own cutting-edge research, provides them with some of the finest training pastures available. We hope you like the results: super, natural clergy.[4]

Yet such a sketchy and skeletal outline of the priorities for theological education affords considerable licence to any ecclesial tradition and its training institutions. What then, can be said about Anglican theological education? And what of formation and training for rural ministry? Few, if any clergy are now able to focus on a single parish for ministry. Many now preside over multi-parish benefices, often with several villages and churches to care for. Spiritual engagement is stretched and challenged, perhaps as never before. For some, this is deeply frustrating. As Denham Grierson suggests, 'the seminary gives you an

---

4   Text from a Cuddesdon student T-shirt.

ideal picture of the church – it is difficult, in the light of all that we are told about the church to accept what the local congregation really is'.[5]

Context and Challenge

That the Church of England faces a crisis is hardly news. It does so in every age, and those that face ours are both new and familiar. However, there is considerable reason to be realistic about the issues the church will need to address, if the church is to continue being resilient as an institution, a vital spiritual resource for the nation and a rich reservoir of religious hope for generations to come. Yet some recent statistics for the Church of England (2010/11) are instructive. They reveal an alarming fall in baptisms, weddings and funerals, as well as Sunday attendance and the numbers of full-time clergy. Few places record any measurable numerical growth. But there are other fascinating statistics too, revealing that less than half of our churches have toilets and kitchen facilities, and less than half do anything involving the community on church premises. So whilst we worry about mission and evangelism strategies, and fret about and the declining numbers in the pews, we seem to have simply forgotten to engage in the complexity of theology (and community ministry) in the public square, which might inspire a wider public.

Clergy numbers are also a cause for some concern. There are just over 5,000 full-time paid clergy (i.e., Vicars, Rectors, etc.) in parish ministry at present caring for the country's 50 million people. This means that each full-time vicar will be looking after an average of three church buildings in 2.5 parishes containing 10,000 people between them, with 200 regular (once a month or more) worshippers. They will take an average of 29 baptisms a year, see five new people confirmed and take 12 weddings and 34 funerals per year. And they'll each have roughly one church school, no doubt with a 'tradition' that the vicar is chair of governors. And they'll be encouraged to develop 'fresh expressions of church' as well.

So the scale of challenge in ministry is rooted in facing the context of that ministry – honestly and squarely. Visions for growth, coupled with targets and plans, are all well and good. But the church needs to engage with what it actually is and faces if it is to be transformative. Indeed, this is an essential prerequisite to

---

5   Grierson, *Transforming a People of God*, p. 18.

the process of trans-formation that ministerial formation is concerned with, and perhaps especially in rural contexts. Church growth, when it happens, at least in the developed world, can often a by-product of religious competition. Indeed, it cannot escape being an outcome of capitalism. Competition in healthy climes, means more and better choice, even in religion. But this tends not to work in rural areas where there is little choice – the same applies to the US, although mobility is usually better. Likewise in deprived urban areas, where few may venture, and one denomination may function as the 'church for all'. Likewise in cultures and communities (especially, perhaps those that are rural – including North American) where choice, competition and individuation may be less valued.

Church growth thinking and practice, of course, *does* work in capitalist and consumerist societies; and, critically, in prosperous urban and suburban contexts. But as Gibson Winter pointed out several decades ago in *The Suburban Captivity of the Churches*, our churches can lose senses of time, patience, depth and relationality when they become subject to programmes originating from suburban contexts, and invariably rooted in assumptions about growth and effectiveness. Thus, and as James Hopewell perceptively observed:

> Rather than assume that the primary task of ministry is to alter the congregation, church leaders should make a prior commitment to understand the given nature of the object they propose to improve. Many strategies for operating upon local churches are uninformed about the cultural constitution of the parish; many schemes are themselves exponents of the culture they seek to overcome.[6]

One might add a loud 'Amen' to such sentiments. But what exactly does Hopewell mean when he suggests that clergy are often 'uninformed about the cultural constitution of the parish'? One fertile notion that comes from the vocabulary of sommeliers might be helpful here. 'Terroir' is a Gallic word for which there is no English equivalent. The term refers to the combination of factors that make one wine slightly different from another, even when they are geographically proximate. Sunshine and temperature; north or south facing, and the amount of rainfall; the height of the land and the drainage, the type and acidity of the soil, the types and subtypes of grape, and their progeny; local know-how

---

6   Hopewell, *Congregation*, p. 11.

and human skill; the amount of time permitted for a wine to mature, and the types of barrels chosen: all combine to make wines taste different.

This accounts for why one Burgundy tastes quite different from another, even though they might be from the same village. And this analogy has something to teach theologians as they reflect on the composition of local ecclesial identity. On one level, church is church, just as wine is wine. Yet to the refined palate, the differences are detectable and telling. The ecclesial history and ethos of one rural church might be composed through all manner of stories, buildings, forms of organisation, ecclesial and theological accents; and an adjacent church, in a similar context, might turn out to be entirely different. And arguably, it is only through deep and patient immersion and reflection – the refining of the palate, in effect – that good mission can be undertaken.

The 'ecclesial terroir', in other words, is something that a minister needs to be able to read sensitively and deeply if they are to cultivate congregational life and offer connected parochial ministry. Moreover, if a minister is overseeing several rural churches, their clustering together, for organisational purposes, will seldom disguise the fact that although roughly proximate, each congregation will have a slightly different feel, flavour, history and dialect. (Rather as in anthropological terms, neighbouring tribes in a given place can be very different. Indeed, the surfacing and expression of difference is what makes identity possible.) So ministerial formation and training will, at this point, need to find ways of providing deeper forms of discernment that enable ministers to move beyond the surface or presenting task of demand-led organisation, and make time and space to read each congregation and parish as a semi-discrete but related locally distinctive expression of Christian faith.

These brief remarks are perhaps especially suggestive for rural ministry, but also for formation and theological education more generally, whether in residential or non-residential contexts. Context may indeed have a direct bearing on theological output. In other words, theology can be a rather 'slow' discipline; it takes time to accrue wisdom for the journey. Part of the process of formation is to comprehend the vision for theological reflection, which is attending patiently and deliberately to all kinds of material. This means helping ordinands to 'loiter with intention' (or 'deep hanging out', as one anthropologist puts it) within issues and over encounters; to consciously and purposefully dawdle in their deliberations, so that clarity and wisdom come to fruition. Theology is not a discipline for hurrying.

Re-Thinking Growth

Arguably, Karl Barth understood something of the necessary patience required in rural ministry, and from his Swiss canton penned these words:

> The true growth which is the secret of the upbuilding of the community is not extensive but intensive; its vertical growth in height and depth ... It is not the case that its intensive increase necessarily involves an extensive. We cannot, therefore, strive for vertical renewal merely to produce greater horizontal extension and a wider audience ... If it [the Church and its mission] is used only as a means of extensive renewal, the internal will at once lose its meaning and power. It can be fulfilled only for its own sake, and then – unplanned and unarranged – it will bear its own fruits.[7]

But what might Barth mean by this? He has several things in mind, I suspect, but for the purposes of this brief chapter, three merit noting. First, that rural churches and ministries may need to be genuinely patient and resilient. They have vested interests in continuity and perpetuity. This means that a (quick) results-orientated immediacy often has to be set aside in favour of something more natural, organic and slower. Sustaining and maintaining is as important as changing. Second, there is a sense in which Barth clearly understands our earlier reference to utility-extensity and market-intensity models of the church. And theologically, Barth graciously points out that that intensity cannot be adopted in order to produce extensity. Third, Barth goes some way to redeeming the notion of intensity, by suggesting that a more concentrated focus on God is at the heart of all good ministry, but that this does not necessarily lead to the kind of extensive growth one might witness in a city or suburban context. Quality of discipleship, in other words – the sheer faithfulness of ministries – may not necessarily lead to quantifiable results.

---

[7]   Barth, *Church Dogmatics*, IV, ii, chap. 15, p. 648.

So what of a vision for formation and training for ministry in rural contexts? Jesus, interestingly, offers quite a range of powerful organic or 'natural' metaphors that may be of some help to us here. But I want to focus on just two for the moment – yeast and salt: 'He told them still another parable: "The kingdom of heaven is like yeast that a woman took and mixed into a large amount of flour until it worked all through the dough"' (Matthew 13:33). Here, Jesus tells us most of what we probably need to know about ministry. He suggests that the kingdom of heaven is like yeast that is mixed in with dough. Yeast? That microbe fungi? That discard-able and forgettable material that is, oddly, the key to so much of our lives? It would seem so. For yeast is what ferments the wine and beer; and it makes the dough rise to make the bread. It is the tiny, insignificant catalyst for our basic commodities and the formation of our communities. The leaven in the lump; the difference between bread and dough; juice and wine; refreshment and celebration.

Yeast is, of course, small. Moreover, it is lost and dispersed into the higher purposes to which it is given. And when Jesus talks about the kingdom of God as yeast – and our ministries too – he is not advocating the concentrate of *Marmite* in a jar: yeast for the sake of yeast. Rather, in Jesus' imagination, we are invited to purposely disperse. To lose ourselves in something much bigger. But not pointlessly. Rather, in 'dying' to our context, we activate it. We become the catalyst that brings flavour, strength, depth, potency and growth. Without yeast, there is no loaf; just dough. Literally, we die to ourselves for growth. We are the ingredient that makes bread for the world.

But this is not a call to dying or dissolving. God wants us alive, not dead. (Actually, the more alive the better.) So the notion of our ministry is not that we are the yeast, *per se*; but rather that we offer a yeast-like type ministry. It is about being the agent of transformation that is often small, or even unseen. It is about being immersed so deeply in the world and the parish that the depth of growth is often unquantifiable. As Einstein once said, that which truly counts in life can seldom be counted. The work of yeast is one of deep fission.

Baking bread, if you have ever done it, is rewarding work and very therapeutic. But it also offers us a rich analogy for what we are about. John Paul Lederach, in his *Moral Imagination*, offers a rich meditation on our calling to be yeast. Consider this. The most common ingredients for making bread are water, flour, salt, sugar and yeast. Of these, yeast is the smallest in quantity, but the only one that makes a substantial change to all the other ingredients. Lederach says you only need a few people to change a lot of things.

So yeast, to be useful, needs to move from its incubation and be mixed into the process – out of the seminary and into the parish. Clergy (like the proverbial manure), do the most good when they are spread around. But yeast also needs to grow – it requires the right mix of moisture, warmth and sugar. And it initially needs covering and cultivating before it is ready to do its work. (The analogy for training and formation could hardly be more fruitful here.) Only then should the yeast mix with the greater mass. In bread, it is kneaded into the dough; it requires a bit of muscle. And it also requires someone else to light the fire to make the oven. Bread, in other words, is not just about the yeast, but about a context – one of feeding, desire, need and the skills of others. So in talking about small fungi that produce change and growth, Jesus is asking us to imagine his kingdom – one in which tiny spores mixed in to the social mass can make a massive difference. One of my predecessors at Cuddesdon had this to say about 'classic' parochial ministry:

> Confronted by the wistful, the half-believing and the seeking, we know what it
> is to minister to those who relate to the faith of Christ in unexpected ways. We
> do not write off hesitant and inadequate responses to the gospel. Ours is a church
> of the smoking flax, of the mixture of wheat and tares. Critics may say that we
> blunt the edge of the gospel and become Laodicean. We reply that we do not
> despise the hesitant and half-believing, because the deeper we look into human
> lives the more often we discern the glowing embers of faith.[8]

Similarly, Jesus also invokes his disciples to be the 'salt of the earth'. Matthew 5:13 reads: 'You are the salt of the earth; but if salt has lost its taste, how can its saltiness be restored? It is no longer good for anything, but is thrown out and trampled under foot.'[9] In interpreting this text, most preachers and many bible commentaries work with a false assumption: that the 'salt' in this text is the white granular chemical we know as sodium chloride, normally found in a condiment set or kitchen cupboard, where its purpose is to add flavour to foods, or occasionally to act as a purifier or preservative.

---

[8]   Avis, *A Church Drawing Near*, p. 18.
[9]   *Holy Bible: The New Revised Standard Version.*

Yet the fact that Jesus refers to 'the salt *of the earth*' ought to immediately alert us to another meaning for the text. The 'salt' (*halas*) mentioned in the text is hardly likely to be table salt, since it is a chemical and culinary improbability that sodium chloride will lose its flavour. Any salt that is extracted from food, water or any other substance remains 'salty'; even if it loses its form, it retains its essence, as many a spoilt meal and frustrated chef can bear witness.

The substance of Jesus' words are, in Greek, *to halas tes ges*, 'the salt *of the earth*', with the word for 'earth' here not referring to the world at all, but rather to soil. In other words, the 'salt' that Jesus is referring to here is probably a kind of salt-like material or mineral such as potash or phosphate. These *halas* elements were available in abundance in and around the Dead Sea area of Palestine, and were used for fertilising the land and enriching the manure pile, which was then spread on the land.

There are further clues as to why our usual understanding of this text is in some respects flawed. The word 'taste' that features in most English versions of this passage is actually a poor translation of the Greek word 'moranthe', which literally means 'to become foolish'. (The English word 'moron' is derived from the term.) A number of translators render the word as 'tainted', but 'loses its strength' is probably the best way to translate the word: loss of strength and foolishness would have been synonymous in Jesus' age. Moreover, and ironically, although paved paths also have their uses, Jesus' salt is arguably never 'useless'.[10]

The soil, of course, contains many different elements, all of which are intertwined. 'Soil', then, is a kind of cipher for the particular cultural contexts (i.e., religion, culture, ideology, etc.), in which Christians are to 'be salt'. The many soils of the world carry, in various degrees, qualities of empowerment and disempowerment within cultures. Moreover, in a post-modern world, we can now see that culture is being increasingly homogenised through globalisation, which has brought with it materialism, individualism, consumerism and hedonism, with the undesirable result of suffocating the life-giving force of the earth.

The empowering mission of the Church, like the salt of Jesus' parable, has a consistency of power. However, that power, enculturated into contexts, does not

---

[10]   For a fuller discussion of this passage see Shillington, 'Salt of the Earth?'. Cf. Luke 14:39. Interestingly, the *New Jerusalem Bible* is the only modern translation that renders the Greek correctly with 'you are the salt *for* the earth'.

lead to uniformity. Rather, it leads to considerable diversity of expression, growth and human flourishing. The salt has always to respect the type of earth in which it is situated. Diverse cultural sensibilities have to be taken into account in the mission of the Church. The soil can also be inhospitable: it may be rocky, thorny and adversely affected by climatic conditions. Under these circumstances, the task of being the salt of the earth is more demanding.

A key to understanding the relationship between Church and culture rests on a tension. On the one hand, Christians are to be engaged in the world and influence it, perhaps in ways that are not easily identified as specifically 'Christian'. The power of salt is that it is pervasive, and nourishing. Here, the church accommodates culture; Christ is therefore, in some sense, *for* culture. On the other hand, Christianity also proclaims God's Kingdom – a radically 'other' culture that will sweep away the present order. This is the beacon of light set on a hill: it illuminates the present, but points to a new order. This is the Christ who is above or against culture. The church seeks a kingdom that is to come, and it therefore resists the standards of the world.

Accommodation and resistance are, of course, closely related. What they share, in character, is resilience. We might say that accommodation is a 'soft' form of resilience: flexible, pliable, adaptable and so forth. Whilst resistance is a 'hard' form of resilience: concrete, unyielding and defiant. The true character of ecclesial resilience – construed in almost any local church context – will show that most congregations will simultaneously resist and accommodate culture. The church, albeit unconsciously for the most part, understands that it lives between two cultures.

This way of understanding the *halas* (salt) of Jesus' metaphor changes the sense of the text significantly. In fact, it completely undermines the most conventional translations and expositions. The 'salt' is not to be kept apart from society, and neither is it to be used as a purifier or as an additive stabiliser. Ministers are not to be simply preservers of the good society, and neither are they merely agreeable folk adding flavour to either an amoral or immoral society. More powerfully and positively, true religion, as salt, is a life-bringing force giving itself to an otherwise sterile culture.

Thus, the 'salt' of Jesus' metaphor is a mutating but coherent agent that is both distinct yet diffusive in its self-expenditure. As a result of individuals, communities, values, witness and presence – the *halas* – being literally dug into society, the earth or soil will benefit, and many forms of life can then flourish. Correspondingly, salt that loses its strength (rather than its 'flavour' – the more usual translation) is only suitable for making paths, as the biblical text confirms. Thus, the salt of Jesus' metaphor is not only counter-cultural; it enriches 'the earth' and many more things besides, by being spread around and within it.

So there is an irony here. The 'task' of the salt is not necessarily to maintain its own distinctiveness, but rather to enrich society through diffusiveness. There is a temporal dimension here: what must begin as distinct to be useful ends up being absorbed and lost. Of course, this reading of the metaphor makes sense of Jesus' own self-understanding, which in turn is reflected in his parables, teachings and other activities. So, if the church or the disciples of Jesus are the salt of the earth, they will begin by being a distinct yet essential component within society, but who will ultimately fulfil their vocation by engaging self-expenditure.

Conclusion

What, then, are the practical implications for training and formation in rural ministry arising from these two organic metaphors? Three brief points can be made by way of conclusion. First, the yeast is suggestive insofar as it reminds churches and ministers that Christianity is about change and conversion. But that such transformation is often natural and organic, rather than traumatically disruptive. Nonetheless, the church is to be a catalyst, not just a catacomb. Second, the salt suggests that a patient vocation of nourishing lies at the heart of many rural ministries. To actively engage in the nourishment of the soil is to be committed to a time-consuming and costly process that will *not* yield instant results. Moreover, the 'salting' of the soil is about broad coverage – a deep and extensive parochial exercise rather than something solely concentrated in congregations or in confessional particularity. Third, ministers need to develop a wisdom that can both resist and accommodate culture, but set within a broader understanding of how the church (and its tradition, the gospel, etc.) remains fundamentally resilient. Training in colleges, courses and in post-ordination schemes therefore needs to continually develop forms of theological reflection that help ministers surface the tensions and changes that are part and parcel of rural life. It also needs to equip ordinands to be animators and mobilisers in mission, as well as providing pastoral enablement and consistency. The call for clergy is, in other words, to be agents of change as well as continuity. For both change and continuity are at the heart of the gospel, just as they are the very centre of good, balanced rural mission and ministry.

And finally, to return to Elmdon. A community that is seemingly unchanged, and yet now enjoys a plethora of identities. And arguably has never been broader in its composition; the inhabitants ranging from commuters, those working more locally to those who have retired to the village because of its relative proximity to Cambridge. It has also been ministered to as a single community, and now as part of a team. And with ordinands from nearby theological colleges adding to richness now provided by Readers, NSM clergy, associate and retired priests, as well as laity and other kinds of support.

It is ironic that this new breadth and emergent diversity in Elmdon – seen by 'real villagers' as the apparent fragmentation of its true identity – now presents the church with a fresh opportunity. To be the gathering place in a community that needs to find new and old purpose in being knit together. To bring 'locals' and 'strangers' together; to foster relations between established families and newcomers; to create a genuine community of worship that expresses the complexity and richness of the parish, in its emerging composition. Kinship is indeed at the core of this. But it is the kind of kinship of the kingdom that Jesus speaks of that is to be fostered; something in the world, but not exactly of it.

Chapter 4

Pitching Tents: Formational Sketches
on Sacred Space

In *The Illusionist* (French: *L'Illusionniste*), an animated film directed by Sylvain Chomet in 2010, and based on an unproduced script dating from 1956 by the French mime, director and actor, Jacques Tati, we encounter a modern parable of religion and public life. Of sorts. The main character in the animated version of the Tati story is an illusionist (magician), who plays the theatres and music halls of France and London. But much to his puzzlement, he is rapidly watching his career give way to rock and roll, and to the emerging popular culture that would come to dominate the 1960s. In the film, this new mood of modernity is represented by the advent of modern technology, and specifically electricity – guitars, lighting and amplification – none of which the illusionist requires for his trade.

We see the illusionist head off to new virginal pastures, unsullied by the advances of modernity and technology, and the animated story follows him to a community that bears more than a passing resemblance to the Island of Iona. Here, he books in to a guest house – the Abbey Church clearly visible in the background – and that evening entertains the Gaelic community with his repertoire. The villagers are awestruck. We sense that the illusionist has finally found a place that will truly appreciate his talents – disappearing rabbits in hats, bouquets of flowers pulled from coat sleeves and coins found behind children's ears – an environment where he is no longer competing with modernity.

The evening is a great success. But as the illusionist soon discovers, the whole community has not come together to marvel at his magic. They are there in the bar to celebrate the ceremonial turning on of a single light bulb. Electricity has arrived on the island. And before the evening is over, the pub landlord has pulled out a brand new juke box from the cellar. Everyone dances – not to the sound of the Gaelic fiddle, but to the new sounds from the juke box, and under the perpetual lighting that is now strung across the bar. There is, it seems, no place left on earth where the illusionist can hold people in awe with his magic. Technology and modernity are in the ascendancy.

The illusionist leaves Iona. But he is followed by a young girl who is smitten with his art, and they go to Edinburgh together. Here the illusionist tries to ply his trade again, but all we see are a few old people and a tiny number of children. His magic no longer holds people in any kind of thrall. He is forced to get a job in a garage to make ends meet, whilst the young girl tends to their lodgings. There is a brief revival, of sorts. The illusionist is hired to do magic in a shop window for passing customers, but it is schematised around the products the store is promoting. The work soon goes awry, and our last glimpse of magic at work in the public sphere is a turbaned magician (a Turk – perhaps representing Islam?), who sticks at the job well, but with ever-depleting audiences. The story ends with the magician leaving the girl, who has found love with a boy of her own age. The message of the film is that illusions do not work: only love is real, and we must seek it and find it.

I should say at the outset that Tati's intention in writing the story was almost certainly autobiographical. Conjecture from theorists suggests that he wrote the story for the daughter he had become estranged from (Helga Marie-Jeanne Schiel). So the story is not a romance, but rather a complex narrative about a father and daughter, and one that both apologises for and partly justifies the absent father.

And yet I think Tati, and especially the interpretation given by Chomet, is also capable of being read parabolically. Tati set his original script in Czechoslovakia. Chomet's choice of Scotland, and Iona indeed, in the 1950s, is therefore intriguing. Moreover, the resonances with the story of religion in late European modernity can hardly go unnoticed. The illusionist is applying a kind of priestcraft, and as modernity and technology advance, he is driven in to more rural, marginal and basic communities where his work still captures the imagination and inspires awe. When even this fails, he is reduced to aligning his magic to a more subservient end, namely commercialism. But by now, religion (in the form of magic) is truly marginalised. Only the very old and the very young are watching; the rest are indifferent.

The film's ending sums up the apparent fate of religion in public life and space. There is no mystery and awe in a world shaped by modernity and technology. There is only love and each other – and this is the rather hopeful and hopeless note the film leaves the viewer with. The illusionist retires, in an echo of T.S. Eliot's poetry – motoring and modernity have taken over. Religion can no longer enchant and hold the public spaces as it once did.

I am well aware that this is a contentious and rather forced reading of Chomet's animated film. Yet it serves to highlight how easily space is taken for granted, and what the empty or filled places of modern life might be saying about religious purposes and Christian identity. With reference to three brief sketches, I intend to highlight how we can see and imagine space differently – and in a theologically literate way – that resonates with the insights and imagination we commonly find in the writings of Richard Giles. His work has had a significant impact on clergy and churches in recent years, and most especially for his theological considerations and observations on sacred space

This is not, however, a direct engagement with his books and lectures on the uses of space for worship and enchantment. Rather, this chapter is an intentional analogical expansion of Richard Giles' work, and is therefore an invitation to the reader to begin to read spaces and places in ways that are theologically literate and culturally prescient. Inevitably, this is tendentious in places – but my sense of Richard's writings is that this very same cadence and timbre is detectable in the analytical descriptions we find, for example, in *Re-Pitching the Tent: Re-Ordering the Church Building for Worship and Mission* (1999) and *Always Open: Being an Anglican Today* (2005) – and this chapter is inspired and prompted by the kinds of theological fusions and accents that Richard expresses in his work. I also owe a debt to Stephen Pickard's reflections, and especially his paper, 'Church of the In-between God: Recovering an Ecclesial Sense of Place Down-Under' (2009). Here, Pickard teases apart the dialectic of space and place more formally, to reflect on how the places of Australian Anglican identity are shaped by the spaces they inhabit. In this chapter, I use the space–place dialect more broadly.[1]

---

[1]   See also Inge, *A Christian Theology of Place.*

Sketches on Space, Place, Ministry and Meaning

To that end, we turn to three brief sketches. And we begin by noting that the very nature of contemporary parochial ministry in England can place a demanding onus on institutions preparing individuals for the ministry of the church. Despite the undoubted decline in church-going, opinion polls and surveys consistently show that anything from two-thirds to over three-quarters of the population believe in God. In recent history, this has comforted many clergy, who have understood the English to be 'believing without belonging', and worked their parish ministry within that paradigm. Of course, it is now no longer as simple as that. Contemporary cultural commentators tend to talk excitedly of 'pastiche spirituality'; academics, more reservedly, of 'religious pluralism'; and church leaders, nervously, of 'syncretism'. Many mainstream Christian denominations no longer enjoy the coherence of a homogeneous culture: movements *within* them are trying to transform them. The 'New Age', growing exposure to other religions, globalisation and privatisation have driven many to interrogate their faith, and then adapt it.

Thus, and in spite of the numbers of people who claim to believe in God, the undeniable reality is that England is shifting from being a 'Christian nation' to a spiritually diverse society. Moreover, there is evidence to suggest that individuals are beginning to be more inventive with their spiritual lives, assembling private faiths from religious bits and pieces; what is created has meaning and coherence for its creator. Quite simply, the term 'spiritual' has now become rather spongy: it seems to lack definition, and yet soak up virtually anything and everything.

So the spiritual relationship between individuals, communities and their buildings is perhaps an even more complex one in the twenty-first century, and one that merits some elucidation in terms of implicit theology. Even a simple shared space such as a student or community common room can suggest a complex nexus of theological formation and ecclesial participation. For example, I am often struck by how students, spouses and children inhabit the common room at our college in Cuddesdon – the place where Richard Giles was initially trained, educated and formed for ministry.

There are three entrances or exits to the room, a small bar and a variety of different types and heights of seating – fixed benches, comfy (and rather worn) sofas and easy chairs and some upright chairs positioned informally around tables. The room is arranged in such a way that it is easy to move in and out, yet also linger and chat. Smaller and larger conversations are possible, and the room as a whole manages to feel both snug and open – helped by a fireplace that is one of just several focal points. The room, in other words, is a kind of parable of Anglicanism: it embraces commonality and diversity. It is neither circular nor square; but rather a kind of parallelogram that invites movement and circulation. It is also a place of both settling and journeying; literally a *via media*, expressed in architectural form. The layout of this one room is also matched by the overall architectural layout of the buildings – open in texture, facing outwards to horizons both near and far, and yet sufficiently composed to convey a sense of being apart from its environment as well as within it.

Whether or not the architect (G.E. Street) designed the buildings to somehow be a lived parable of (idealised) broad Anglican identity cannot be known. But what can be said is that the way in which the rooms and spaces are occupied is a matter of deep interest to those who are concerned with the articulation of implicit theology. Here, how space is inhabited and understood has a deep impact on formation and identity, and on composition and vocation. If further proof were needed of this, one need only observe how other similar spaces are used in other institutions, yet in very different ways.

At a neighbouring theological college, the common room has only one entrance. The chairs – all of one kind – are laid out to both sides of a rectangular room, with a path dividing the chairs; an aisle within a nave comes to mind. Students therefore tend to cluster (if standing) in the aisle, or sit in small groups with their backs turned to other groups if they occupy the seats. It is the very antithesis of the first room described. Standing in the centre means that pathways are blocked; but being seated is also, potentially, an exclusive decision. The layout of the room, in other words, is uncomfortable for ambivalent lingering, and forces people into choices. The composition of the room (matching theological ethos), is somewhat divisive in character.

These remarks are perhaps especially suggestive for parochial ministry, but also for formation and theological education more generally, whether in residential or non-residential contexts. Quality may need to be valued more than quantity; pace, solidarity and connectedness more than haste, energy and apparent achievement.

It may be important to encourage ordinands to see that the worth of affirming the resonance of the past may have a higher spiritual value than the apparent obviousness of the need for relevance and progress.

Indeed, one can sometimes suggest that Cuddesdon – and here this is shared with many other theological colleges – is a parable that dwells on unity and diversity. The buildings of Cuddesdon are mostly hewed from the honey-coloured stone that is common for many Oxbridge colleges. There is a pastoral warmth in the hue and density of the stone, which the sunlight catches and illuminates at certain times of the day. The actual stones are, on closer inspection, arranged in an ordered way, but not a uniform way. Every stone wall testifies to the mantra that unity is not the same as uniformity: diversity of size, shape and sequence is easily found.

And then there are the wings. Cuddesdon, as a College, looks like a singular building. But looked at more carefully, one can see subtle differences in the stone work of Gore, Liddon, Rashdall and Major – and where these have been joined. And such differences are now more apparent in the Edward King Chapel, and Harriet Monsell House, both of which are more contemporary in design, and newer additions. The chapel is shaped like a coracle, expressing the motif of a pilgrim faith. Inside, the wooden pillars, reminiscent of gothic arches, lift the eyes to natural light that pours in, and to the heavens beyond. The sense of pure, warm, natural light bathing light-coloured wood is cleansing and prayerful. Harriet Monsell House, nearby, is both an education centre and a home to a small community of nuns, who help to shape the prayer life and spiritual heartbeat of the community. The building is shaped like the hull of a great ship – another hint at the pilgrim's progress: the soul in transition. The buildings as a whole appear to form a composite. But on closer inspection, one sees that the different centuries have each brought their own contribution to the collective sense of the college. The different nuances of architectural style create a sense of completeness, but also testify to the mixture of traditions that have formed not only the college, but also those students who have passed through the place for training and formation.

The buildings as a whole, in other words, expresses unity and diversity – the many different eras that have shaped its life and witness. It is one, yet many; diverse, yet singular. It is, in short, a parable in stone that speaks of Anglicanism. Moreover, I hold that this kind of deep relational engagement with spaces and places may have a greater missiological impact than overt evangelistic schema and initiatives. And clearly, the ministerial 'blend' of being and doing (i.e., the clergyperson as both contemplative and activist) may need to be adjusted in any transition from urban or suburban contexts to rural ministry. Context may have a direct bearing on theological output. Theology has an in-built intentional slowness about it. There may be flashes of insight, and epiphanies. But it is about travelling the way too – finding God in the journey and the pilgrimage, and not just getting to the end point as quickly as possible. This is not ecclesial subterfuge either. The Christian tradition reveals disciples who slowly comprehended the resurrection. And a church that only developed its creeds and core beliefs centuries after the events happened, including the spaces and their possibilities, and buildings and their potential meanings. This means helping ordinands to 'pause with purpose' in spaces and places, noting how issues and encounters surface in different environments. Indeed, good training might help clergy to purposefully dwell and dawdle in their loci, so that deliberations can inhabit the spaces they need, and so that clarity and wisdom might more easily come to fruition. Theology cannot be a discipline for hurrying.

Yet it is a discipline that should lead to action. I recently found myself on the other side of the world from Cuddesdon, and in Macau, as a guest of the Anglican Province of Hong Kong. Macau was, for centuries, the gateway for Christianity to enter China. Matteo Ricci, Francis Xavier and Florence Li Tim Oi (the first ordained woman in the Anglican Church) all have associations with the island. The feature that will strike any visitor to Macau, however, is its Portuguese heritage.

Settled by traders and missionaries from Portugal in the sixteenth century, Macau quickly became a place of distinctive fusion – cultures, faiths and trade combining to shape architecture and identity. Macau became a Portuguese colony in the nineteenth century, and in 1999 was handed back to China – although it remains, like Hong Kong, a 'special' territory of the motherland, still with its own currency, police and laws.

A walk in Macau's densely populated city and suburbs is a surprising experience. Many streets lead into public squares – the kind one would typically find in Portugal and Spain. Originally, these squares had several functions. First, it was a liminal meeting place immediately outside a church, and could also be used for trade, meetings and relaxation. Often the *Communidade* (administrative building) was also to be found flanking the square, and then prominent families would build their residences to provide further flanking, with the school (usually run by the clergy) completing the enclosure of the space.

In common with Mediterranean and Latin Catholic Europe, these squares evolved into places where boule could be played, villagers or townsfolk could gather and children could play. And in Macau, these spaces have indeed been faithfully recreated. However, where Macau is different from Portugal is in the density of population. The houses and flats on Macau are tiny, and overcrowding in family dwellings a significant problem across the territory. At the same time, the main source of income in Macau is gambling, with almost 40 licensed casinos. These are substantial in size, and gambling takes place on an almost industrial scale. (A walk in one of the larger casinos was not unlike the experience of stumbling into a vast battery-chicken farm – except filled with humans at tables and machines, in their many thousands, seemingly unaware of the date, time and climate outside.)

The Anglican church that day was introducing me to a new kind of space in Macau. The Taipa Youth and Family Integrated Service provides space for development in a city that has little room to develop the (moral?) character of its inhabitants. The main work of the centre focuses on youth and family work, offering what must seem, to many westerners, a rather innocuous set of services. There is a television lounge that families can book to watch a DVD. And a small library, karaoke room, dance studio and arts and crafts rooms. There are also rooms set aside for education, catering, counselling and simply meeting.

This project is government supported but church-run, and it recognises that in a place where there is little private space, and what public space there is is often commercialised, simple space for youth and families that is adequate for developing social skills and moral character is at a premium. The community halls and church rooms that many western Christians might take for granted are simply not there in the same way, so the Shen Kung Hui Macau Social Services Coordination Office provides a valuable service to the community by simply offering adequate space that enables families to meet and relax in such a way that many homes cannot offer or afford. This is a deep ministry of social engineering, generating moral capital through the provision of a pace and space that is affordable, commodious, non-commercial and unthreatening.

Of course, other ministries are on offer too – with specialist advice for young people, school counselling, addictions (gambling and alcohol) and family mediation all catered for. Yet the striking thing about the place is the space in the place – for Taipa is one of the most crowded new cities in the Far East, and here the church offers a simple (Benedictine-style) ministry of hospitality, that is mostly a form of 'anonymous Christianity'. Yet it is a remarkable ministry, born out of a vision for how open spaces and places can transform the lives of those who have little space, and little sense of the identity of the place to which they now belong. In some sense, then, the Taipa Youth and Family Integrated Service provides the same kind of environment that the Portuguese no doubt intended with their original public squares in the older parts of Macau. A space and a place to be together – gently watched over the by the church, surrounded by good neighbours and with food, drink and education all near to hand. All the things needed for life, in an open, yet bounded space.

For our final sketch, we turn to St Paul's Cathedral in London. Situated on Ludlow Hill, which is the highest point in the old City of London, the present building was constructed by Christopher Wren in the late seventeenth century, after the Great Fire of London of 1666. It is generally thought to be the fifth cathedral on that site, the first being built by St Mellitus in AD 604. The cathedral is one of the city's most distinctive and recognisable sights, standing at 365 feet (or 111m) high. From 1710 until 1962, it was the tallest building in London, and its central dome remains one of the highest in the world.

Wren was given the task of re-building the cathedral in 1668, along with dozens of other city churches destroyed by the fire that began in Pudding Lane. There were several design stages for the new cathedral, with at least four design schemes rejected on either practical, ecclesiological or theological grounds. By the time Wren came to complete the ultimately successful fifth design, he had resolved not to publish his drawings in advance, as consultation was proving to be divisive and time-consuming. The final design incorporated concepts drawn from the Renaissance, fused with a more Gothic style, and drawing some inspiration from St Peter's Basilica in Rome. The first stone of the cathedral was laid in 1677, and the cathedral came into use 20 years later. It was finally completed in 1708 ('topping out'), some 42 years after a spark from Farryner's bakery had caused the Great Fire of London. At the time of completion, some remarked that it was 'un-English', whilst for others there was an air of 'Popery' – the sense of the space and the dome being unlike anything seen before. Yet this extraordinary space may have another origin, rooted in Wren's childhood, and the religious and political settlements that emerged in the late seventeenth century.

Ask any school child what the most traumatic and violent period of English or British history was, and the chances are that they will say the First or Second World War, or possibly the Black Death, or perhaps even the Great Plague. Yet without doubt, it was the English Civil War – which of course extended to Ireland, Scotland and Wales, and lasted from 1642 until 1651 – and with sporadic violence and repression continuing until the restoration of 1662. Family members turned on each other. There was betrayal, death and suffering on an unprecedented scale. The war waged not only over the right form of governance for the country (monarchy or democracy), but on the theological vision that builds societies, and shapes human behaviour.

The statistics for the Civil War, insofar as they can be deemed to be reliable, are startling. The English suffered a population loss of almost 4 per cent as a direct result of violence (these figures do not include those who perished through disease or neglect), which is a greater percentage per head of population than the First and Second World Wars combined. The loss in Scotland eventually stood at 6 per cent, and in Ireland, where Cromwell conducted a vicious and visceral campaign, may have been as high as 40 per cent; a figure that is more than twice that of the losses suffered in the great famines of the nineteenth century. Or, put another way, more than double of the losses the Soviet Union incurred in the Second World War. Whilst the Irish statistics are disputable, there is no question that the scale of loss and atrocity was considerable, and Cromwell's name and legacy remains a permanent feature etched into the Irish psyche.

As a teenager, Christopher Wren was caught up in all of this. He was a teenager when Charles I was executed. His father was Dean of Windsor, and deprived of his living and housing under the Cromwellian reforms. His uncle was Bishop of Ely, and spent a good deal of the Civil War in the Tower of London. He survived – but as an emaciated and broken man. The deep psychological trauma of the Civil War has had a lasting impact on the British psyche. It was in fact three wars that took place over a nine year period. And it was, let us not forget, a religious war. It led to new ideas in religion (e.g., Levellers), breakthroughs in medicine (Harvey and blood circulation – far too much opportunity for field work), weaponry and techniques in war (some of the first POW camps).

The outcome of the war, however, is perhaps what is most interesting in relation to Wren's project at St Paul's, and the emerging settlement under the reign of Charles II. In a decade of some of the most brutal and bloody conflict seen on British and Irish soil, the English learned some important lessons about religion – lessons that had begun in the Reformation and Counter-reformation of the previous century. What were these lessons?

The first had been rehearsed in the Reformation, namely that you cannot change people's beliefs by beating them or persecuting them, or through war and violence. This would lead to a new accent in English Anglican identity. It led, for example, to the emergence of 'dinner party rules' for religion – we can worship together, but we don't talk about it afterwards. This was a new extension of the Elizabethan settlement – you cannot make a window into men's souls. The second lesson was a harder one, and Anglicans still live with this agenda. We, as a nation, found out the hard way, that we prefer peace to truth. The war was essentially over imposing truth as a precondition for peace. We realised that you cannot do that. Peace is the priority, because truth is contestable and contingent. Third, and because of this lesson, the eventual settlement of English identity is one where an uneasy peace is usually valued over and against settled and theistic solutions; because the latter, as the English learned, led to division, hatred and violence. It is better to live in love and charity with our neighbours, and disagree with them, than to try and impose our truth on them through indoctrination or violence. The lesson of the war was simple: it can only be done at a cost – and that cost is too high.

So the post-1662 Settlement is, essentially, a liberal one. But not liberal in the sense of campaigning or winning victories against conservatives or fundamentalists. Liberal, rather, in the sense of being open, tolerant and capacious. Politically, such liberalism will express itself in a coalition rather than a government of one single party. It will consist of allowing different viewpoints to flourish, including ones it does not agree with. In this sense, English or European Christian liberalism is rather different to the kind of 'party' or campaigning liberalism one might find in the USA. This side of the pond, liberalism tends to seek peace, not victory. In contrast, liberalism in the USA is more of a party matter; it has a tendency to want to win, seek vindication and not to compromise.

So how does all this have any kind of impact on a space like St Paul's? Whilst there is clearly a history to the design – a fusion of gothic and renaissance styles – the striking thing about St Paul's is the sheer size of the space, and the relative absence of décor and ritualistic focus. Wren's psychological response to the trauma of the English Civil War – one in which stained glass windows were blasted by muskets, people died for their faith and churchgoers argued intently about surplices, altars and lecterns – was to produce a capacious space in which all can co-exist but find little to focus their disagreements on. In some sense, the cathedral expresses the new English need for sufficient space, yet enclosure – something achieved by Wren in height, length and breadth of the project. It is an inclusive space, with an oddly early enlightenment feel to it. It is no accident that the Book of Common Prayer project (1662), which was now in its third edition (after 1549 and 1552) and was an attempt to be universal and inclusive, should also find expression in stones and spaces.

So, in St Paul's we have a huge dome, with not too much in it to cause unease or controversy. A big space; indeed, rather sterile, perhaps? A place to be, but devoid of controversy and ritualistic or symbolic foci. Indeed, perhaps the dome should be seen as a singular weaning breast? Or perhaps we can see the space as an expression of Newton's early thinking on space, and the Enlightenment's interest in the possibility of new life in new spaces. Australia, after all, was 'terra nullis' (empty space) for some while before it became populated and colonised.

So Wren's architecture, following the English Civil War, is clean, uncontroversial, tidy and neat. True, the inspiration for the canopied dome, drawn from Ely Cathedral, dazzles with colour. But if you look up, you see light. And whilst Nonconformists in England would continue to be oppressed for decades to come, there is nonetheless a something about the space in St. Paul's that welcomes and embraces everyone. It is the proverbial Big Tent. It is charity and capaciousness in stone. It is not filled with objects that mediate many messages; but a space that invites new possibilities for thinking and being. It is, in short, a space of Religious Enlightenment. Then it all begins to make sense. Especially when you discover that for a few brief years, whilst a student at Westminster School, Wren sat next to a child called John Locke, one of the fathers of the Enlightenment, and therefore of open and inclusive liberalism. It is a space that, as the theologian Dan Hardy would have said, is like so many churches: it is layered, and interwoven with many meanings, which all point to the infinite expansiveness of God, which is his wisdom.

Conclusion

We began this chapter with some observations about Chomet's interpretation of Tati's tale. Granted, this was a tendentious reading of *The Illusionist*, yet it served a purpose, namely to suggest that one of the challenges faced by faith groups today is the marginalisation of religion in public life – the pressure placed on belief (and the space the practice takes) to move into the shadows and corners of modern life. This is partly due to the gradual weakening of the capacity of faith to offer enchantment. Yet our three sketches – Cuddesdon, Macau and St Paul's London – are, in their different ways, all rooted in a vision of faith that is public, alive and central. For Cuddesdon, the space exists precisely because the clergy of the nineteenth and twentieth centuries needed new forms of training, education and formation that would enable them to contribute to the increasingly compressed and oppressive spaces of industrialisation and urbanisation. It was also a response to their own perceived sense of marginalisation in these new secular spheres. The church centre in Macau is, in a different way, a counter-cultural space in another kind of secular sphere. Not only symbolically, but also as a place where the advances of capitalism and urbanisation can be resisted. St Paul's, as we have seen, represents a form of space that articulates a new form of peace after the trauma of violent social and religious division; settlement and orthodox liberalism that aspires to be inclusive rather than divisive. In each case, the church has sought to pitch a tent in the age in which it is set. Each kind is a Big Tent in every sense; one that serves God, society and the needs of the church (and in that order).

Our age has a high view of freedom and variety, and a low view of habit and discipline. It is also an age where regular, frequent committed church-going – and indeed belonging to any other kind of voluntary institution – is struggling against the weight of secularisation, consumerism and individualism. Religion in the developed world is adapting – mainly by placing a greater emphasis on spirituality rather than institutional religion. Regular week-by-week church attendance (dispositional and disciplined) has had to concede significant territory to more episodic forms of faith, such as pilgrimages, celebrations and shrine-based worship. These are more intensive and personal; but less time-consuming too – suggesting, perhaps, that religion has been quietly pushed into the corners of modern life.

We have been here before, of course. The no less traumatic revolution or civil war that took place in France at the end of the eighteenth century, and saw a variety of experiments with monarchy, republicanism and democracy before the current settlement, also finds expression in religious and civic places. The Pantheon of Paris is partly a church, and partly a secular space for national heroes. Unlike Westminster Abbey, it has been unable to find a unity of purpose (note, not uniformity). The Pantheon bristles with tensions: religious paintings competing with clean, empty spaces that memorialise philosophers and writers who would more readily be recruited to the secularist cause. Yet in the middle of the Pantheon sits a vast dome – the same kind of space that Wren had conceived of – in which co-existence is both taught and caught. Wren's clock tower at St Paul's is replaced in the Pantheon by Foucault's pendulum. The message is clear. Take time and space.

In an influential essay by Dan Hardy, he writes that

> The task of theology, then, is to begin from common practice and examine its quality in open trial by the use of natural reason in order to discover the truth of this practice, by a truth-directed reason ... (including) practical reason. And the outcome ... should be an agreement on the proper organization of common life which would actually promote the practice of society ... The concern is public ... the use of public reason, open trial of the truth and the achievement of truly social existence.[2]

In creating the sense of time and space – whether at Cuddesdon, in Macau or in St Paul's, the Christian cadences that are present in the provision of this space actually help to form, create and recreate new possibilities for sociality. This space may be pastoral or performative; or peaceable and prescient. Yet the spaces and places testify not only to a story about their origins, but also one of aspiration. This is the congenial sense of community at Cuddesdon which carries

---

[2]   Hardy, 'Theology through Philosophy', p. 33.

a message about the reality and possibilities of the Anglican Communion. It is the emergence of alternative space in a church-based project in Macau that affirms family and youth, and resists the tide of commercialism and individualism that otherwise might reign in the city. It may be Wren's extraordinary domed cathedral that quickly complemented the spirit of the Book of Common Prayer with a sense of common space that was intended to be non-divisive and all-inclusive.

The burden of such places, and the vision for such spaces, is not simply that they serve the church, or even that they are at the disposal of their local communities. It is, rather, that as holy and inhabited places, they actually make for a better society. As Hardy says, the outcome 'should be an agreement on the proper organization of common life which would actually promote the practice of society'. It is here that we may find the coalition of Christian belief, practice and artefact (i.e., spaces and places) can be at its most dynamic, and truly shape the common practice of our social life. This is partly what it means to pitch God's tent in every age. But such a vision for the world, under God, to be enabled and achieved, requires a real sensitivity to the character and nature of the spaces and places we inhabit, and the people we serve. When we begin to reflect deeply on what we have, we can start to glimpse some of the possibilities for the church and world that God might intend. This is only part of what it might mean to re-pitch the tent. But to do so requires some vision, courage and adventure on our part: as well as faith, hope and love.

PART II
Commitment and Mission

Chapter 5

Many Rooms in My Father's House:
The Parish Church

Some years ago I was asked to fill in a questionnaire for a school survey run by some children. The question was this: 'what is the church?' My answer was as follows:

Partly a building
Partly people
Partly an ideal
Partly complete

The idea of partiality to describe the church is fascinating, especially when compared to the Kingdom of God that might be glimpsed on the other side: 'the heavenly city, coming down like a bride, complete ...'; or, 'in my father's house there are many rooms ...'; so no need for extensions, then. It is enough; it is finished. But as though we need reminding, we as a people are not; we remain deficient and incomplete. And neither is our church ever the finished product. And yet God accepts us, and continually beckons us to his house – the heavenly place where there is room for all.

Speaking of room for all, we remember too, that this is the vision behind what it means to be a Parish Church. The word 'parish' is never used in the New Testament, but it is, interestingly, an ancient Greek word, which literally means 'those outside the house': not the insiders, but the outsiders. The Greeks used it to refer to the areas of a city where the non-citizens lived – those with few rights, who were non-Greeks, and therefore excluded. So a Parish Church, in an ideal world, is not an exclusive place, but an inclusive place for the local stranger; for those who don't know the way, the truth and the life; for those who don't know they have a place in the heart of God, and who are ignorant of their room reservation in heaven. It is the inside place for the outsider; the only club that exists for non-members, as William Temple once quipped.

Set alongside this theological vision is the realisation that the English Parish Church is part and parcel of the cultural furniture of the nation. To some it is a place of denominational worship; for others it is the natural focus of the community; for still others, a place of Christian *witness* within a community. These idealist descriptions of the Parish Church all have their merit. But what does it mean to talk about a Parish Church today?

The question is a timely one when one considers the various subtle and inimical forces that appear to have eroded the identity of the concept. Religious pluralism has been a feature of the landscape of English religion since the Reformation; a Parish Church is no longer the sole focus for the religious rituals of its people, nor for their spiritual aspirations. Changes in population, and church-going habits have also left their mark.

Yet there have been other periods when parochial sustainability and viability seemed threatened. For example, Winchester could once claim to be the most over-churched city in England, with, in the twelfth century, a cathedral, two monasteries and at least 57 churches for a population serving no more than 8,000 people; that is one Parish Church for every 130 people. What did 8,000 people *do* with 57 churches and a cathedral? It would appear that these churches were made up of congregations serving relatively small communities. By 1535, the number of Parish Churches in Winchester had a fallen to just 13 – a quarter of the number for the twelfth century.

I will reflect on the identity of the English Parish Church and explore some of the ways in which the pressures it now faces are particular and specious. In order to do this, it will first be necessary to 'de-bunk' the myth of secularisation. Most sociologists of religion no longer accept that modernity necessarily ushers in a less religious era. Religion in the modern world does not suffer as one might immediately suppose; granted, it mutates, is squeezed into new shapes, and patterns of religious affinity and belonging are certainly altering. But the world is *not* a less religious place with the onset of modernity. People continue to possess and express what we scholars of religion variously call 'innate', 'folk' or 'common' spirituality, or 'vernacular religion'.

The concept of the Parish Church has some apparent ambiguities: the very idea of a Parish Church can be said, to some extent, to be a bit of an accident. The Saxon age is the first phase in the development of the concept. Minster churches – hundreds were dotted around England – devolved spiritual responsibility to smaller units – 'Parish Churches' – that were charged with the task of ministering to local communities. A community now defined as a parish was an economically viable community that could not only pay its secular taxes, but also afford its spiritual duties. Even then a system of tithing existed to support the ministry and fabric of the church, which was to survive well into the nineteenth century.

In short, the viability of a church was deeply connected to the viability of a community; church and parish lived in a relation of intra-dependence. Payment of fees to the church meant that the poor were cared for, sacramental ministry provided, the dead buried honorably and that the moral welfare of the community was generally catered for. The church needed a parish; and the parish needed its church. But this relationship began to bifurcate even before the Reformation, and so the waning and mutating identity of a Parish Church has (at least initially) nothing to do with secularisation. With these observations in mind, the questions that this chapter is concerned with are as follows. With the collapse of parochial identity in contemporary English culture (a process that appears to pre-date the Reformation), what can a Parish Church offer to its environment and to its people? And to what extent can a space such as a Parish Church be meaningfully spoken of when many people have lost their conscious sense of belonging to a parochial space?

The Myth of Secular England: A Brief Sketch

One the great paradoxes of late modernity is that churches believe in the steady decrease of public faith almost more than any other group. During the last half of the twentieth century, it has been popular to believe in a new credo: secularisation. Promoted by a few busy sociologists in league with disenchanted voices in the media, the faith is simple enough. The more advanced or modern society becomes, the less it looks to the spiritual and the religious. Ergo, church attendance declines, and the once golden age of Christendom, at least in the West, is coming to its end. The thesis appears to be supported by statistics; less people go to church than, say, 100 years ago, so the long-term prognosis seems to be correct.

As with most things, the truth is not nearly so simple. We now know enough about church-going habits to make a more sober, less bleak judgement about the Parish Church. It doesn't take a mathematical genius to figure out that church-goers who once went 52 times a year (and on high days and holy days), but now only go 47 times a year (allowing for vacations) leads to a 10 per cent drop in attendance. But there are not 10 per cent less people attending church; what has changed is the performance of the worshippers. It may be the case that more people come to church less frequently, and that *regular* church-going is in decline, but the appetite for occasional church attendance seems undiminished. Granted, less people belong, formally, to a Christian denomination when compared to the inter-war or Victorian periods. But almost all forms of association have declined steeply since those days. Associational disconnection is an endemic feature of modern life, but, ironically, churches are holding up far better than many of their secular counterparts.

For example, today there are fewer Scouts and Guides; Trade Union membership has waned; and there are now fewer members of the Conservative Party than there are Methodists. Bodies such as the Freemasons, Round Table, Townswomen's Guilds and Women's Institutes have noted steep declines in membership; but the Mother's Union has held out rather well by comparison. Recreationally, there are fewer people in our cinemas and football grounds than 70 years ago – yet no-one can say these activities are in decline. Indeed, it is a sobering thought that in so-called secular Britain, there are still more people turning to God each weekend at a church than watching a game of football.

Another problem with secularisation is that after sociologists and the media, the body that believes in the thesis most passionately is the churches themselves. Many, if not most, have bought the idea that modernity leads to the gradual and incremental loss of faith. Correspondingly, various interest groups emerge, hoping to make some capital out of the perceived crisis. Liberals propose stripping the faith to its bare essentials in order to make religion more credible. Evangelicals also strip the faith to its essentials, and promote 'the basics' of religion through courses like *Alpha*. But most Christians (though it is never easy to say *who* these people are, nor exactly what their faith consists of), who are in the middle ground are rather bewildered by these approaches to faith and society. For in their day-to-day Christian existence, no matter how intense or nominal, they do not encounter a 'secular' world at all, but, rather, one in which spirituality, religion and questions of faith remain public and widespread. In short, they do not believe in the modern 'disease' of secularisation, and consequently, they are un-persuaded by those groups that seek to promote their panaceas. As we noted in the Introduction, whatever kinds of secularity there may be in the modern world, they do not seem to produce secularisation, *per se*, in the developed world. Rather, the conditions of modernity, overt and tacit forms of secularism appear to be squeezing faith and spirituality into new shapes and arenas. Religion changes; it morphs and adapts, as people continue to seek meaning and values that may be ultimate, and experiences and anchors that speak of the transcendent. As Charles Taylor has argued in *A Secular Age*, the supposition that science would displace is no longer valid. All modernity does is relocate religion and spirituality – often to private spheres – but also such that they continue to be publicly accessible.

But surely there is some truth in the idea that fewer people are turning to official or mainstream religion? Yes and no. To a large extent, it depends on what periods in history are being compared to the present. For example, the Victorian period saw a revival of religion and religious attendance that lasted for about 40 years. Yet the beginning of the eighteenth and nineteenth centuries were eras that were very much the opposite of this: church attendance was, on the whole, derisory.

The Medieval and Reformation periods are often characterised as ages of great faith. However, the general scale of apathy and antipathy should not be underestimated. The eleventh century monk, William of Malmesbury complained that the aristocracy rarely attended mass, while the very poor – then as now – hardly attended church at all. There have been very few periods in English history when everyone went to Church or Sunday School, knew right from wrong and absolutely hung on every word their parish priest uttered. Detailed readings of parochial records from almost any age can illustrate the pragmatic, amateurish nature of 'official' English religion.

The Archdiaconal Visitation of 1578 for Bedfordshire (published by the Bedfordshire Historical Records Society, no. 69) shows its Parish Churches apparently in a poor state of repair, with theft of lead and timber being relatively commonplace. Meanwhile the clergy appear to be mostly absent from their churches, squashing the myth that every parish was (until recently) well served by its own parish priest. In many cases churches in Bedfordshire had not seen a priest for months or even years. And the concerns of the churchwardens are similar to the same concerns expressed today by the churchwardens of the twenty-first century. Namely, when will we get our next vicar, bishop? And what is to be done about the state of our church? The agenda for the Parish Church is as old as the hills: without staffing and proper maintenance, there is a fear for the identity and viability of the community as a whole.

This haphazard, semi-secular, quiet (but occasionally rowdy and irreverent) English Christianity continues well into successive centuries. James Woodforde's *Diary of a Country Parson* provides an invaluable window into the life of the clergy and the state of English Christianity in the eighteenth century.[1] Whatever secularisation is, it is not obviously a product of the Industrial Revolution. Woodforde clearly thinks it is reasonably good to have 'two rails' (or 30 communicants) at Christmas or Easter, from 360 parishioners. Such figures would be low by today's standards in some rural communities. Woodforde tells us that the only time his church is ever full is when a member of the Royal family is ill, or when there is a war on. Generally, the context of his ministry is one where he baptises, marries and buries the people of his parish, but the week-by-week Sunday attendance is not something that would get many ministers into a frenzy of excitement. But Woodforde is not bothered by this – not because he is especially lazy – but because the *totality* of his contact with his parish constitutes his ministry. He is *with* his people in all their trials and tribulations, not just his congregation. He is their man for all seasons; an incarnate presence in the midst of a community that waxes and wanes in its religious affections.

What needs to be stressed at the end of this short section is that the Parish Church and the ministry that issued from it was, generally speaking, greatly valued by the parish. However, that valuing did not necessarily translate into frequent and intense church attendance on the part of the masses. Mostly, it seems that the English have tended to *relate* to their Parish Churches in a variety of ways; it partly reflects a relationship of affection (sometimes grudging), of vicarious

---

[1]   Woodforde, *Diary of a Country Parson*, p. 38.

religion (of having others to believe in those things that one can't quite be so certain of – 'say one for me, padre', etc.), and of 'believing without belonging', to borrow the oft-quoted maxim of Grace Davie. Statistical surveys continually support the thesis that England is a place where the vast majority of the population continues to affirm their belief in God, but then proceed to do little about it. So church attendance figures remain stubbornly low. Yet this is not a modern malaise, but is rather a typical feature of many western societies down the ages. Granted, there have been periods of revival when church attendance has peaked. But the basic and innate disposition of the English is typical of Western Europe – one of believing without belonging; of relating to the church, and valuing its presence and beliefs – yet without necessarily sharing them. Or, as the ageless witticism expresses it: 'I cannot consider myself to be a pillar of the church, for I never go. But I am a buttress – insofar as I support it from the outside.'

The Contemporary English Parish Church: An Ambiguous Identity?

With these brief reflections in mind, we now turn to the ambiguity of the Parish Church in contemporary English culture. What does it stand for? Whom does it serve? As many ministers of religion already know, the shape and content of parish ministry has altered radically over the last century. It is true that rates of church-going were buoyant during the Victorian era, but the peaks and troughs of church attendance figures have nearly always depended as much upon cultural factors (e.g., the shifting population from agrarian to industrial contexts, or in the case of the Billy Graham evangelistic campaigns of the post-war era, the shift from cities to a new suburbia) as they have on the intensity of engagement between a church and its parish.

Parish Churches and their ministers throughout the nineteenth and twentieth centuries were, in effect, being forced to re-invent their connectedness to the parish. The obligation of tithing was withering, if not altogether defunct, which meant that the parish now had no necessary economic relationship with its church (besides which, other denominations had received legal recognition since 1689). The 'church-rate' that levied a tax on local people for the upkeep of the Parish Church was abolished by law in 1864, leading to the present anomalous situation, whereby the whole parish has access to the Parish Church for baptisms, weddings, funerals and other rites, but only the congregation are obliged to pay for the upkeep of the building. The experience of Victorian parochial ministry was one of more intense engagement as the parish and the church underwent rapid bifurcation, with the parish – as a space – ceasing to be recognised, except as a division of boroughs and civic authorities. Or, to put it another way, the increasing loss of the parish as a recognised 'place' that began in Victorian England – a product of industrialisation, capitalism and early globalisation – led to the Parish Church becoming a more intensely and exclusively spiritual space.

The continuing development of modernity has carried on changing the nature of locality. Air travel has led to a decline in passenger shipping, which has isolated many remote island communities. Thus, whilst for some the world is more compressed and globalised, for others it is increasingly lonely and fractious. Technology also reduces spatial distances – fax, e-mail and video-phone – yet many still travel many miles just to collect water. The city may be alive and well, with everything 'within easy reach'; yet the pensioner can still be living in a bed-sit, their presence or absence going undetected for many months. In other words, the mobility of some, whilst destroying the identity of the 'local' for many, can equally leave many depending even more heavily on their immediate environment and community for support.

But let us return to the relationship between the Parish Church and the parish locality. I noted at the beginning of this chapter that their identities had begun to undergo a process of bifurcation that can be dated from the Reformation, and in all probability well before that. For example, even from the early Middle Ages, it became increasingly difficult to order and police growing populations through the auspices of the local church. Courts of Law, the rise of civic authorities and guilds, the need for better transport infrastructures and the like meant that many people looked beyond their immediate parochial boundaries for their livelihood. As we observed earlier, in small cities such as Winchester, what passed for 'parochial worship' was essentially congregational in character – a Parish Church may just have consisted of a few extended families worshipping together, and whatever sacramental ministry they could afford. In turn, this dynamic emerged afresh in the wake of the Reformation, when religious services could easily be said at home, presided over by the head of the house and gathered around the word, and not sacramental worship – what we could identify as an early form of vernacular spirituality.

Furthermore, the economic ties that bound parishes to their Parish Churches were beginning to break down as commerce became increasingly cosmopolitan. Increasingly, the local mattered less and less as people became more mobile. These trends, present long before the Renaissance, never mind the Reformation, could only increase during the Industrial Revolution.

Two areas are particularly significant: birth and death. Under the Saxon Minster system, minster churches had once monopolised the rite of baptism; it was a sacrament undertaken by patronal churches, and the origin of the phrase 'mother church' partly lies in this fact. Other chapels and places of worship belonging to the Minster rarely had fonts of their own. The fight to acquire the status of Parish Church was often about local autonomy and prestige against the interests of the Minster. To be a Parish Church meant owning a font, and this in turn enabled the local church to be truly a community in its own right. Parish Churches symbolised not only the presence of God in the midst of a community; they also made a powerful economic and social statement: this is a viable, living community that can support itself and support its God. A chapel said something different: we are dependent on another area for our welfare.

Baptism is only one half of the equation that allowed medieval chapels to make the uneasy transition to Parish Church. The other space that was required was a graveyard. Burials too allowed the community to 'own' their place of worship in a very particular way. The identity of a community could be entirely tied-up with the location of the dead, and how the living memorialised them. The right to bury the dead signified that this 'place' was not transitory, but established. Not only was it a viable economic community, it was also a place that had a history and a right to a future.

I make these observations about Parish Churches in Saxon and medieval times because they were clearly important in maintaining a sense of place and in creating a kind of local identity, which was secular, sacred, religious, civic, local and catholic. Many Parish Churches today struggle to 'connect' with their locations in ways that are similar. In the case of births, baptismal rates have dropped steadily in England since the turn of the twentieth century, the trend accelerating with noticeable speed from the 1960s. The response of the churches, interestingly, to this loss of *extensive* connection, has been to reify baptismal rites into a more *intensive* form of religious experience. Gone are the accommodating cultural customs of bygone eras in which the clergy baptised large numbers of children at times that were mainly convenient to families (i.e., Sunday afternoons). Baptism ceases to be a social rite of passage – even the term 'Christening' is discouraged – and is replaced by something more definitive, with the baptismal service now more usually being situated within a normal Sunday morning service. The effect of this is hard to measure, but it would not be unfair to say that the Parish Church, in its loss of extensive connectedness with its own locality, has attempted to re-engage its disparate community by becoming more intense in its religious expression and by sharpening up its spiritual identity.

Another dynamic can be seen in relation to death. For most of the twentieth century, new churches that were built did not provide graveyards; gardens of rest for interred remains are a relatively late innovation. Death has moved, sociologically and culturally, from a commonplace event that was central to the life of all small communities and localities, to becoming something that is removed from the mainstream of society, and placed on its margins. Most deaths occur in hospitals, hospices or residential and nursing homes. The vast majority of funerals are conducted in anonymous crematoriums that form no spatial, spiritual or social attachment with the bereaved. The memorialisation of the dead – once the main point and function of a Parish Church – has been speedily eroded by the contemporary utilitarian forces that have tidied death up (in the name of clinical cleanliness) and swept it into the corners of modern life.

Predictably, the responses of the English Parish Churches to this have been pragmatic and pastoral. Remembrance Sunday refuses to die, long after its veterans have all been mourned. The festival of All Souls has undergone a renaissance in recent years, as churches have sought to restore the memorialisation of death and the reality of bereavement, as well as speaking of resurrection, into a relationship with the communities they serve. The spaces and places for death may no longer exist in the way they once did, but there is always the compensation of calendrical ritual. And, as many churches discovered after 11 September 2001, or after the death of Princess Diana of Wales, an open church, in which to light a candle or say a prayer and sign a condolence book is still the first port of call for many people, and preferred to posting a message on the web.

The Future of the Parish Church and Its Identity

Our reflections so far have hinted that the gradual bifurcation of the life of the Parish Church from the life of the parish community was a process that began prior to the Reformation, and has been as much about economic realities as it has about anything we might call secularisation. We might also add that the gradual atomisation of public space – a feature of modernity stretching back to the Industrial Revolution – has forced the Parish Church to reconsider its own sense of place. It is not that long ago that Parish Churches were the only places within a community that could house debates, discussions and social gatherings. But their monopoly has been broken by the endemic pluralisation of public space: taverns, cinemas, community halls, as well as competing denominations and a host of other arenas. Arguably, the media, as the purveyors of information, recording and memory are the new public space. It would appear then, that Parish Churches are beginning to lose their point.

But it would be premature to sound the death knell for the Parish Church. My narration of the Parish Church in English cultural history clearly suggests that its identity has always been evolving, so there is arguably little cause for alarm. Every generation of churchwardens has had to face an apparently insuperable set of problems ranging from apathy to poverty through to clerical negligence and absence. All that we may say here is that the Parish Church is losing its identity because the concept and feel of parish-type communities has been lost first. The next line of defence, then, is for the recognition of *local* churches, and that is arguably the key mutation of modernity for the Parish Church: its identity is shifting from the parochial to the local – as the church that people know and identify with as their own.

Perhaps the churches need to panic a little less about the apparently bleak statistics, and their apparent loss of identity, and concentrate a little more on maintaining religion as something that is public, accessible and extensive, whilst also being distinct, intensive, and mysterious. I have five general comments to make by way of conclusion.

First, even in the most modern societies, there is still demand for religion that is public, performative and pastoral. Many churches have seen a rise in numbers since 11 September 2001. Religion mutates and lives on; churches, to take advantage of this, must continue to try to be open to the world and extensively engaged with their communities. Churches are often the only bodies that provide public and open places within a community for tears, grief, remembrance, laughter and celebration.

Second, religion is remarkably resilient in the modern age. Much of our 'vernacular religion' – such as the celebration of Christmas – reveals a nation that still enjoys its carols, nativity plays and other Christian artefacts that long ago moved beyond the control of the church to become part of the cultural furniture. Religion is still in demand. And here, Parish Churches have particular responsibilities to connect with vernacular religion, nascent spirituality and local cultures that show some yearning for the transcendent.

Third, the churches can respond to the challenge of an apparently faithless age with a confidence founded on society (yes, society), which refuses to leave religion alone. Often the best that churches can do is to recover their poise within their social and cultural situations, and continue to offer a ministry and a faith to a public that wishes to relate to religion, without necessarily belonging to it.

Fourth, the future of the Parish Church cannot be disconnected from its ecumenical context. Increasingly, Parish Churches have to come to terms with the different and similar ministries offered by other Christian communities within the same area. Granted, competition can be the engine of increase. But increasingly, collaboration, and actively working to preserve a dynamic mixed economy of ministry, looks like a worthwhile missiological strategy. Parish Churches, rather than stretching themselves to the limit in all things, may be able to contemplate a degree of specialisation within a culture of collaboration.

Fifth, although the accent of this chapter has been very much centred on places, there can be no question that the more contested, fluid and ambiguous spatial identity becomes, the more vital it is to make sure that ministries engage with people. This may mean congregations and parishes taking a more adventurous (and risky?) look at the intentional building of faith communities within particular niches. This may involve fresh expressions of chaplaincy (e.g., in the workplace), or new ways of being church that may not have an obvious spatial rootedness. The church, after all, is constantly seeking the lost, the dislocated and those who have no place – those who feel no tie or loyalty to their immediate environment. There must be a church for them too – further expression of Jesus' love.

So the recipe for the idea of the Parish Church might look like this: cultivate a relaxed awareness of the opportunities that surround us all; have faith in the resilience of God and the church; but also respond to the many tests of faith that dominate every age with tenacity, compassion and wisdom. Be confident in the buildings too; they are 'signs' of God's presence in the community. A tatty church suggests a neglected God. A neat, modern, comfortable (but otherwise invisible building) might suggest a private God. But a beautifully kept building, fit for few other purposes other than worship, suggests, funnily enough, life and otherness – something in the world, yet not of it. The Parish Church and the Christian faith have many more supporters than members. We do not live in a secular age: our era continues to be a time of questions, exploration, wonder and awe. The offering of an open building, and an outward-looking worshipping community, remain dominant signs on the cultural landscape, pointing to nothing less than the deep generosity and openness of God, who promises his people that 'there are many rooms in my Father's house'.

The gradual atrophy in the pivotal power of the English Parish Church since the Industrial Revolution is, in one sense, undeniable. At the same time, a detailed history of Parish Churches shows that their success and failure, prior to the Industrial Revolution, is not linked to secularisation, and that spirituality and vernacular religion persist, waxing and waning, with or without due regard to the provision of parochial places of worship. Having said that, with Parish Churches no longer linked to the *local* economy and what that space generates in terms of wealth and income, Parish Churches may have to re-invent themselves as places of worship, offering both intensive and extensive connectedness.

The Parish Church has always been a complex pottage of competing convictions and interests, brought together in the focus of a building and a ministry, the ownership of which has always been open to interpretation. What the Parish Church needs now, arguably, is to continually rediscover its ministry, one that engages with culture in creative ways. The shift from the *parochial* to the *local* might not be entirely deleterious. In the future, patterns of ministry will no longer be configured solely through geographical space and its constraints. For the church to find its place in the modern world, it will have to create new spaces for new communities and different opportunities for differentiated niche groups. Such a vision might appear to threaten the very concept of a Parish Church; but it might also be its saviour. To be a Parish Church, a church must find a community and locate itself within it, incarnating the life of God there in ways that are both local and catholic. In the complex, porous and ambiguous spaces of our future, the church will need to find its places in society once again, if it is to continue to offer a religion that is public, performative and pastoral.

Chapter 6

Mind the Gap: Mission, Youth and Generational Change

On the whole, you don't hear of many clergy boasting about the number of older people they have in church, Sunday by Sunday. It would a rare thing to meet a priest who, sitting comfortably at a Chapter Meeting with their fellow clergy, sat back and waxed lyrically about the rising number of pensioners that were now attending his or her church. Such bragging, were it to take place at all, would be read by most as a trope of some sort, or perhaps interpreted as a kind of wistful sardonic irony that was trying to make some other point. This may immediately strike one as being rather odd when one considers that many churches are actually (but quietly) rather good at attracting the older person. Older people give time, money and expertise to churches. They tend to be its most loyal and constant supporters. But typically, the discussion about the future of church attendance is shaped around anxieties relating to the young:

> Young people are important members of the Church today, and they also hold the future in its hands. This future is by no means certain. To quote just one statistic, churches lost 155,000 teenagers between 15 and 19, from 1979 to 1989, a loss far greater than the decline of 15 to 19 year olds in the general population.[1]

There are good reasons for these types of anxieties being expressed, to be sure. Concerns about young people and the church are perfectly legitimate missiological issues that need to be addressed. But having said that, one might note that the work of the church with the young has a curiously brief history. True, in the 'golden

---

[1]   Collins, 'Spirituality and Youth' (quoting Brierley, *Act on the Facts*, p. 214), p. 221.

age' of pastoral ministry (from the Reformation through to the beginning of the Industrial Revolution), many parish priests catechised the young as part of their priestly duties, although there was no particular or specialised outreach to young people worthy of note. George Herbert (1593–1633), for example, advises that children be admitted to Holy Communion as soon as they can distinguish between ordinary bread and consecrated bread, and when they can recite the Lord's Prayer: he estimates the age at which these things come together to be at around seven. Similarly, Parson Woodforde (1740–1803), whilst clearly showing an awareness of young people in his parish, has nothing remarkable to offer them in his ministry.

But lest this sound too complacent, the advent of the Industrial Revolution caused many parents to begin to dread Sundays. As the only day that was free of the toil of the factories (in which the children also worked a six day week), church services became increasingly rowdy. With traditional village and rural ties broken, the 'new generations' of children were also less likely to be inducted into any kind of religious instruction or church custom, and there was general concern about the lapse of the young into crime and delinquency. In Gloucester, England, Robert Raikes (1735–1811), the owner and printer of the *Gloucester Journal*, decided to establish a 'Sunday School' for the children of chimney sweeps, housed in Sooty Alley, opposite the city gaol. The School began in 1780, and was an immediate success, offering general and religious education to children from the working classes. The idea of the schools spread with astonishing rapidity. By 1785 a national Sunday School Organisation had been established, and many thousands of children were attending in most major cities.[2] In 1788 John Wesley wrote that: 'verily I think these Sunday Schools are one of the noblest specimens of charity which have been set on foot in England since William the Conqueror'.[3]

Sunday Schools continued to spread and develop throughout the nineteenth century, with their aims and objectives altering in the course of their evolution. By 1851, three-quarters of working class children were in attendance, and many adults too.[4] In Raike's original scheme, social action and evangelisation had been the primary motivation in the formation of the schools. Yet by the mid-1800s, some scholars assert that the primary focus of the Sunday School had become a

---

[2]   Kelly, *A History of Adult Education in Liverpool*, pp. 74–6.
[3]   Trumbull, *The Sunday-School*, p. 118.
[4]   Laqueur, *Religion and Respectability*, p. 44.

means of expressing emergent working class values (e.g., thrift, communalism, self-discipline, industry, etc.). In other words, the Sunday Schools had become a means of providing some generational continuity and identity. Moreover, the 'associational' character of the Sunday Schools also provided a significant social environment in which young and old, male and female, could meet and interact. Thus, Joseph Lawson, writing in the 1890s, notes:

> Chapels are now more inviting – have better music – service of song – which cannot help being attractive to the young as well as beneficial to all. They have sewing classes, bazaars, concerts, and the drama; cricket and football clubs, and harriers; societies for mutual improvement and excursions to the seaside.[5]

Lawson's observations from over a century ago are illuminating because they draw our attention to the fecund associational nature of Victorian religion. Indeed, this lasted, in all probability, well into the twentieth century, with religious bodies providing significant social capital, the means whereby malevolent and anti-social forces were overcome by the purposeful encouragement of 'mutual support, cooperation, trust, institutional effectiveness'.[6] Religion, in its many and varied associational forms and offshoots, provided social capital that was both bridging (inclusive across different social groups, trans-generational, gender-encompassing, etc.) and bonding (exclusive – clubs and societies for particular groups, boys' clubs, girls' clubs, etc.), and was therefore part of that new social culture which now obviated the generational gaps that had first awoken the reformers of the early nineteenth century. But the mid-twentieth century was to mark further changes for the churches. As Putnam notes of North America, in the 1950s roughly one in every four Americans reported membership with a church-related group, but by the 1990s that figure was cut in half to one in eight. Americans now devote two-thirds less of their time to religion than they did in the 1960s.[7]

What has led to this change? There are a variety of theories that offer 'generational change' in religious affiliation as a way of framing the causes

---

5   Cunningham, *Leisure in the Industrial Revolution*, p. 181.
6   Putnam, *Bowling Alone*, p. 22.
7   Ibid., p. 72.

and trajectories, and the insights, although of a fairly general nature, are useful. Putnam, for example, states that:

> The decline in religious participation, like many of the changes in political and community life, is attributable largely to generational differences. Any given cohort of Americans seems not to have reduced religious observance over the years, but more recent generations are less observant than their parents. The slow but inexorable replacement of one generation by the next has gradually but inevitably lowered our national involvement in religious activities.[8]

For Wade Clark Roof and William McKinney, the transition is marked by movement from formal religious observance and membership to 'surfing' from congregation to congregation, not belonging strongly to any one particular body of believers, and an increased appetite for spirituality:

> Large numbers of young, well-educated middle-class youth[s] ... defected from the churches in the late sixties and seventies ... Some joined new religious movements, others sought personal enlightenment through various spiritual therapies and disciplines, but most simply 'dropped out' of organised religion altogether ... [there was a] tendency toward highly individualised [religion] ... greater personal fulfilment and the quest for the ideal self ... religion [became] 'privatised' or more anchored to the personal realms.[9]

We might add to these observations a remark from Margaret Mead, that 'the young cannot learn in the old ways' and that 'the old are outmoded rapidly' in the speedily advancing and saturated world of media, science, questing and consumerist cultures.[10]

Speaking of culture, we might also mention Callum Brown's *The Death of Christian Britain*, in which he argues that the very core of the nation's religious culture has been irrevocably eroded. More unusually, however, he argues that the process known as 'secularisation', whilst gradual and endemic, is not the Industrial

---

[8]   Ibid., p. 72.
[9]   Roof and McKinney, *American Mainline Religion*, pp. 7–8, 18–19, 32–3.
[10]   Mead, *Culture and Commitment*, p. 78.

Revolution or the Enlightenment. Rather he argues that it is the catastrophic and abrupt cultural revolutions of the post-war years, and most especially those trends and movements that began in the 1960s.

Charting the growth of institutional religion in Britain from 1945 to the early 1960s, Brown contends that it is the change in the role of women that has done for Christianity, rather than scientific rationalism. The apparent feminisation of religion in the Victorian era led to a resurgence of family values in post-war Britain, in which various bourgeois standards rose to the surface, and were equated with 'religion' (e.g., Sabbath observance, drinking in moderation, etc.). What undid this cultural trajectory was a combination of liberalism and feminism – Brown cites The Beatles and the end of the ban on *Lady Chatterley's Lover* as examples. Brown's book is full of insight, and his appeal to cultural forces of late modernity as a corrosive influence on religious adherence, have far more nuance than those that are normally to be found amongst the pages of secularisation theorists:

> It took several centuries (in what historians used to call the Dark Ages) to convert Britain to Christianity, but it has taken less than forty years for the country to forsake it. For a thousand years, Christianity penetrated deeply into the lives of the people, enduring Reformation, Enlightenment and the industrial revolution by adapting to each new social and cultural context that arose. Then really, quite suddenly in 1963, something very profound ruptured the character of the nation and its people, sending organised Christianity on a downward spiral to the margins of social significance. In unprecedented numbers, the British people have stopped going to church ... The cycle of intergenerational renewal of Christian affiliation, a cycle which had for so many centuries tied the people however closely or loosely to the churches and to Christian moral benchmarks, was permanently disrupted in the 'swinging sixties'. Since then, a formerly religious people have entirely forsaken organised Christianity in a sudden plunge into a truly secular condition.[11]

Brown's assertions appear to confirm the underlying thesis that we have so far been sketching in this opening section, namely that large-scale disaffection with organised religion is primarily a post-war phenomenon in both Britain

---

[11]   Brown, *The Death of Christian Britain*, p. 1.

and America. Furthermore, the changes are due to broader cultural streams that the churches have no direct control over. These cultural changes might include the rise of the 'post-associational' society, consumerism, individualism, an accentuation of generational identity and familial atomisation. However, it is important not to allow such descriptions to become the only frames of reference for determining reality. To this end, some problems with the historical narrative are worth pointing out.

First, it needs to be remembered that our ways of talking about generations – especially childhood – do not have fixed points of meaning. Historians of childhood often quip that a child over the age of seven in medieval times did not exist. The term 'teenager' and the very idea of adolescence are comparatively recent 'discoveries'. The emergence of a 'buffer zone' of development between childhood and adulthood is something that is mostly attributable to economic and social conditions that can afford such space for maturity and advancement. The cultivation of such a zone as an arena for further specific forms of consumerism only serves to concretise and consecrate such identities. (Today, in many developing countries, a 'child' of 10 can be the main 'bread-winner'.) Before the onset of the Industrial Revolution in Western Europe, it should be recalled that the churches could not claim to be doing any special work with children. As Heywood points out, prior to 1800, there was 'an absence of an established sequence for starting work, leaving home and setting up an independent household'.[12] Indeed, it is only the child labour laws and schooling that provide 'age-graded' structures for social ordering at this level, and such provisions are less than 200 years old. Often, the work of churches went hand in hand with educationalists, and a newly perceived need to provide 'nurseries of Christian character' at every 'stage' of childhood, from infancy through to the age of 20, in order to advance civilisation and good social ordering.[13]

Second, generational change in religious adherence does not necessarily mean the rise of secularisation. Brown, for example, cites 1963 as the beginning of the end for the churches. So how long would it be before Britain becomes 'truly' and wholly secular? Brown does not say, but the teasing question draws our attention

---

[12]   Heywood, *A History of Childhood*, p. 171; see also Goldscheider and Goldscheider, *Leaving Home before Marriage*.

[13]   Kett, *Rites of Passage*.

to his rhetoric, which contains in-built vectors of decline: 'ruptured', 'downward spiral', 'disrupted', 'forsaken' and 'sudden plunge' suggest a mind already made up. Whilst it may be true that the 1960s, with its revolutions of popular culture, social liberalism and political upheaval did more to question and shake the foundations of institutions than in previous generations, it would appear that Brown is also guilty of shaping his facts around his thesis. Whilst it is clearly helpful to assess religious adherence down the ages through the lens of generational change, it simply does not follow that if the present generation is uninterested in religion or spirituality, then the next will be even less so. Moreover, is it not the case that many religious movements began in the 1960s? Ecumenism, charismatic renewal, the New Age movement and a variety of sects, cults and new religious movements were part and parcel of the culture of experimentation that dominated the 1960s. Would it not be fairer to say that, far from turning off religion, people were rather turned on by it, and tuned into it in new ways (e.g., spirituality) that simply reflected the emerging post-institutional and post-associational patterns of post-war Britain?

Third, far from seeing generational change as a threat to the churches, the cultural forces that shape debates should be seen in the wider context of general social change. In a capitalist and consumerist culture, it is probably reasonable to go along with Putnam's hypothesis that the late twentieth century has seen a dramatic collapse in many forms of civic association, and a corresponding rise in individualism. However, churches have tended to hold up rather well under this pressure when compared to their non-religious counterparts. That said, changes in the way people spend 'free' time do appear to have had a deleterious effect on associational forms, and in all probability no agent of change has been more influential than the television. Initially, the creation of the 'electronic hearth' was a family-bonding and generation-bridging experience. But as consumerism and individualism has steadily increased, this phenomenon has changed. In the USA, the average adult now watches almost four hours of TV per day. As the number of television sets per household multiplies, watching programmes together has become rarer. Television has evolved into an example of 'negative social capital'; it is the new public space through which the world speaks to us, but it means that we no longer talk to one another. This has increased further with technological development: tablets, personal computers and other devices now enabling individuals to watch TV programmes on their own and at time of their choosing.

Watching TV has now become a partially solitary and individual activity – even in a house full of people (and perhaps multiple TV sets, few of which now need using to watch TV programmes).

Putnam points out that 'husbands and wives spend three or four times as much time watching television as they spend talking'.[14] Similarly, Putnam points out that 'unlike those who rely on newspapers, radio and television for news … Americans who rely *primarily* on the internet for news are actually *less* likely than their fellow citizens to be civically involved'.[15] But of course, this does not mean that technology spells the end for civic life, associations and religious adherence. Rather, it suggests a new mutation of social and religious values, and it is to the discussion of this that we now turn.

Generations and Mission

Every generation that has ever lived has done so within its own modernity. Each new generation that faces its past, present and future does so with a sense of being on the cusp of time. Continuity between generations may be valued; but it is also evaluated as it is appreciated, and then perhaps subjected to alteration. But how true is it that the cultural and social forces being addressed at the present are more problematic than those faced in the past? Can it really be said that the transformations of the late twentieth century are more disruptive than those experienced in the Industrial Revolution, or in the wake of the economic and social re-ordering that followed the Black Death in medieval England?

In general, it would be imprudent to argue (historically) that one generation has struggled more than another, and that the forces shaping religion and society are now more or less inimical than another period. It is important that in any sociological and cultural analysis, proper attention is paid to (proper) history, before engaging in any kind of speculative futurology. There is a well-known aphorism that needs heeding by every would-be cultural commentator: 'sociology is history, but with the hard work taken out'. To avoid the endemic sociological habit of generalising, it is important that any discussion of the generations is

---

14   Putnam, *Bowling Alone*, p. 224.
15   Ibid., p. 221, emphases mine.

rooted in a sound grasp of historical enquiry, and, where possible, married to data, ethnography and other forms of intellectual garnering that are rooted in methodological rigour. Two examples are offered here that paint slightly different pictures. The first is a Roman Catholic and North American perspective, and the second is a British one.

Roman Catholics are a diverse body of believers in the Third Millennium, and the relationship between 'official' and 'operant' in American Catholic religion is under increasing academic scrutiny:

> Most observers agree that there is a great deal of diversity among American Catholics ... While there was a certain amount of diversity in the 1940s and 1950s ... the beliefs and practices of American Catholics have become increasingly varied since then. Studies done during the 1950s and 1960s indicated that there was more uniformity among Catholics than among mainstream Protestant groups ... More recent research, however, suggests that American Catholics' beliefs and practices are now more diverse than they were prior to the Second Vatican Council.[16]

Williams and Davidson, in their study of American Catholicism, offer a generational explanation for the seismic shifts of the last 50 years. The pre-Vatican II generation (born in the 1930s and 1940s) viewed the church as an important mediating force in their relationship with God. When asked why they were Catholic, many participants in the Williams and Davidson study replied that it was because 'it was the one true church'.[17] The Vatican II generation (born in the 1950s and 1960s), however, were more circumspect about the nature of the church and its absolutist claims. Interviewees were more inclined to see their priest as representing 'official' religion, which, in turn, was only one religious source that fed and nurtured their private and individual spirituality. In this sense, the Vatican II generation is pivotal, since the post-Vatican II generation (born in the 1970s and 1980s) has tended to be even more liberal and open. For this generation, Mass attendance is not a priority; being a good person is more important than being a

---

[16] Williams and Davidson, 'Catholic Conceptions of Faith', p. 70.

[17] Ibid., pp. 75–6.

good Catholic; faith is individualistic and private – 'what really counts is what is in your heart'. Williams and Davidson conclude their study with these words:

> One thing is certain: the hands of time cannot be turned back. Societal changes, as well as changes occurring within the church, leave no doubt that tomorrow's Catholics will be very different from previous generations. The children of post-Vatican II Catholics will receive their religious education from those who never read the *Baltimore Catechism*, and are likely to know little about the changes brought about by Vatican II. The conceptions of faith post-Vatican II Catholics are apt to pass on to the next generation will look decidedly individualistic in nature.[18]

In a similar vein, Sylvia Collins bases her assessment about the future shape of spirituality and youth on just such foundations. Her research is not motivated by confessional or denominational anxiety, but is rather located in the quest to discover how young people are changing in their attitudes to belief. Contrasting 'baby boomers' (those born between 1945 and 1960) and 'baby busters' (those born after 1960), Collins skilfully notes and narrates the changes between the generations. On balance, 'boomers' tended towards radicalising religious traditions in the wake of post-war settlement. This was to include an emphasis on liberation, justice and political involvement, but was also coupled to an increasing tendency to experiment with religion (e.g., innovative 'sects', New Religious Movements, Communitarianism, etc.). Thus, the

> baby boomer generation … saw spirituality among young people move in line with social change from its location in one main tradition associated with the old established order, through to a new spirituality that sought to break the bonds of establishment and set the self free to reach its new potential. Even more widespread, however, was a growing apathy and indifference towards the spiritual realm altogether in favour of materialistic self-orientation in terms of hedonistic consumption.[19]

---

[18]   Ibid., p. 75.
[19]   Collins, 'Spirituality and Youth', p. 229.

Collins argues that 'baby busters' followed up and extended these changes. She notes, in common with other sociologists such as Francis and Kay, Walker and Hervieu-Leger, that the late twentieth century has seen 'a thorough-going fragmentation in lineage of Christian memory', that 'gospel amnesia' has set in, as society has come to observe the fragmentation of belief and decontextualisation of spirituality.[20] But lest this sound too pessimistic already, Collins points out that religion has merely mutated rather than disappeared:

> spirituality ... has moved from the self-spirituality of the boomer generation to a more aesthetic spirituality, a spirituality which is focused on pleasure and experience in and of itself ... Successful churches, it seems, offer an atmosphere and intimate experience of God over and above doctrine ... the spirituality of intimacy of the millennial generation will be deeply bound up with the consumerism that has increasingly concerned youth throughout the post-war period.[21]

Collins' analysis is persuasive on many levels; her descriptive arguments appear to be a good 'fit' for young people and spirituality at the dawn of a third millennium. However, one important caveat should be mentioned, namely that of change. Interest in, or even a passion for 'an intimate experience of God over and above doctrine' is not necessarily sustainable over a period of time. It does not follow that those things that are valued and cherished in teenage years or one's early 20s will even be regarded in one's 30s or 40s. For example, many young people are enchanted by the discipline, fellowship and spiritual atmosphere of a Christian Union (UCCF) whilst at college or university. But large numbers of students will quietly forsake this type of commitment for a different *attitude* to belief in later years: something altogether more mellow, temperate, open, ambiguous – a faith that can live with doubt.

This transition from the early 20s into 'young adulthood' raises some intriguing issues for the consideration of generations. Wade Clark Roof notes that 'in times of social upheaval and cultural discontinuity especially, generations tend to become more sharply set off from one another'.[22] The added power of consumerism in

---

[20] Francis and Kay, *Teenage Religion and Values*; Walker, *Telling the Story*; Hervieu-Leger, *Religion as a Chain of Memory*.

[21] Collins, 'Spirituality and Youth', pp. 233–5.

[22] Roof, *Generation of Seekers*, p. 3.

late modernity reinforces this sense: niche marketing to almost every age group for every stage of life is not only prevalent, but also highly successful. And in the early years of adulthood, the desires appear to be less clustered around fulfilment and more around authenticity. As Parks notes, there is a 'hunger for authenticity, for correspondence between one's outer and inner lives ... a desire to break through into a more spacious and nourishing conception of the common life we all share'.[23] Parks' work is one of the few treatments of faith and belief in the '20-something' age group, and her work is a prescient consideration of how generational change evolves within itself, even to the point of questioning the contemporary bewitchments of consumerism and self-fulfilment.

The idea that changes take place *within* generations, and not simply between them, is an important one to grasp in the consideration of the future of religion, spirituality and the churches. Personal and communal beliefs have to be sufficiently robust to cope with all stages of life (if they are to last), and they also need the capacity to be able to negotiate the standard ruptures in mundane reality that raise questions about meaning and value. Such occurrences are typically located in the traditional turning points; moments of life such as birth, death and marriage.[24] And of course, as we have been inferring throughout this chapter, cultures themselves can undergo rapid changes that make adaptation essential, particularly for institutions, with which we are also concerned.

The idea of churches adapting to culture is as old as the hills. There is no expression of ecclesiology that is not, in some rich and variegated sense, a reaction against, response towards or the attempted redemption of its contextual environment. Churches may choose to regard themselves as being primarily for or against culture (following Niebuhr), but as I have argued elsewhere what mainly characterises ecclesial responses to culture is their *resilience*, either in the form of resistance or accommodation, but, more usually, by combining both in its strategic survival and mission within late modernity.[25] This observation is important here, for it reminds us that religion is both deeply a part of and also totally apart from culture. Its sheer alterity is what gives it its power, as much as it is wholly incarnated within space, time and sociality. In other words, religion

---

23   Parks, *Big Questions, Worthy Dreams*, pp. 9–16.
24   See Kett, *Rites of Passage*; Goldscheider and Goldscheider, *Leaving Home before Marriage*.
25   Percy, 'Mind the Gap'.

is that material which generations will attempt to fashion and shape around their needs and desires. But the power of religion will also fashion and shape its 'users', causing them to question, reflect and wonder. Religion evokes awe; the numinous inspires; the spiritual invites a quest of ceaseless wandering.

That said, many theological, ministerial and ecclesial responses to the rapid cultural changes of late modernity, coupled to the apparently dynamic differentiation between generations, has caused the spilling of much ink. Christian bookshops are awash with literature on how to reach the young, how to engage with secular culture and how to reach those who are 'spiritual but not religious'. Typically, the character of these works is conditioned by a general sense of panic and fear, with churches engaging in ever-more neuralgic responses to the perceived crisis: flight, fright and fight would not be too wide of the mark. This is especially true in the arena of 'popular culture', where, ironically, spiritual motifs, symbols and ideas are plentiful: one trips over such 'cultural furniture' all the time in the somewhat haphazard assemblage of late modern life. There are, of course, more sophisticated attempts to read 'the signs of the times', and come up with compelling and thoughtful responses to the apparent 'generation gap'.

Paul Albrecht, for example, offers a serious theological and ecclesiological programme for the churches that was pregnant with prescience for its time – the crucible of the early 1960s.[26] More tangentially, Milton Rokeach provides a way of understanding how human values are translated and learnt from one generation to the next, and from group to group within institutions.[27] Indeed, there is now an abundance of works that could be at the service of the churches, helping them to read cultural and generational change.[28] But on the whole most theologians ignore such tasks, leaving the arena free for smaller confessional voices to shout and narrower tribal interests to be developed.

From earliest times, Christians have carved out their faith in a pluralist world, settled churches in alien cultures and adopted their practices and customs that have eventually become 'tradition'. I suspect that the litmus test for assessing the extent of generational change and its implications for mission can probably be best understood by speculating about death and memorialisation in the future.

---

[26] Albrecht, *The Churches and Rapid Social Change*.

[27] Rokeach, *Understanding Human Values*.

[28] See for example Zaltman, *Processes and Phenomena of Social Change*; Thompson, *Cultural Theory*; Hall and Neitz, *Culture*; Strinati, *Popular Culture*.

If our cultural commentators – who speak of 'gospel amnesia' and 'a thorough-going fragmentation in lineage of Christian memory' – are right, then what will a funeral visit look like in 50 years time? At present, many ministers conducting funerals can be confident that, unless otherwise requested, there will be Christian hymns and prayers at the ceremony. The Lord's Prayer may be said, and is still mumbled by many in traditional language. Some hymns – a number of which were learned at school – can be sung, and it is just possible that certain passages of scripture and collects will be familiar to a number of the mourners. But what of the future, where prayers, collects and hymns are not likely to have been part of the schooling for the vast majority of mourners? What types of religious sentiment will be uttered by the generation that is, in all probability, non-conversant in the language of formal religion, but fluent in the many dialects of spirituality?

To partly answer my own question, I turn to an analogy drawn from the world of art history. Restorers of paintings sometimes talk about the 'pentimento', the original sketch that is underneath an oil painting beginning to show through as the painting ages. The pentimento is a kind of skeletal plan (the first lines drawn on canvas): where paint falls or peels off, the earliest ideas for the picture are sometimes revealed. The analogy allows us to pose a question: what will the spiritual pentimento of millennial children look like when it comes to their funeral? It will, I suspect, at least at a church funeral, be primarily Christian, provided we understand the term 'Christian' broadly. It will be a kind of vernacular, operant (rather than formal), folk Christianity, not that dissimilar from what many ministers already encounter. But it will also be a more spiritually open and evocative affair, with perhaps readings from other traditions. It will also be more therapeutic, centred less on grief and more on celebration. In all likelihood, the funeral of the future will be able to tell us just how much change there has been between the generations. There will be gaps, to be sure, but they are unlikely to be unbridgeable. Previous generations have always found a way through to the next; there is no reason to suppose that this generation will lack the wisdom and the tenacity to do likewise. After all, the original etymology of religion comes from two Latin words, meaning 'to bind together'.

Futurescape: Opportunities and Challenge for the Churches

In this brief and final section we can do no more than suggest some further avenues for exploration. It is a fact that generational change and its implications for mission is an under-researched area, and that the churches, with what research data are available, have been reticent to read and react. As we have already indicated, this is probably motivated by fear as much as anything else. Churches are afraid of what David Ford terms 'the multiple over-whelmings of modernity', and this then characterises their responses to rapid social change and the apparently inexorable rise of popular and consumerist culture. And yet as we have seen, in the midst of these conditions, spirituality appears to thrive, although there is apparently now a greater gap between formal religion and the beliefs and values (operant religion) of the present generation. Having said that, it must be remembered that beliefs and values are not fixed in generations or between them; change is here to stay. With these remarks in mind, there are five points to make by way of concluding.

First, Putnam's analysis of the 'post-associational' society raises some intriguing missiological questions for the churches as they seek to shape their ministry. Similarly, Grace Davie's well-known mantra 'believing without belonging' has been used to characterise British church-going habits since 1945, and the statistical data tend to bear out her thesis.[29] The question for the churches is, therefore, how they can operate in a climate where people accept the message but don't respond with commitment? Of course, *insisting* on commitment is one way forward, but it is unlikely to be enough. Increasingly, churches will have to accommodate a society that expects and demands a reflexivity in its patterns of belonging. Moreover, it is likely that churches will have to provide associational opportunities for a society that is marked by diversity and mobility, and is less concerned with territoriality. This shift can be characterised as a move from the dispositional to the episodic. Whereas parochial or local churches once assumed that they operated within fairly settled and identifiable communities, these same churches will now have to work for the many different (and sometimes transient) groups within the community. This will demand more creativity, tenacity and flexibility in local mission, and less stress on the apparent 'given-ness' of a community.

---

[29]   Davie, *Religion in Britain since 1945*.

Second, Putnam's work also questions the extent to which churches are too broad in their appeal. Whilst a number of evangelical churches and other Christian traditions have enjoyed considerable success with 'family worship', there may also be room for specific services and meetings that target particular ages. There is nothing new here: pram services, Sunday Schools and the like have been practised for more than a century. But churches may need to put more energy into considering how they appeal to individuals in their 20s and 30s who may not have families, pensioners and those who have retired from work and other niche groups. With the increasing atomisation of the generations within society, churches can both swim with the culture as well as acting counter-culturally. They can meet specific generational needs (bonding), but also provide environments for generational bridging. But again, this will need to be done across a social landscape where diversity and mobility are increasing, and where people may belong to several different places and interact with a multiplicity of communities.

Third, and to return to Heywood, churches need to see that the debate about how to minister to the generations is not best served by the old 'traditional-progressive' or 'conservative-liberal' divides.[30] Heywood's history of childhood shows us, for example, that when history is done properly, feminism has not eroded the traditional status of mothers. Many mothers had a miserable time in eighteenth- and nineteenth-century industrial Britain; rates of bastardy were high, as were those of neglect, abandonment and infant mortality. Mothers had to work to survive; orphanages were filled to overflowing when either one or both parents could not work, or there was economic decline. The generation of 'stay at home wives' whose sole duty was to care for their children is but a brief blip on the landscape of social history, at least in Western Europe and America. The churches can help understanding across generations by not siding with one against another, but by educating each successive generation into properly understanding how they have come to be (e.g., values, beliefs, ideals, etc.), and how it might live out the gospel in its own time.

Fourth, if the history of generations and the churches is done properly, we can also see that the churches' 'success' with the young is relatively brief, and is also linked to wider social and civic aspirations. This is important, for children often mean different things to different congregations: they symbolise something to

---

[30]   Heywood, *A History of Childhood.*

present generations, and this is often subject to change. For some, children are a sign of spiritual strength and fecundity. Others display them in worship prominently, whilst others 'school' them quite apart from the church (and quietly).[31] But lest this sound too laissez-faire, the churches will have to work harder to reach each new generation, because, if Brown is right, the 'cycle of intergenerational renewal' has indeed been disrupted in late modernity. We cannot assume that our children will want, do, believe or behave as we have. No one can afford to be complacent. But no one should be overly pessimistic either.

Fifth, there are still certain occasions that reach across the generations, of which religion is likely to remain an intrinsic part. And this is where established and national churches – Anglicans in England amongst them – come into their own. To return to funerals, we can see this most clearly at times of national disaster. The funeral of Diana, Princess of Wales; the memorialisation surrounding the attacks in Washington and New York on 11 September 2001; the outpouring of vernacular spiritual grief for the victims of Hillsborough, Heysel – or almost anywhere else one can think to mention. At such times, the churches can often provide an inclusive act of supra-memorialisation which bridges the generations, unites in grief and hope and expresses the latent prayers and spiritual pentimento of a people that want to be together when it matters most. It is here, in these situations, that the churches must continue to reflect on how they provide the *something* that is much more than 'something for everyone'. For it is in these moments that generational gaps are bridged, wounds healed and shared understandings and memories begin to emerge, surpassing those particularities that are specific to ages and groups. It is at this point that some kind of generativity is born for the generations. Finally, there is something we can all talk about; something that we can all recollect and locate ourselves through; there is something to pass on; and something to shape the future.

---

[31]   Hopewell, *Congregation: Stories and Structures*, p. 8.

Chapter 7

Opportunity Knocks: Church, Nationhood and Establishment

There can be little doubt that times are changing, and with them, definitions and perceptions of 'establishment'. Most hereditary peers have lost their automatic right of place in the House of Lords. (A number of seats are reserved for hereditary peers, with a smaller group elected from their number.) The nation, as a whole, is markedly less deferential to what is collectively known as 'the establishment' and its culture. In turn, this has implications for a Church that is 'established by law', especially when it is only in one country (England), within a Union of countries that enjoy (increasingly) a degree of devolved power. (The (Presbyterian) Church of Scotland has been the established church in Scotland since the late Reformation period. The Anglican Church was disestablished in Ireland during the reign of Victoria, and disestablished in Wales in 1923.) Central to any enquiry relating to national churches is the use of the word 'establishment': the term normally highlights the intimate relationship between the Church – or particular churches – and individual nation states. That relationship is expressed in markedly different ways throughout Europe – an unsurprising result of geography, history (both ecclesiastical and secular) and the general cultural diversity of Europe. And yet behind the constitutional questions, there is also a cluster of theological issues connected to establishment (such as the relationship between the monarchy of God and the social legitimisation of authority in power), not to mention the hegemonic structures present in any sociality, which might include class, race, gender, wealth and birthright. Quite simply, the agenda is enormous.

Yet the agenda needs to be addressed precisely because the very sense of the culture of establishment in the United Kingdom is now self-consciously subject to variables, and is of course beginning to unravel itself and be deconstructed at a faster rate than has hitherto been previously known. The gradual but on-going reforms of the House of Lords, general public questions about the appropriateness of the Church of England colluding with such structures, not to mention more general questions about privileged positions and their relations to a democratic national state at the turn of the century, all play their part.

It is not possible here to engage in a comparative discussion of other European member states and their church/state relations; such a detailed exercise belongs to another discussion. But we should note that there is no European country that treats religion as purely a private matter. There is no European country that does not address it constitutionally, in law.[1] Equally, it must be stressed that a comparative survey of Europe does not present a neat balance sheet of establishment and disestablishment in member states. The issues, as we know only too well from England, Scotland and the rest of the United Kingdom are too complex, and interact in unexpected ways. For a start, there is an odd sense in which the legal position is often out of step with aspects of the actual practice. The hub of the wheel turns slower than the rim.

If there is any doubt about this, consider for a moment the 'normal' arrangements surrounding the coronation of a new monarch. As soon as the king or queen has died, the Earl Marshall is supposed to collect the keys to Westminster Abbey from the Dean. The Abbey remains locked until the coronation service. Meanwhile, one of the Dean's jobs is to visit the Royal Apothecary in Bond Street, to order the oils for the anointing of the head, hands and breast of the new monarch. The coronation service has at its heart Communion according to the Book of Common Prayer, attended by the crowned heads of Europe and hereditary peers of the realm. In today's multi-faith nation, it is hard to imagine anything so apparently exclusive and elitist being repeated.

And yet, just as one might think that 'establishment' is waning, events conspire to contradict us. The recent memorialisation after the Queen Mother's death revealed a nation that was relatively happy to shuffle off its disenchantment with monarchy, and put its faith in the virtues that it can embody: service, duty, representation, charity and continuity. No less significant were the recent celebrations for the Queen's own diamond jubilee. Over a million people crammed into the Mall

---

[1]   'Religions in European Union Law'; Doe and Hill, *English Canon Law*.

leading up to Buckingham Palace in early June 2012. Thousands enjoyed a music festival inside the palace grounds. Millions watched the celebrations on television. The Queen expressed her pride in the nation; the nation reciprocated with street parties, beacons and almost unparalleled celebration. As for the modest 'Republican' movement in the United Kingdom, and those who would like to see the monarchy reformed or even scrapped altogether, there was the steady haemorrhage of support. Britons, it would seem, like their monarchy more than even they knew; better the devil you know.

The tapestry we observe now – at royal funerals or at the jubilee – may be fragmentary in a pluralist and modern state, but the customs, rituals and protocols still provide some social cohesion in a picture that is as yet unfinished. It seems highly unlikely that England, or Britain, is ready to jettison the monarchy or the establishment. It sees its value, and it sees that it embodies values, freedoms and virtues that are not necessarily present within the democratic system, or readily apparent in consumerist cultures. There is some appetite for reform; yet this has been around for several centuries, and there is no reason to suppose that the current forms of establishment are entirely redundant in a modern democratic state. What seems striking about the current context is how *little* public call there is, either against the monarchy or church establishment.

The practice of establishment is, strictly speaking, a nest of contested issues and theories that is not easy to disentangle. Seen from various perspectives, an established church can be a form of religious elitism; or, perhaps an acceptable mode of representation in which one Church represents a wide variety of faith interests in political and national life; or an outdated hegemony that owes more to privilege and social capital than it does to faith; or a necessary and contingent part of the state that enables vital ethical questions and transcendent values to be referred to at most levels of society. But support for this relationship is by no means unanimous. Yet at present, there can be no doubt that the concept of 'establishment' – in its widest cultural meaning in Britain and the Commonwealth – is rapidly unravelling. The tapestry seems to be fraying. Respect for non-democratic forms of authority can no longer be counted upon (e.g., hereditary peerage). The governance of the Church of England itself, and its identity, is not immune from such prevalent cultural suspicion. Correspondingly, there are potential dangers for any national church if its power and privilege is seen to flow from elitist forms of authority that are now regarded as outmoded. Europe offers several relevant case studies over the centuries, ranging from the extreme – one thinks of the French Revolution – to the more recent and waning affections for Roman Catholicism in Spain, Italy, Portugal and Ireland, and to the fairly rapid changes in attitudes to church taxation in Sweden and Germany (following reunification).

Privilege within a devolved union of democratic countries is another key issue to reckon with in the current debate. The Church of England is the only church – out of all the democratic countries in the world – to enjoy guaranteed representation within Parliament or its equivalents. But how necessary is the presence of bishops within the House of Lords to guarantee a truly *national* church? Can English bishops 'represent' Scotland, Wales or Northern Ireland? What is the justification for one denomination, or one faith, enjoying such a singular political and social privilege? Have Britons now reached the point when such privileges, within a self-consciously plural society and devolved Union, look culturally problematic to the majority of people?

The main issue I therefore want to consider here is nationhood. Many more issues could be taken up, but space does not permit. This is an immensely complex arena for study and debate, where the social, political, cultural, theological, ecclesiological and national issues are intertwined, and virtually inseparable. As we shall now see, it is rarely possible to talk only about the nation without, at the same time, including the established church, the constitution of the state, and indeed, God.

So, let us examine the heart of the matter. Can one national or established church be justified in a pluralist and multi-faith society? How can one church represent the divergence of contemporary society? Does the very idea of establishment nurture elitism and privilege? Does the culture of 'high' establishment inhibit the national witness of the church at local levels? And how can mono-establishment be reasonable and warranted within the emerging federalism of the European Union and the devolution of British nation states?

The idea of a Christian Commonwealth – promoted by, amongst others, Coleridge, Arnold and Gladstone – seemed to have had little difficulty with particularities of unity in the midst of plurality.[2] Granted, the nineteenth century was not as pluralist as the twenty-first, but the confidence of the Victorian and

---

[2]   Nicholls, *Church and State in Britain since 1820.*

Edwardian theologians and politicians is worthy of attention, not least because it assumed that sociality needs 'high' symbols and ideals for the proper ordering of society. This partly accounts for why the separation of church and state is argued against by such authors. For them, separation would have led to social anarchy, reflected in the European countries around them that were, so it seemed, permanently in the turmoil of revolution. Correspondingly, the idea of the Empire (and later the Commonwealth) was simply a socio-political and theological framework for settling pluralism. Establishment was therefore defended by Archbishop William Temple and others well into the twentieth century (mainly drawing on the works of Richard Hooker) in the interest of the common good.[3]

But where do citizens or subjects obtain their freedom? In part, it is acquired through democratic processes and other features of the emerging public sphere mentioned earlier; governance is chosen. Yet the notion of freedom is also underwritten by a reticulate system (e.g., law, monarchy, rights, religion, etc.) that is no less at the service of the nation. This 'system' is deeply inter- and intra-related to democracy, and yet it is also capable of standing slightly apart from it. Like democracy, 'it' declares itself to be under God, and at the service of the people. The link between sovereignty and freedom is similarly expressed, such that monarchy may be said to 'represent' metaphysical values in society that partly guarantee the rights and freedoms of individuals and communities. The socio-sacramental paradigm of monarchy can also embody civic virtues such as voluntarism and charity. As Bradley notes, Coronation is sometimes referred to as 'the eighth sacrament'.[4]

Yet at the same time, we must note that the sacral integrity of the monarchy is no longer something that monarchs can claim of right. Where it exists in modern Europe, it is *conferred* by the Church rather than acclaimed by the people. In other words, the sacral relationship between the monarchy and the established church is, increasingly, and certainly in England, something that looks like an obscure artefact, in which two outdated and formerly public and dominant institutions – Church and monarchy – prop each other up through a process of mutual legitimisation. For many people, its only present justification is to identify the link as an embodiment

---

[3]   For two interesting counter arguments from the period see Figgis, *Churches in the Modern State*; Dawson, *Religion and the Modern State*.

[4]   Bradley, *God Save the Queen*, pp. 73–93.

of continuity, service and other civic virtues. But the more secular the monarchy becomes (as well as de-mythologised, popular, accessible, with less mystique and sacral charisma), the more problematic 'established' religion becomes, because the power of the crown is insufficient to sustain one Church in its hegemonic position. A link with the state, however, remains a viable avenue; but that is a *national* Church, not an established Church. And to be the latter, any church, including the Church of England, could only justify and maintain its public role by being open, free and accessible to all peoples, at all social levels.

At present the Church of England does fulfil this mandate – in effect, a National Spiritual Service. But to sustain this, it needs to guard against its own brand of congregationalism, caused by, amongst other things, evangelical or catholic sectarianism, and the pecuniary rationales that increasingly focus the funding and output of ministry upon congregations rather than parishes. I am not the first to claim this. Coleridge distinguished between *ekklesia* and *enclasia*, the latter being a description of those who are called *into* the world, and are to remain there for the common good.[5]

In view of this, I would argue that the function of a national church – even one that is tied into an evolving monarchy – might still represent a viable form of Church–State relations in a modern state. The idea of (Christian) establishment as an essential organic and living part of national identity that still has a valuable role to play in local, regional, national and international life has plenty of life left in it. Whilst pluralism, subsidiarity, devolution and other changes to the demographic, social and political culture of the nation do question the place of an established church, the presence of an established religion within a reticulate and complex ecology of establishment ensures that questions of value, ethics and justice can be raised within the midst of the governance of Parliament, and in the very heart of a consumerist society. This prescient, mildly prophetic role is still valued (but like so many features of establishment, not elected by society), and is essential for the common good and social flourishing.

In other words, freedom is guaranteed through sovereignty; sovereignty is a form of service, and not necessarily the obvious elitist hegemony that many assume it to be. As Werner Stark notes:

---

[5]   Nicholls, *Church and State in Britain since 1820*, pp. 24–31.

the societies in which monarchical religion flourished were, by and large, communities ... they were unities rather than diversities; they were collective rather than individualistic ... this primacy of the whole needed to be made visible, to be symbolised, and its visible image, its commanding symbol was the sacred monarch.[6]

So, to a point, a single concentrated (Christian) tradition may better represent and serve the interests of the many, than can other forms of democratic representation in which all have a voice. Or, put another way, sovereignty, rightly constituted as sacramental service (following Jesus), provides a paradigm for Church and monarch alike to continue being set aside to provide for the spiritual and civic needs of all the people.

If monarchy – rather like a sacrament – points beyond itself to the majesty of God, then the task of an established Church must also be to witness to the eternal in the midst of the temporal and transient. The role of a national, established Church may therefore be primarily sacrificial and sacramental in character. Incarnate, it must live with its ambiguities, lack of definition, mystery, distinctiveness and power. It actively seeks intra- and inter-dependent social, political and constitutional relations for the sake of social flourishing, to bear witness to the incarnation, and to anticipate the Kingdom that is yet to come.[7]

So, I am suggesting that churches can only be the social form of the truth (or the social transcendent body) if they ensure that they remain public bodies. This form of engagement is of course a risk, but no more so than the incarnation itself. This is about being prepared to see truth being embodied socially, contextually and temporally, in order that grace may abound. In such a situation, the Church cannot guarantee its own power absolutely, neither be sure of entirely protecting truth, nor be certain of the outcomes of its intercourse with society. But it can at least be there, and continues to speak as of right as a public body, and as a social incarnation of transcendence, mystery and morality.

In a paper written some years ago for DEMOS, Bhikhu Parekh, outlines a new paradigm for a relationship between religion and the State.[8] First, he argues

---

6   Stark, *The Sociology of Religion.*

7   See Percy, *Salt of the Earth.*

8   Parekh, 'When Religion Meets Politics'.

that instead of marginalising religion (as many secularists might have), its distinct contribution to public life should be recognised, and faith given a stake in maintenance of a free and open society. He is aware that religion can sometimes do the opposite of this, but suggests that the more openly dialogical a religion becomes, the more it is able to foster moderation and respect within itself: society can 'civilise' the church. Second, when religion enters politics, it has to accept the constraints of political life. This includes speaking in a 'public' language that is intelligible to all citizens, and accepting 'the burden of public judgement' which sometimes requires people to live with deep disagreements. Third, religion plays an important and direct role in moral life, and the community therefore has a deep and collective interest in the well-being of churches and their beliefs. For this reason, religion should be taught in school in the same way that children are politically educated. The teacher is neither to subvert nor convert, but discuss beliefs in an open, respectful, comparative and analytical manner, recognising that religion is a distinct form of human consciousness and experience.

To give Parekh's arguments a slightly different slant, I would argue that being a Christian in the twenty-first century cannot simply be about belonging to a Church, but should rather be seen as equally consisting of being a certain type of citizen within society. 'Civil religion' therefore becomes more than the 'social glue' or 'the spiritual dimension' to society. Rather, it also becomes bound up in the actual aspirations of society which are related to the common good. Andrew Shanks' work takes this at least one stage further:

> A genuinely 'open' church ... would be an open forum: reproducing within itself, the full range of (thoughtful) moral conflict characteristic of the surrounding world; excluding nothing except intolerance; and differing from the world only in the exemplary manner in which it tried to process these conflicts.[9]

Shanks continues by arguing that the church must move beyond simply providing pastoral remedies for personal sin, which he says can no longer make the church, priest or pastor a focus for communal unity. Instead, the clergy needed to be gifted in tackling the phenomenon of structural sin on behalf of the community: they

---

[9]   Shanks, *Civil Religion Civil Society*, p. 90.

need to be issue-raisers, prophets and protagonists. In this respect, he sees the Christian spirit as being invested in a new form of mission:

> the stage which Christianity has now reached is to recognise that the church-phase of its development is over, and that the Christian Spirit has entered into its ethical, or political, maturity ... the innermost essence of Christianity drives it out beyond the Church; it has to seek embodiment in nothing less than the body which encompasses the entirety of human life, namely the state.[10]

Yet Shanks, like Parekh, knows that churches need to be maintained as distinctive bodies, independent of the State and the public, if they are to be the yeast and salt of the Kingdom of God. The Church is there to help fund civilising strands within society. But it does not own society, and neither does it entirely own the moral strands which might guide and make sociality. The church does not possess a monopoly on the moral impulses of the nation; but what it does have is a vital voice in contributing to the common good. As Coleridge suggested almost two centuries ago, the Church of the nation is not quite the same as the Church of Christ, yet it is there to secure and improve the moral cultivation of its people, 'without which the nation could be neither permanent nor progressive'.[11] The Church is therefore not a world to come, but another world that now is, whose role is to combat political evil, not just institutional defects.

In precisely this vein, the current government, like others before it, seems to be looking for a church that provides vision, as well as a prescient prophetic voice, and is socially rooted. To be 'established' cannot be simply about history and privilege. I, as an Anglican in England, must continually *earn* (not just own) the right to be the Church for all people. Anglicans must move from achieving this episodically – such as enabling and focusing the mourning and funeral for Princess Diana – to *living* it dispositionally. This does not necessarily entail compromise, but rather pursuing an agenda where we strive to participate in the flux and flow of civil life at its very centre. This requires the Church to risk being deeply embedded in society. Rather than counting the potential cost of such social intercourse, one

---

[10]   Ibid., p. 114.
[11]   Newlyn, *The Cambridge Companion to Coleridge*, p. 167.

might want to ponder the gains, and be alive to the collective social and spiritual losses if we refuse to participate.

This kind of agenda, by the way, also occupies the minds of other faiths. In his recent *Islam and Liberal Citizenship*, Andrew March asks how Muslims can be both good citizens of liberal democracies and good Muslims. He is mindful that some Muslims would argue that separation of religious loyalty and political loyalty is not part of the Islamic tradition, and therefore participation in an open and pluralist society is not possible. Other Muslims – perhaps more extreme – might argue that all believers should oppose non-Islamic forms of government, and strive to implement Islamic law.[12]

Yet using the theory of John Rawls, March argues that there is a tradition that is both consistent with orthodox Sunni Islam and also compatible with modern liberal citizenship, which is rooted in the idea of 'overlapping consensus'.[13] This, suggests March, might be found in the synergy between a public conception of justice, and religious or ethical outlooks. Indeed, he argues that the more religious traditions are engaged with, the more likely it is that consensus with public concerns will be found. There can be, therefore, an alliance of interests between secular and sacred. Indeed, through engagement with public life, religious traditions may not only shape society: they may also discover some deeper truths on how they in turn are shaped.[14]

So what should the churches and faiths try to do about the current debate on Church and State, and religion contributing to the shaping of public life? A defence of the *status quo* is neither desirable nor practical, because there has always been change. An explanation of the organic, living, breathing nature of establishment is, however, highly desirable. It should be possible to articulate a modern type of establishment that 'fits' with the modernising of the constitution, and yet preserves the values, freedoms and ideals that are already embodied in sacramental/sacrificial service to the nation at all levels, either through religion or through the monarchy. But an exercise of this kind has yet to be undertaken.

However, Vernon Bogdanor hints at some intriguing possibilities in his analysis of the British constitution. He reminds us of the Prince of Wales' oft

---

[12]   March, *Islam and Liberal Citizenship*.

[13]   Rawls, *A Theory of Justice*; Rawls, *Political Liberalism*.

[14]   For further discussion, see Percy, *Engaging with Contemporary Culture*; Percy, *Shaping the Church*; Percy, *The Ecclesial Canopy*.

quoted statement that he would like to be regarded as 'Defender of Faiths' and not 'Defender of the Faith'. In other words, the Protestant monopoly on the crown would be broken, or perhaps freed up to become, once again, a socio-sacral and religious-civic focus for the plurality of faiths in modern Britain, and their voice within the public sphere.[15] Bogdanor also defends the idea of a national church (not an established one), in which the Church of England remains, for the non-religious, an 'Apostleate of the Indevout', valuing folk religion, rites of passage for all and generally providing a National Spiritual Service.[16] At the same time, Bogdanor notes that if the Church of England were to disestablish, the effect on the monarchy would be profound. Equally, if the monarchy becomes more secularised or more pluralised (e.g., repealing the Accession Oaths, which currently require the monarch to be an Anglican and not to marry a Roman Catholic), then the Church of England would lose its establishment, but might still have a claim to be a national church.

And yet, some rather stout defences of the *status quo* remain. Tariq Modood has argued that from the perspective of minority religions in Great Britain, 'establishment' remains a sign of hope:

> The real division of opinion is not between a conservative element in the Church of England versus the rest of the country, but between those that think religion has a place in secular public culture, that religious communities are part of the state, and those who think not...the minimal nature of an Anglican Establishment, its proven openness to other denominations and faiths seeking public space, and the fact that its very existence is an ongoing recognition of the public character of religion, are all reasons why it may seem far less intimidating to the minority of faiths than a triumphal secularism.[17]

Here Modood shows that a practical argument for establishment remains powerful and reasonable, even for someone who doesn't share 'the faith of the nation'.[18] And from older theological resources, there are some surprising advocates for the 'tapestry' of Church, State, nation and faith. For all the accusations of fideism and

---

[15]   Bogdanor, *The Monarchy and the Constitution*, p. 230.
[16]   Ibid., p. 231.
[17]   Modood, 'Introduction', p. 4.
[18]   See also Hastings, 'The Case for Retaining Establishment', p. 41.

imperialism levelled at Karl Barth, he turns out, ironically, to be a rather doughty defender of the inter-weavings that some have come to dislike, or even mistrust:

> The only possibility that remains – and it suggests itself compellingly – is to regard the existence of the state as a parable, as a correspondence and an analogue to the Kingdom of God which the church preaches and believes in. Since the state forms the outer circle, within which the church, with its mystery of faith and gospel, is the inner circle, since it shares a common centre with the church, it is inevitable that, although its presuppositions and its tasks are its own and different, it is nevertheless capable of and reflecting indirectly the truth and reality which constitute the Christian community.[19]

All of which is another way of saying that the church does have an interest in keeping a positive stake in the articulation of the social consensus, and that any neutrality towards the state is undesirable. However, any partnership with the state sometimes comes at a cost – perhaps even, temporarily, to that of being the Church of the nation. Oliver O'Donovan contends that, to pass beyond suspicion and the totalised criticism of politics, and to achieve a positive reconstruction of thought, theology must reach back behind the modern tradition, achieving a fuller, less selective reading of scripture, and learning from an older politico-theological discourse which flourished in the patristic, medieval and reformation periods. Central to that discourse was a series of questions about authority, generated by Jesus' proclamation of the Kingdom of God.[20] So high and low forms of establishment, together, for all the potential and actual flaws, may be a better arrangement than the alternatives. Perhaps it is for this reason that writers such as Jeffrey Stout describe the current situation as a kind of 'moral bricolage' – a kind of miscible state of being in which we accept a blend of consensus, compromise and pragmatism in our Church–state–nation–monarchy tapestry – but only because the alternatives are probably worse.[21]

So, if a monarch could choose their faith – and this is not so very far from what Prince Charles appeared to be suggesting some while ago – then one established

---

[19]   Barth, *Against the Stream*, section 14.

[20]   O'Donovan, *The Desire of Nations*.

[21]   Stout, *Ethics after Babel*.

church could, conceivably, give way to a new kind of national church, in which representation in Parliament may not be guaranteed, whilst at the same time the state would have less to say in the affairs of the Church. It would seem, then, that constitutional reform and the gradual secularisation of the monarchy, something that Blanning claims began in the seventeenth century, may have more of a say on the evolution and reform of Church–State relations than the Church itself.[22] This remains to be seen. The future beckons; and an opportunity knocks.

---

[22] Blanning, *The Culture of Power and the Power of Culture*; see also Hazell, *Constitutional Futures*.

Chapter 8

Old Tricks for New Dogs:
A Critique of Fresh Expressions

Fresh Expressions has come to prominence since the publication of *Mission-Shaped Church*, a ground-breaking report from the Church of England that argued for new and complementary forms of evangelism that would work alongside parishes in their ministries. Fresh Expressions abounds. No self-respecting diocese is without one, and in most cases, each will have several. Resources have been poured into the movement, with many dioceses and Methodist districts having dedicated officers. In some Anglican dioceses, individual deaneries have set aside income and resources to cultivate distinctively local Fresh Expressions. Thus, there are Fresh Expressions for clubbers, Goths, Mums 'n Tots, silver surfers, post-Evangelicals, pre- and post-Christian folk, generation X and Y and more besides.

Indeed, the very idea of targeted or niche church seems to have captured the attention of most denominations: a 'shape' of church that reaches out to those who lack a specific 'connection' to church is the primary driver for a plethora of rhetoric that appears to respond sensitively and resourcefully to a range of neuralgic concerns about the place of faith in public life. Thus, a phrase such as 'mission-shaped church' will often accompany a theological construction of reality such as 'being church'; and 'staying fresh' will be a spiritual and missiological imperative. Cultural relevance – and by implication, something that 'ordinary' churches can no longer truly accomplish – is elevated as the primary mode of engaging with contemporary society. Thus, and in his critique, *Mission-Shaped Church: A Theological Response*, John Hull argues that he can register his anti-nuclear Christian protest group as a Fresh Expression of church. In his politicisation and radicalisation of the term, he is drawing on the liberation theology base communities of South America.

The self-narration of the groups though, does reveal a fascination – even obsession – with being new and alternative. That is, ironically, not an especially fresh development within the sub-culture of 'soft' or 'open' British evangelicalism, which has an established tradition of continually re-inventing modish associational models of the church. None of this is new, of course. Paul Weston, writing on Lesslie Newbigin, highlights the contrast Newbigin makes between 'associational' (or congregationalist) models of the church with the parish system. Whilst recognising the power of the associational, Newbigin remains firmly committed to the parish model.[1] That same tradition has been gently experimental with a variety of dense and intense forms of congregationalism in the post-war era. It has also tended to derive its ecclesiology from biblical roots (usually accessed in a hermeneutically direct rather than nuanced manner) that focus on either the (alleged) pre-institutional state of the church (e.g., Book of Acts, Jesus and his disciples, etc.), or, the configuration, organization and ethos of the model has been centred on an apparently obvious biblical grammar and theological construction of reality that assumes the New Testament church (which presumes that its shape and identity could be easily agreed) was somehow its ideal and complete (or even revealed) form. Ergo, the more *like* a New Testament church a group can appear to be, the better, purer or more original it is held to be.

This, in part, accounts for why many Fresh Expressions resemble small church 'home groups' or early versions of House Churches – but with a slightly enhanced ethos and sense of identity. The groups are trying to return to a kind of (mythic) primitive and intimate fellowship that, it is held, the New Testament primarily advocates as the 'model' for the church. Here, the size of the group will not matter especially. What binds the members of such groups together is the sense that they are participating in something that is simultaneously fresh, new, original and culturally relevant on the one hand; and on the other, securely located in the past (i.e., the scriptures).

What follows from this is that 'church' – as an institution – emerges as the problem, rather in the same way that the early House Church Restorationists used to read and interpret scripture and the complex sweep of church history. As Andrew

---

[1]   Weston, *Lesslie Newbigin*, p. 141.

Walker pointed out, early Restorationist leaders believed that church history had rarely witnessed a 'pure' version of the church.[2] The first four centuries up until Constantine, and the reformation period (significantly, both anti-establishment eras) were deemed to be times when the Holy Spirit was 'active', and unencumbered by the established nature of an institutional church. Early Pentecostalism (i.e., pre-denominational) was affirmed, as was Restorationism itself, which of course did not regard itself as an expression of denominational identity, but rather a restoring of the kind of Christian fellowship that is allegedly narrated in the New Testament. For it is the church, with all its trappings, miscibility, complex structures and organisational baggage, that is held to have masked or corrupted an arrangement of people and ideas that should be fairly simple, and in some ways quite virginal. For this reason, I note with interest that very few participating within the Fresh Expressions movement add the rider 'of church'. The second part of the phrase has been quietly, innocently and unconsciously parked by most adherents, leaving only the proponents (who need the resources and income of the church to sustain the movement) as the ones using the full phrase.

But what evidence might there be that the Fresh Expressions movement is a form of collusion with a contemporary cultural obsession with newness, alternatives and novelty, rather than the recovery of a lost theological, missiological or ecclesiological priority? We are on tricky ground here, to be sure. Yet a sketch of recent 'open' evangelical history in England might lend some gentle support to this hypothesis. To help us here, I wish to introduce two fictional friends, whom we shall call Geoff and Anne, and who have been leaders within English charismatic renewal and related evangelistic movements for around 40 years. Geoff and Anne are 'into Fresh Expressions in a big way right now'. They speak for the movement, and are closely aligned with its agenda.

We first meet Geoff and Anne in the early 1970s, and are immediately aware of their interest in the Fisherfolk and other experimental Christian communities. The Fountain Trust, Michael Harper, Colin Urquhart and other pioneers of early charismatic renewal also feature in their interests and conversations during this time. During the 1970s and 1980s these foci develop apace: the church growth movement (Donald McGavran, Eddie Gibbs, etc.), as well as a number of individuals who are beginning Christian healing ministries such as Jean Darnell,

---

[2]   Walker, *Restoring the Kingdom.*

Jackie Pullinger, Doreen Irvine and David Pawson. The work of John Wimber then emerges as something of a breakthrough, following a close interest in David Watson's ministry and 'conversion' to charismatic renewal. First Geoff and Anne sign up for 'power evangelism'; then 'power healing'; closely followed by the third and fourth waves of the Holy Spirit, before the Kansas City prophets and the Toronto blessing.

There were other interests too: Disciple a Whole Nation (DAWN), Alpha Courses, Jesus in Me, Minus to Plus, church planting, cell churches and many more movements and initiatives besides. As the millennium approaches, their interest with Wimber fades, and they begin to follow the revival at Pensacola, and also become more absorbed with neo-Pentecostal figures such as Benny Hinn and Reinhard Bonnke. The early years of the twenty-first century see Geoff and Anne being drawn into the new alternative of the cell church movement, and then Fresh Expressions.

I do not mean to offer a cynical or even critical perspective. But Geoff and Anne's spiritual trajectory prompts several questions. Is it the case that Geoff and Anne have been on the cusp of every micro and major wave of the Holy Spirit over the last 40 years? Or, that they are simply part of an associational church or congregationalist culture that is almost instantly absorbed and captivated by whatever seems to be new, fresh and alternative? Or that, in the late-modern elevation of the individual in relation to God, religion and faith have become consumable commodities, which constantly require updating, some discarding and regular (novel) replenishment? (In other words, the very character of believing and belonging follows the traces of all other 'fashions'?) And what does all of this tell us about the missiological drivers that might be underneath the surface of an apparently innocent movement, such as Fresh Expressions? In the commentary that follows, we shall seek to flesh out some of these concerns in a little more depth, in order to try and engage in some empathetic yet critical decoding of the Fresh Expressions movement.

Commentary

English church-going has always been a complex and ambiguous phenomenon, and it is no less so in contemporary culture. The movement away from 'utility' models where the church serves all the population that identifies with the denomination (independent of their church-going habits) has gradually been replaced with 'market' models, where religious and spiritual consumerism has meant that individuals now subscribe to their chosen church or denomination. The first model (utility) is extensive in outlook, claiming all who make any kind of claim to belong, no matter how weak or tenuous. The second model (market) is intensive, and recognises only those who fulfil the criteria of membership – whether financial support, or tangible patterns of belonging. The two models are related, of course – and remain the primary paradigms of European church-going. However, we should also add that in the middle of the two models, what also seems to be flourishing is the 'episodic' rather than the 'dispositional'. The latter refers to believing (of variable salience), but not necessarily active belonging; the former, to intense-but-occasional forms of belonging, but with believing again of variable salience. The current boon in cathedral worship is one example of episodic belief on the rise: well-attended high quality religious services by increasing numbers, but with little evidence that this leads to an overall rise in actual Church of England membership. Indeed, what seems to flourish in modern European mainline denominational Christianity is pilgrimage, memorialisation and celebration, all of which are episodic in character, rather than intrinsically dispositional.

If one accepts these hypotheses, one becomes immediately aware of a tension and ambiguity around the identity of the Fresh Expressions movement. It uses all the rhetoric of extensity, outreach and engagement. Yet it is largely composed through intensity and in-reach; apart from some notable exceptions, it would seem that many individual Fresh Expressions are made up of Christians who are weary of the church as an institution, but still desire fellowship and individual spiritual sustenance. This suggests that the Fresh Expressions movement, despite its claims to the contrary, is a form of collusion with the post-institutionalism that is so endemic in contemporary culture. Some exponents openly admit this, and point out that this is 'church' for people who no longer join bodies or associations. But the risk here is clear. Belonging together in a body with higher purposes places demands on individuals and groups, including those of duty and service; this is discipleship. Demand-led groups, in contrast, may just service people's desires for more meaning and fulfilment, whilst vesting this in the language of purpose, connection and even sacrifice.[3]

On a recent visit to a church that has spawned a large number of 'cell churches' and Fresh Expressions, a map on the wall in the foyer illustrated the problem more starkly. Maps, of course, as any anthropologist knows, are representations of reality. They require the reader to collude with scales, symbols and other codes to develop a sense of what is on the ground. But the map is not reality; the same applies to any description of anything – it must also be interpretative. This particular map placed itself at the centre of the city it was ministering to, and from the centre, ribbons flowed out far and wide to the suburbs, which were then pinned in a significant number of peripheral locations. It was a kind of web-like image, if you will. The message of the map was clear: we have the city covered.

Yet I was well aware that a number of the identified locations were far from obvious. To be sure, there could be no question that groups of Christians, who attended this church, were meeting in these neighbourhoods, week in, week out. They were praying for these localities too: 'naming and claiming' whole streets in passionate and concentrated extemporary prayer meetings. But I also knew where these gatherings were held, and that, with one or two rare exceptions, the vast majority of the inhabitants of these neighbourhoods (including those that attended their own ordinary local or parish churches) were ignorant of these gatherings. In other words, for the church in the city centre, there was a map and a story that spoke of widespread engagement with all these different neighbourhoods. Yet on the ground, there was little evidence to support this. Thus, the city centre church continued to feed off and promote its rhetoric of *extensity*. Whereas the actuality – in missiological terms – was one of *dispersed intensity*. The two are not, of course, the same. Dispersed intensity lacks the complex social engagement that can really only come about through dense and reticulate institutional structures that emerge out of churches that are committed to deep local extensity. (Of course, the genius of the Deanery system – a legal collation of parishes in the Church of England – is that it consists of a range of extensive and intensive models, and an assortment of hybrids. This ensures that a relatively small area offers different types of parish ministry. The mixed ecclesial economy arguably offers a strong missiological foundation.)

---

[3]   On this, and for a critique of fulfilment-centred church growth exponents, see Schmiechen, *Saving Power*.

So, based on what we currently know about the Fresh Expressions movement the following brief comments may be salutary for the majority of examples under consideration. First, the local church is under severe pressure from both outside and inside the church. Ironically, the proliferation of the Fresh Expressions movement may threaten the relationship between religious and social capital. But if the Fresh Expressions movement turns out to be an expression of post-associational-ism, there may be serious trouble ahead.[4] The lack of 'thick' connection between a Fresh Expression and local commitment (i.e., duty, obligation, etc.) may diminish social capital, despite many claims to the contrary.

Second, and as Bellah notes, multiple-choice ('niche spirituality') 'suggests the possibility of million[s of] American religions – one for each of us'.[5] So does the Fresh Expressions movement collude with pluralism and individualism – whilst cloaked in the rhetoric of 'alternative', 'new' and 'fresh' forms of church? If it does, then the survival of the 'community of memory' is at risk – replaced by 'empathetic sharing' by loosely associated individuals. Faith is privatised; it becomes the property of a sect that sees itself as engaged with but apart from society.

Third, faith in the Fresh Expressions movement may lead to 'over-specialization' in the 'faith sector'. 'Quasi-therapeutic blandness' sets in, which cannot resist 'the competition [with] more vigorous forms of radical religious individualism, with their dramatic claims of self-realization, or the resurgent religious conservatism that spells out clear if simple, answers in an increasingly bewildering world.'[6] Put another way, the Fresh Expressions movement may represent a conservative, therapeutic and individualist *retreat* from the world, whilst cloaked in a rhetoric that emphasises the very opposite of this: namely 'cutting edge', 'radical' and so forth. Correspondingly, Linda Woodhead and Paul Heelas, in *The Spiritual Revolution* argue that formal religious organisations are now giving way to individualistic and relational forms of spirituality and sacralised therapeutic insights.

Fourth, it would seem that the insights of Putnam concur here. He notes how the (apparent) 'community building efforts of the new denominations have been directed inward[s] rather than outward[s]'.[7] Thus, members of the Fresh

---

4   Bellah, *Habits of the Heart*, ch. 6; Putnam, *Bowling Alone*.
5   Bellah, *Habits of the Heart*, p. 113.
6   Ibid., p. 113ff.
7   Putnam, *Bowling Alone*, p. 123.

Expressions movement may well join important (and of the moment) politically active or campaigning groups to achieve certain ends, at local, national and international levels. But the investment in the complex relationship between spiritual and social capital will often be lacking (e.g., paying church quotas that support a vast and complex ecclesial infrastructure – parish coverage, sector ministry, education, prison ministry, etc.).

Fifth, 'the primary objective of 'brandscaping' is not to sell the product but to generate a fascination with the brand; to get the customer to identify the world of the brand, creating a brand awareness and providing it with a deep emotional core'.[8] One can conceive of the Fresh Expressions movement as a 'brand', but not a product – in fact, it is not clear what is actually being sold. But the brand creates the sense of 'fresh' starts, horizons and newness: just one 'expression' of something existential and grounded. It is all very post-modern. Almost anything can be a fresh expression – a Book of Common Prayer service; a drop-in centre; a toddler group with some prayer and choruses. None of these are 'church', *per se*; but they have a new 'brand' that offers hope, newness and the simulation that in-dwelling the novel will somehow take us somewhere different, and better – it is a pure but subtle form of consumerism. The websites seem to confirm this, offering an array of soft, subtle and toned spiritual choices.

Sixth, the rhetoric of 'alternative' is also problematic, because it is overly dependent on (a mostly) docile but larger 'host' body to support the implied contrast. But there are dangers here for the Fresh Expressions movement. After innovation and charismatic authority has waned, bureaucratisation inevitably emerges as a strategy to cope with potential disenchantment. One also questions the cultural relativity of modish quasi-ecclesial rhetoric. For example, the attention to 'steps' and 'programmes' in health, wealth and prosperity movements (deeply rooted in American pragmatism, but only thinly and derivatively connected to gospel values). Or take the emphasis on 'power', 'expansion' and 'growth' in more mainstream Protestant churches in the 1980s – precisely correlating with capitalist culture, producing congregations obsessed with the latest [apparent] biblical, experiential or ecclesial steroids: how to get maximum growth with minimum effort; how to be bigger and better than your neighbour.

---

8   Riewoldt, *Brandscaping*, p. 10.

Seventh, the Fresh Expressions movement is a curiously bourgeois phenomenon. One website advertises prayer mats inspired by 'our [leaders'] visit to Tuscany', and a 'souk' that sells/exchanges home-made bags, purses, broaches, belts and other items that 'express [our] creativity'. There are meals, walks in the park, holidays, days out, art galleries, exploration and journeys. The imagery is telling – stones, rivers, sunsets, sky; children, young people and families. No old people, death, images of decay or hardship. The language is born of a middle-class 30–40-something age-group beholden to 'fresh' and 'organic' concepts (including nutritional advice); a God of the *Gap* or *Habitat* consumer. One idea for prayer suggests 'it's the holiday season – and if you can, go for a swim. If that's not possible take time to enjoy the sensation of water on your body as you shower'.[9]

Eighth, the Fresh Expressions movement is somewhat Janus-like in its missiological outlook. Is this movement the new highway to mission, or rather a series of new intricate cul-de-sacs? For example, what is a Fresh Expression doing when it designates their leader 'Abbot', and key or core members as 'Guardians'? Can it really be much more than hubris that such a dense and traditioned concept as 'Abbot' is appropriated for what is still a new, thin and rather un-tested group? The danger is that we are all too easily immersed in a semi-detached and sacred meaning-making enclave within consumerist culture. Left to its own devices, the Fresh Expressions movement may actually be deeply collusive with consumerism, offering alternatives and affirmations simultaneously (but note, not critiques). As Jackson Lears notes, 'under certain circumstances [the marketplace holds] out a vision of transcendence, however fleeting'.[10]

Conclusion – Ecclesiological Reflections

The purpose of this short reflection has been to challenge the relationship between contemporary culture and apparently new forms of Christianity such as the Fresh Expressions movement. The ecclesial analysis that emerges from this brief discussion suggests that many examples of Fresh Expressions are symptomatic of contemporary culture, which has typically adopted the rhetoric of 'new',

---

[9]   MayBe website.
[10]   Lears, *Fables of Abundance*, p. 9.

'alternative' and 'fresh', which in turn is rooted in increasing individualism, and the inward turn to fulfilment and personal enhancement. This, in turn, represents an uncritical absorption of post-institutionalism within the movement, that is further vested in a rhetorical cluster of tropes – 'local', 'cell', 'fresh' come to mind – which legitimise the retreat from the duties (and occasionally drudgery) of supporting and sustaining larger organisations that seek to offer something to society through utility-extensive models of service. The plethora of Fresh Expressions – dispersed forms of intensity – masks this, and in so doing critically undermines the very host body that sustains it. This is indeed ironic. The core body appears to be too weak to resist the onslaught of 'alternatives'; yet the alternatives can only survive if the core body is sustained.

Of course, it may be possible to counter the current momentum of the Fresh Expressions movement with a number of commonplace observations. For example, new is not necessarily better than old; fresh is not necessarily superior to established; and effervescence is not a substitute for substance. One might also add that in theological terms, innovation should be judged by tradition. (However, this is a complex argument to mount in both Anglican and Methodist ecclesiology.) Perhaps a better way of putting this would be to underline that 'emerging church' is not likely to be superior to the emerged church; infancy is not better than maturity; that innocence (and its assumed accompanying purity) is a starting point, not a goal. Moreover, that simplicity is not better than the demanding and dense complexity of wisdom.

Defining the turn of phrase 'fresh expressions' on its own terms of reference can also be illuminating. Definitions of 'fresh', from just about any dictionary, include the following: not salted; untainted; pure; new, novel, additional; recent, newly made; not stale; lively; not faded or fatigued. 'Fresh' implies 'consume immediately' and/or 'discard after sell by date'. The question, therefore, is how long before we speak of 'traditional fresh expressions'? And then what? Similarly, the definitions of 'expression' include: the action of pressing or squeezing out; character or feeling; an act representing something in a word or symbol; an appearance; sentiment; a sign or token. The question here is, I suppose, does this have sufficient density to be church?

Part of the puzzle of the Fresh Expressions movement is that its newness and lack of settled identity allow it to point in several directions. There is clearly an enormous amount of energy and vision to admire and commend. The diversity of projects, encounters and ideas seems to be almost limitless, suggesting that the identity of the movement is very much caught up in the sense of this being centred on evangelism for a post-institutional generation. (And perhaps post-ecclesial; but not post-spiritual or post-Christian?) This must partly account for why the official Fresh Expressions website is rather coy about ecclesiology. It acknowledges that definitions of the church are 'difficult', and that Fresh Expressions are therefore not easy to define.

This is one of the more puzzling features of the movement. In discussions with some of the advocates of Fresh Expressions, there is some reluctance to identify Metropolitan churches (i.e., where the primary focus is gay and lesbian membership) as Fresh Expressions. (This suggests that the insights of Bellah and Putnam are illuminating. Fresh Expressions do not gather individuals around overt campaigning or left-wing agendas. They are not like the base communities of South and Central America, which are birthed in liberation theology. Rather, Fresh Expressions are mainly right-of-centre and bourgeois, or individualistic and apolitical – which is, of course, anti-political.) On the other hand, some Christian Unions at colleges or universities, whilst clearly operating as Christian associations and *not* churches, appear to be regarded as Fresh Expressions. So a gathering of a few like-minded and similarly aged persons can apparently register as a Fresh Expression (of church). Yet many Christians will at least be able to make an innate cultural distinction between 'going to church' (and all that this implies in terms of likely social mix, obligation, diversity, etc.) and 'attending an act of worship' (even one repeated regularly each week) – which may of course have little to do with belonging to a church.

But underneath a rather playful ambivalence about what may or may not be 'church', there lurk some potentially serious dangers. Some of these are rooted in the constituency that Fresh Expressions has primarily drawn upon, namely individuals who have been weaned on associational patterns of the church, but are now expressing their spirituality in a post-institutional culture. One consequence of this is that individual Fresh Expressions may be able to demonstrate a thick surface commitment to social and political engagement (e.g., Jubilee, a variety of ecological concerns, etc., will feature as organisation supported by individual groups). Yet this is all a matter of conscious choice – the selection of issues and projects that further galvanise the identity of the Fresh Expression in question. But these same groups will not usually be engaged in helping to sustain the institutional church in all its miscibility and complexity. Put more sharply, how does a Fresh Expression or one of its members *invest* in ordinary, serious, extensive ministry? Whether that is prison ministry, church schools or simply ministry in an unremarkable place that needs sustenance and engagement? The danger for the Fresh Expression movement is of colluding with post-institutionalism: legitimising support for preferred causes (with the promise of immediacy, and a clear return on a focused investment); but it does not help the organisations that sustain our social and spiritual capital.

A further question can be put here: can this new type of post-institutional associational model really Christianise and convert society? Some advocates of Fresh Expressions would see the movement as engaging with the 'spiritual, not religious' generation. Laudable though this may be, a potential hazard here is that the movement may collude with contemporary culture in a potentially perilous way. Is there not a danger of weaning a generation of spiritual consumers who are resistant to religious demands?[11] Where, for example, is the self-examination or deep intra-accountability of the Methodist Class systems? People bringing concerns and interests to a group composed through 'shared values' bears no real relation to prayer and discipleship groups of previous generations. Moreover, I have this nagging sense that the line between sacralised narcissism and some contemporary worship is wafer thin. Too much of the spirituality in Fresh Expressions seems to celebrate the self (e.g., 'beautiful me') in a kind of spiritual aspic.

More generally on the subject of ecclesiology, there seems to be little in the Fresh Expressions movement that has evolved beyond the cultivation of the kind of (bourgeois?) niche groups that could potentially be advocated through Donald McGavran's homogenous unity principle (church growth). McGavran argued that differences in economic, social and caste positions (e.g., in India) inhibit church growth. Ergo, by developing 'homogenous units' in which such differences need not be presented or surface, 'like attracts like'. Thus, a church simply for Hispanics, blacks or whites will tend to fare numerically better than attempting

---

[11]   See Woodhead and Heelas, *The Spiritual Revolution*. When asked by a lawyer what he had to do to inherit eternal life, Jesus did not reply 'well, what works for you?') (Luke 10:25–8).

one large inter-racial church. There is no deep difference between the missiology that McGavran advocates and that of the Fresh Expressions movement.[12] For McGavran, the most effective way to numerically grow groups of Christians was to adopt his Homogenous Unit Principle – a section of society (or subculture) in which all members have much in common. Indeed, the lack of reference to McGavran's work in the Fresh Expressions movement is a puzzle, since it is clear that his missiological DNA has deeply influenced the movement.

Fresh Expressions are, primarily, contemporary versions of the homogenous unit principle for church growth that were promoted over 40 years ago, but were subsequently widely discredited by theologians, and also condemned by missiologists for their focus on pragmatism, and their willingness to sanction narrowly constituted groups (on the basis of age, gender, race, class, wealth, etc.) as 'church', which of course then legitimises ageism, sexism, racism, classism and economic divisiveness.

One puzzle here is that very few advocating Fresh Expressions will have ever heard of Donald McGavran's work, or would know why his writings are now mostly treated with a healthy suspicion. In one sense, then, we can say that Fresh Expressions is a case of 'old tricks for new dogs'. Or to paraphrase and adapt G.K. Chesterton's quip, it is not that church has been weighed and found wanting by many in the Fresh Expressions movement. It is, rather, that, it has been found too difficult and not really tried. Many Fresh Expressions therefore constitute a perfect fit for a post-institutional culture that does not want to invest in complex organisations and infrastructure for the common good.

That said, I do think that the Fresh Expressions can make a modest and positive contribution to the mixed economy of church life. At worst, the movement is a distraction – another way of keeping energetic folk occupied. On one level, this is not a problem. Why not have lots of epochs that enhance energy? I can only think of one reason. And that is that many of these movements have one thing in common – they avoid the 'C' word, with a relentless appeal to another 'C' word. It is fine to talk about Christianity: but Church is boring, cumbersome, institutional, messy and difficult. But I think Church is also *deep*. And I am wondering – with all the emerging post-evangelical rhetoric about religion-less Christianity – when it will be realised that Church is actually it. That parish ministry is still the cutting

---

[12]   McGavran, *Understanding Church Growth*.

edge. And that without the institution of the church, all we'll have left is multi-choice spirituality, individualism and innovation. And that this simply won't be enough to sustain faith in future generations.

Then again, the Fresh Expressions movement represents a serious attempt to engage with contemporary culture, and the fact that it can be identified as an enculturated version of contemporary faith should not lead it to be judged harshly. The emerging pragmatic missiology that the movement is producing will help to shape future entrepreneurial leaders: risk-takers who may indeed help to reframe our ecclesial paradigms.

The challenge for the church will, I suspect, lie in maintaining the extensive, utility and parochial forms of mission that go on each day, and are often unsung; yet also allowing the effervesce of new movements (usually associational in outlook, market-driven, intensive, etc.) that will continue to both challenge and feed the institution. What the church will need to avoid is falling in to the trap of imagining that spiritual forms of post-institutionalism hold out any long-term hope for the future of the church. I am sure they do not. What is now deemed to be fresh cannot last, by definition. The task of the church, sometimes, is just to wait, and hope, pray and work for better times. It is, after all, one of the major themes of the Old Testament: waiting. We know that the period of exile may indeed be very long. But the answer is not to be found in turning our gaze to the new gods of a very different kind of Babylonian captivity.

PART III
Communion and Polity

Chapter 9

Herding Cats: Leadership in the Church of England

'Leading the Church of England is like trying to herd cats.'

Traditional Proverb

Leadership in the Church of England is a complex business. At the parochial level, and as a distinct community of practice, churches may contain a range of employees who are 'professionals' of sorts (i.e., trained clergy, etc.), who preside over and work with volunteers who also have significant interests and power within the said ecclesial polity. At a macro level, bishops may be said to hold some ultimate authority within an ordered hierarchy, but this is still within the context of a largely voluntary organisation. Then there are synods, with their distinctive mission in representation and leadership. And finally there are the accoutrements of power associated with being an established church. The monarch (a layperson) is the Supreme Governor; no ordination or consecration can take place without an oath of allegiance. The Church of England is, in at least one real sense, the property of the crown, and held in trust for the people. Establishment prevents the church from imagining that it belongs to itself; it is a national treasure rather than a project, programme or product of the Archbishops' Council.

Small wonder, then, that many who hold authority within the church can often be heard to complain that they are often hamstrung when it comes to making decisions or offering decisive leadership. The very nature of the organisation – a complex spaghetti of democracy and autocracy, synodical and Episcopal, local and national, clerical and lay, voluntary and professional – seems to militate against clarity of purpose and direction. Indeed, the church protects and perhaps honours the tradition of loyal dissent; the church embodies too many views to be too easily led. Leading it is, in common parlance, like trying to herd cats. Little can be driven; much must be coaxed. (Indeed, even at Cuddesdon, there is a tradition of Principals vesting obligatory requirements placed upon the community being vested in the more coded language of there being 'a firm expectation' that members will subscribe to or comply with a request.)

But given that the nature of the Church of England's ecclesial polity is obvious, we could be forgiven for asking why, exactly, those who find themselves in positions of leadership and authority are so frequently frustrated? Should it not be apparent that the organisation is *not* shaped for easily defined aims, objectives and goals? Indeed, is it not obvious that the Church of England is, in a profound sense, a community of practice bound together more by manners, habits and outlooks than it is by doctrinal agreement. Indeed, one could argue that Anglicanism, at its best, is a community of civilised disagreement.

In this chapter I want to explore what it might mean to talk about leadership within the church, by focusing on the nature of theological education. I should say at the outset that this is not a theology of leadership *per se*. It is, rather, a preliminary attempt to sketch just some of the contours that I believe to be characteristic of good theological education and leadership – either of a parish or a diocese. Fundamental to my thesis is the assumption that listening and learning from congregations (and I mean deeply here) is an essential pre-requisite for any teaching and directing. As James Hopewell puts it in his seminal study: 'church leaders should make a prior commitment to understand the nature of the object they propose to improve ... many strategies for operating upon local churches are uninformed about the cultural constitution of the parish'.[1]

Hopewell's commonsensical observation is rather understated. Books and programmes that purport to be able to shape and direct the church are a dime a dozen. But guides that educate ministers into a deep engagement with their congregation are few and far between. The assumption is – no doubt generated from the womb of many theological colleges or seminaries – that the congregation is an essentially passive body to which the 'professional' Christian leader is called to minister. I hold this to be an impoverished view of churches (operant religion or grounded ecclesiology), which is supported by a flawed educational philosophy,

---

[1]   Hopewell, *Congregation*, p. 11.

which falsely constructs and then divides the teacher from the learner, and the leader from the led. (I should add that we do try, at Cuddesdon, to teach through education, training and formation, that the congregation or parish is *already* a site of theological reflection and praxis, long before the Curate arrives. For many churches, such reflection and praxis has been going on for centuries, in architecture, ethos and worship.) Correspondingly, a more dynamic and fluid understanding of how congregations are shaped, and how they learn may provide an important key to comprehending how leaders function within a complex ecclesial polity.

Transformation and Leadership

Commenting on the fragmentation and concentration of theological training programmes in the USA, Poling and Miller note how ordinands (or seminarians) are pulled deeply into isolated and disconnected wells of expertise, such as biblical studies, church history and various types of (competing) theologies. In contrast, they argue for a process of

> community formation [establishing] critical awareness of the tradition, focused
> community planning ... reinterpreting the interplay of covenant and tradition ...
> the [Pastor/Priest/Minister] relates so as to stimulate the formation community
> ... [standing] between the interpretive and political processes ... as midwife to
> community formation.[2]

Poling and Miller are conscious that there is a deep problem in theological leadership, education and formation. First, its lack of groundedness in the real or authentic life of the church means that ordinands or seminarians quickly unlearn, forget or distrust all that they have been taught at theological college. Second, this leads to a weakening of their ties with their congregations, because what has been offered (and quickly discarded) was essentially abstract and verbal. Third, the former students learn to distrust not only their teachers but also the idea of teaching: they quickly lapse into 'what works', and, at best, manage a kind of orthopraxy: 'Action and reflection methodologies encourage instant theologising,

---

[2] Poling and Miller, *Foundations for a Practical Theology of Ministry*, p. 147.

quick responses to whatever is offered. The disciplines of scholarship are replaced by agility of response.'[3]

More likely, however, they will be slightly schizoid in theological orientation: cherished theories seldom match practice. The irony here is that the depth of theological formation has probably not gone deep enough. A crisis in leadership is already being shaped at this point. Interestingly, Poling and Miller suggest that the missing element from many theological programmes is any serious attention to the ways in which a sense of *community* is a major part of the process of formation. They also criticise theological colleges for being 'in bondage to upper middle-class interest[s]' and male interests: 'the concerns of blacks, Hispanics ... native Americans, Asian and African Christians are seldom represented'.[4] Rather, it is as and when the community (of practice) or congregation recognises that the environment and context itself is educative that something deeper can commence. Once students realise that the theological college or seminary itself is merely *part* of the schooling process, they can begin to understand how what they are studying relates to whom and where they are, what they are about, and about to become. It is precisely this kind of vision that forms part of the foundation for training and formation at institutions such as Cuddesdon – learning is part of the life and journey of all disciples, and lasts throughout our discipleship.[5] So inevitably, we are drawn to saying that the vast majority of theological education rarely reflects on itself (as a dynamic, process, etc.), and is seldom able to evaluate its performance. This is extraordinary when one considers the all-pervasive nature of theological reflection across faith communities, which is by no means restricted to professional clerics or academics. Edward Farley, in one of the more influential essays in the field of theological formation, calls for a 'hermeneutic of situations' in which the taught and skilled interpreter will learn to

> uncover the distinctive contents of the situation, will probe its repressed past, will explore its relation to other situations with which it is intertwined, and will also explore the 'demand' of the situation through consideration of corruption and redemption ... a practical theology of these activities and environments

---

[3]   Ibid., p. 149.

[4]   Ibid., p. 149.

[5]   For an alternative vision, see Ferris, *Renewal in Theological Education*; Pobee, *Towards a Viable Theological Education*.

will correct their [i.e., the clergy's] traditional pedagogical isolation through a special hermeneutics of these situations.[6]

Again, this approach challenges some of the fundamental assertions relating to the nature of theology. In Farley's thinking, the situations are themselves the crucible for learning and teaching, not something other to which theology is 'applied'. In theological education, therefore, stories, worldview and narrative take on a new significance as the *place* of engagement and interpretation. Or, put more theologically, Christian education and the leadership that flows from that becomes an expression of the incarnate dimensions that it ultimately bears witness to.

But in truth, the problem is deeper and more widespread than is at first apparent. The churches, in valuing their tradition, are not only slow to change; they are also often guilty of resisting it. Proper admiration of the past quickly becomes a dialectical mode: modernity versus the sacred, change versus tradition, and more besides. Paradoxically, transformation can be seen as a sign of weakness, and a lack of depth. In such situations, theological leadership can become extremely difficult, and can often lapse into a series of pragmatic negotiations that end up colluding with and protecting existing vested interests.

Reflecting upon this dynamic more personally, two stories come to mind. First, in attempting to investigate the changing patterns of healthcare chaplaincy in England, I was able to secure a generous grant from a prestigious research body to enable the appointment of a Research Fellow. In the process of designing the research, I naturally approached the Church of England's Hospital Chaplaincy Council to see if they would contribute to or participate in the research. I was surprised to be turned down flat, on the basis that 'we know all there is to know about the field, and we can't really see what you are doing this research for'.[7] The research went ahead anyway, and, unsurprisingly, the Research Fellow discovered a variable and wide range of practices in hospitals related to the delivery of chaplaincy services. Some NHS Trusts had proper systems of accountability, and worked hard to make (state-funded) chaplaincy religiously inclusive by thoroughly involving non-Christian faiths in the shaping of the service and the profession. On the other hand, the Research Fellow also discovered hospitals where the chaplaincy

---

[6] Farley, 'Interpreting Situations', p. 67.
[7] Orchard, *Hospital Chaplaincy*.

service was ill-defined, poorly managed, lacking in sensitivity to non-Christian faiths and generally offering a meagre service to patients and hospital alike.

One can only guess as to why the Church of England should have resisted research into its own performance at this level, particularly when hospital chaplaincy is mainly funded by the state. But the educational implications are, arguably, the more serious issue here. Research-led investigations into ministerial performance (evaluation) could feed directly back into the present state of theological education. One might ask, 'how are Anglican chaplains (who constitute almost 70 per cent of the state funding for hospital chaplaincy) supposed to relate to ministers of other faiths, and build religiously inclusive chaplaincy teams?' It is not as easy as it sounds when one considers that the study of non-Christian faiths (or even, for that matter, other Christian denominations) is not part of the approved curriculum for trainee ministers. Neither does the subject become an issue during Continuing Ministerial Education. In other words, the church is deficient in research-led education to enable processes of transformation. And because of this lack, it resists change, including self-critical reflection that would lead to transformations of its own educational formation.

Second, a similar problem exists when it comes to analysing why clergy leave ordained ministry. Each year, approximately 220 clergy leave full-time ordained ministry in the Church of England. However although the data are collected, they are seldom reflected upon. The educational cost alone of this apparent 'wastage' is surely substantial, and yet researching the phenomenon – which might lead to transformations in selection, training, the management of clergy and so forth – is fiercely resisted at almost every level. Again, one can only guess as to why the Church of England would not wish to look at such an obvious area of research. But the lack of critical self-reflection continues to prevent any kind of transformation. So in advocating a matrix of research, critical reflection and evaluation, I am conscious of its limits, especially in relation to theology and the church. Not everything can be counted; skills are not easily measured; teaching and learning may resist certain types of commodification. True, theology is an art, not a science, and its appeal and argument are more usually aesthetic than systematic. Nonetheless, I hold that the key to the transformation of the church lies in research, evaluation and critical reflection.

In her ground-breaking *Transforming Practice*, Elaine Graham uses the Aristotelian concept of *phronesis* to identify the type of 'practical wisdom' that ecclesial communities need to seek in order to adapt and transform themselves. Using the work of Don Browning as an additional foundation, Graham argues that practical theology as transforming practice can come about when it is reconceived as 'the articulation and excavation of sources and norms of Christian practice'.[8] In other words, theological education needs to take seriously ecclesial communities as a primary *place* and *focus* of theological education. But how would this become transforming practice? Five points need making here.

First, one understanding of practical theology is to enable churches to 'practise what they preach'. To do this, particular attention needs to be paid to the habits, customs and beliefs of churches, in order to identify what it is they value and espouse. Graham argues that this kind of enquiry requires a 'postmodern' methodology of *bricolage*, one that pieces together fragments of knowledge, aware that disclosure of identity is often ambiguous and incomplete.[9]

Second, Graham argues that the postmodern is less of a successor to modernity and more of a complementary and critical corrective to it. It is through postmodern templates that the hubris of modernity can be questioned: its optimism, literalism, imperialism, objectivism and totalitarianism can be interrogated, and its limits probed. From here, the *alterity* of communities (including churches) can move from the margins into the mainstream as their voices are heard afresh.

Third, a focus on the entirety of Christian practice allows for a new opening up of the boundaries and horizons of Christian education. Once *praxis* and *context* is seen to be 'hermeneutically primary', Christian experience is properly re-positioned as the *origin* of theological formulation, and not the application of 'learning' upon experience. Correspondingly, ecclesial communities are once again established as the primary ground of theological education; a critical discipline that interrogates the norms and values that shape and guide all corporate activity, through which 'the community enacts its identity'.[10]

Fourth, practical wisdom, which emerges out of the first three stages, now breaks through the typical theory–practice or abstract–applied dialects, and now

---

[8]   Browning, *Fundamental Practical Theology*; Pattison and Woodward, *The Blackwell Reader in Pastoral and Practical Theology*, p. 104.

[9]   Graham, 'Practical Theology as Transforming Practice', p. 106.

[10]   Ibid., p. 109.

sees all writing, speaking, theorising and activity within churches as performative *practices* that bind communities together, enabling them to share commitments and values. Thus, the *phronesis* of an ecclesial community is both inhabited and enacted. Theological education and spiritual formation is an innate part of the *ordinary* life of the church.

Fifth and finally, Graham's attention to *alterity* (otherness) invites churches to reflect on their diversity and inclusiveness. Distinguishing between disclosure and foreclosure, Graham notes how certain groups, practices, needs, insights and agendas are often overlooked or silenced by the churches. True theological education, therefore, in order to fulfil its transformative vocation, must pay constant attention to 'the other'. This requires not only openness (in terms of boundaries and horizons of possibility), but also a hermeneutic of suspicion that will have the capacity to excavate norms and sources with a critical-reflective mind.[11]

To earth these observations a little more, and to root them in the idea of theological leadership, let us return to an instance that we referred to earlier in this section: clergy leaving full-time ordained ministry. With Graham's insights to hand, we are now in a better position to understand why the agenda (in terms of research, better pastoral care and a review of selection and training methods) is so easily marginalised within the churches. To explore this area would require the registering of pain, the recognition of failure, the hurts and wounds that institutions inflict on individuals, and that individuals inflict on institutions. It is a messy, complex arena to address, and one that could only begin to be approached through narrative *bricolage* (i.e., a sensitivity to people's stories, an acuity for the latent oppression inherent within many practices and organisations, etc.) and methodological *bricolage* (i.e., ethnography, ecclesiology, pastoral studies, etc.).

Furthermore, it requires the church to explore its own types of marginal alterity, and in so doing, revisit its praxis in the light of its conventional norms and sources, excavating their meaning and application. So, we might ask, what does Christian tradition have to say to people who, for whatever reason, fail in Christian ministry? What do the codes and rules of the church say, and, more importantly, what do they *convey* to those who have departed or been forced to leave? How is the pain and grief of the laity who lose a minister addressed or recognised? How is the hope of redemption manifested in disciplinary procedures

---

[11]   Ibid., p. 112.

(occasionally ecclesiastical trials), and other measures that are sometimes taken against a departing minister? It is in addressing the pain, here, in the body of Christ itself, that transforming practice can begin to emerge and offer the genuine possibility of the renewal of theological education.

In other words, theological leadership in this situation requires individuals and communities that are prepared to work within a matrix of evaluation, critical reflection and research. This is a risky, and potentially lonesome, task for true leadership would move quickly from naïve interpretations of the church and its ministry and practice to those that are shrewd (or ironic). But true leadership would have to venture even beyond this into the realm of the revolutionary, since a proper appraisal of the situation requires radical research and a no less radical response.

Education, Liberation and Theological Leadership

These observations take us, quite naturally, back into the field of liberation theology, a term that is loosely used to describe a variety of theologies that makes the specific liberation of a group (marginalised or oppressed by virtue of class, race, gender, sexuality, wealth, ethnicity, etc.) its primary purpose and a theological fundamental. The roots of liberation theology lie principally in Latin American theology and also in the Civil Rights struggles within the USA. But at the very base of these roots lies a theory of education (and therefore transformative leadership and community development) that was first developed by Paulo Freire. For Freire, two approaches to education must be rejected. The first is the traditionalist (or naïve), which '[defends] class interests, to which that faith is subordinated'. Here Freire cites an example of how faith is narrated as something to be 'protected' against the potential ravages of revolution or Marxism. Second, the alternative modernising agenda (or shrewd/ironic) is also opposed, which is deemed to offer reform, but only so as to 'preserve the status quo'. Freire rejects both these options in favour of a prophetic perspective on education that envisages education as 'an instrument of transforming action, as political praxis at the service of human liberation'.[12] For Freire, that will necessarily involve

---

[12]   Freire, *The Pedagogy of the Oppressed*, p. 544; Astley, Francis and Crowder, *Theological Perspectives on Christian Formation*, p. 167.

a further, more radical excavation of norms and sources. Thus: 'They [i.e., the churches] discover through praxis that their "innocent" period was not the least impartial ... [when others] insist on the "neutrality" of the church ... they castrate the prophetic dimension'.[13]

Freire's agenda has been taken forward by a variety of scholars. For example, Thomas Groome argues (rather as we have been), that Christian praxis is the normative form of theological education.[14] This contribution, from a more mainstream (western) theologian opens up the possibility of theology beginning with the praxis of the poor. But at the same time, the more radical edge of liberation theology should not be lost in the milieu of praxis-centred theology, for the *desiderata* of liberation theology remains liberation, not development. There is a perpetual rawness to liberation theology that refuses to be consolidated and consoled by accommodationist strategies that do not fully embrace a radical revolutionary revision of structures and contexts.

Again, this type of assertion about the nature and purpose of theological education takes us back to a fundamental question: the nature of theology itself. What, or perhaps who is it for? There are several different answers to this question, but our purpose in opening up this brief section on liberation with the attacks on neutrality is to show that there is no point on the theological compass, or in Christian leadership, that is non-directive. In other words, an enquiry into the *nature* and *purpose* of theology is an inherently political question that challenges the shaping and ordering of the discipline itself, long before anything is ever 'taught' by anyone, or any church is 'led' by an individual.

That said, liberation theology still stands within a broader tradition of theology: that of the hope of transformation. As Richard Grigg perceptively argues, religion itself can be defined as 'a means toward ultimate transformation'.[15] But although one might try and distinguish between theology and religion – theology being the 'intellectual approach to the infinite' – the distinction barely works in practice, since 'the infinite that theology attempts to understand is just that infinite which can aid us in dealing with fundamental practical dilemmas connected to our finitude ... theological reflection tends always to point to religious practice'.[16]

---

13   Freire, *The Pedagogy of the Oppressed*, pp. 524–45.
14   Groome, *Christian Religious Education*.
15   Grigg, *Theology as a Way of Thinking*, p. 8; see also Streng, *Ways of Being Religious*.
16   Grigg, *Theology as a Way of Thinking*, p. 8.

Grigg extends his theorising to reflect on the particularity of liberation theology, and what is methodologically distinctive about its programme for the field of theological education. Drawing on the work of Robert Long, Grigg identifies six characteristics of liberating hermeneutics.[17]

The first is 'a different starting point'. Instead of beginning with abstract theories, liberation theology commences with the 'experience of being marginalised or excluded'. Second, there is a different interlocutor. Liberation theology does not seek to persuade non-believers with intellectual or philosophical doubts; rather, it works with the people who are oppressed. Third, liberation theology uses different tools. It sets aside metaphysical speculation, and opts for the insights of sociologists, political theorists (often Marxist) and historians. Fourth, liberation theology offers a different analysis. Instead of assuming a harmony between peoples and a degree of neutrality in methodology, liberation theology presumes that injustice is already inbuilt. Fifth, there is a different tone to the engagement. Instead of assuming that there will be a definitive Truth or principle to be arrived at, liberation theology maintains that the struggle for justice and truth will be ongoing, and be known only in perpetual praxis. Sixth, and finally, liberation theology proposes a different kind of theology. Instead of truth 'from above' (that is often then imposed on the world), liberation theology seeks to discover liberating truth in praxis, through a process of critical reflection. It is these six characteristics that, together, will begin the process of transformation that may actually and ultimately enable liberation.[18]

Having briefly discussed liberation theology and education, it is important to state that the promulgation of formation, transformation and liberation as essential characteristics of theological education are by no means confined to the field of liberation theology. Postmodern writers have been quick to identify the agenda as one that is consonant with their own hermeneutics of suspicion in relation to modernity. Consider, for example, the African-American literary scholar, bell hooks:

> To educate as the practice of freedom is a way of teaching that anyone can learn.
> That learning process comes easiest to those of us who teach who also believe
> that there is an aspect to our vocation that is sacred; who believe that our work

[17]   Long, *Theology in a New Key*.
[18]   Grigg, *Theology as a Way of Thinking*, pp. 75–6.

is not merely to share information but to share in the intellectual and spiritual growth of our students. To teach in a manner that respects and cares for the souls of our students is essential if we are to provide the necessary conditions where learning can most deeply and intimately begin.[19]

As Hodgson notes, hooks sees that teaching 'touches, evokes, energises the very depths of the human, liberates peoples to realise their potential and transform the world'.[20] He links hooks' work to that of John Dewey, who maintained that teaching and education has a sacral dimension to it precisely because it is the means by which human beings maintain themselves through renewal.[21] But how exactly is such education the 'practice of freedom'?

Peter Hodgson argues that the tradition is an ancient one, although more implicit than explicit in early theological writings.[22] Gregory of Nyssa, for example, saw Christian *paedia* as renewal, liberation and transformation through individuals imitating Christ. It is here, claims Hodgson, that we first encounter a language of transformative pedagogy. The theme of freedom and education also emerges in the work of Herder and Hegel, with the latter showing particular concern for families and the state and the education of children. Where poor children were put to work at an early age, lack of education meant lack of freedom, and a form of economic slavery. Here, the practice of freedom took priority over the consciousness of freedom: Hegel's work is unavoidably political.

Hodgson develops his thesis by suggesting three discrete areas where theological education and liberation combine to make a richer theology. To some extent these points already echo points we have made earlier, but they merit some further elucidation here, as we seek to establish the meaning of theological education. First, Hodgson agrees with Freire's assertion that liberation is not a deposit made in humans. Rather, it is a form of praxis: 'the action and reflection of human beings upon their world in order to transform it'.[23] As Freire notes, 'The teacher is no longer merely the-one-who-teaches, but one who is himself taught

---

[19]   hooks, *Teaching to Transgress*, p. 13.
[20]   Hodgson, *God's Wisdom*, p. 4.
[21]   Dewey, *Democracy and Education*.
[22]   Hodgson, *God's Wisdom*, pp. 71–80.
[23]   Ibid., p. 75.

in dialogue with the students, who in turn while being taught also teach. They become jointly responsible for a process in which all grow.'[24]

What Freire is saying here is that the subject matter *gives* itself (especially in theology), and that teachers and students are caught up in the dynamic of this gift, which in turn creates, sustains and then transforms their relationships. To be taught, then, means not to be taught *things*, but *how* to think, which alone can then enable transformation and liberation.

Second, education as the practice of freedom is about radical democracy and social transformation. However, this transformation may not only be about resisting and challenging established social norms – it may also involve enabling society to live more peaceably with its many differences and diversities. One of the higher vocations of education is to enable 'the celebration of difference ... [but] persons must learn how to play the politics of difference'.[25]

Third, education as the practice of freedom is potentially conflictual and painful. Education presupposes transformation, and this will necessarily involve clashes with prejudices, habits and 'acceptable' forms of behaviour. In other words, it is only when truth is disputed that truth can emerge. And it is only by entering the debate that a dispute can take place. This takes us back, again, to the character and shape of theology. It is not something settled, signed, sealed and delivered. It is, rather, a way of educating: forming, transforming and liberating. Freedom, then, is not easily attained. The road to liberation (through the practice/ praxis of education) is full of traffic with competing interests and going in different directions. The would-be traveller is not guaranteed a safe and smooth passage. The would-be leader is assured of an uncomfortable journey.

Conclusion

This chapter has sought to show how theological education might be reconceived as a process of transformation and liberation in relation to notions of leadership. We have offered an overview of how this might work, recognising that application of the essentials discussed will take on markedly different characters

---

[24] Freire, *The Pedagogy of the Oppressed*, pp. 66–7.
[25] Hodgson, *God's Wisdom*, p. 77.

in various types of ecclesial communities. However, we have also sought to
show how theological education is a corporate, dynamic and collaborative
exercise, rather than something that is done to or for individuals. Inevitably,
the debate and discussion is political in character, since the excavation of the
meaning of theological education takes us back to challenging the nature and
purpose of the discipline itself. In a community such as Cuddesdon for example,
students quickly learn that the 'politics' of liturgy or theology, and attendant
ecclesial positions, require a greater depth and breadth of charity, generosity
and faithfulness for community life to cohere. It is a lesson – crafted with a deep
intentionality, and part of the hidden curriculum , that may well frustrate students
in the setting of a seminary – through the seemingly endless cycle of tension,
compromise, decision and implementation, for example – that then goes on to
bear much fruit in ecclesial life, when the seminarian has to continue forming
congregational fidelity through the exercise of patience, charity and hope. But
if one can learn to eat, worship and learn together with fellow-seminarians that
we don't otherwise agree with, Christ will be found in the meeting together, and
not divided by theological and ecclesial partiality. The vision for breadth in other
words, at places like Cuddesdon, is rooted in God's own breadth and abundance.

However, we cannot leave the debate at this point, poised as it were, for
an endless number of ongoing political disputes. Hodgson suggests that the
way forward for transformative pedagogy is to recognise that it has a dual
responsibility quite apart from its vocation to challenge and liberate. The first is
to offer 'connected teaching'. Hodgson reverts to the Socratic-midwife analogy.
Teachers draw out truth from their students, and enable the dialogical processes of
education. The creation of this 'space' also enables spiritual formation, and resists
the 'banking' model of education in favour of nurturing, encouragement and trust.
'Connected teaching', in other words, assumes a level of cooperation with the
student; it requires grace, communion, reserve, inspiration and inclusion.

Second, learning is seen as cooperative. Hodgson asserts that teaching and
learning is at its best when the role of the teacher shifts from 'expert and authority
figure to facilitator and coach' – one who 'observes, monitors and answers
questions'. Again, recognition of the shared nature of learning is at the heart of
a transformative pedagogy, and this, in turn, questions many of the prevailing
assumptions about the nature of theological education and leadership that are often

present in most churches. To be sure, the recipe advocated here is one fraught with risk, but it issues a simple invitation. Can church leaders learn to be learners again? And can its leaders learn to truly teach, rather than simply indoctrinate?

Chapter 10

Context and Catholicity:
An Anglican-American Dilemma?

What an interesting year 2008 turned out to be. The world witnessed an election for the US presidency, in which Barrack Obama won a pretty handsome majority in senate and congress, and also won the popular vote by some margin. And just a few months before, the world's media was also invited to be both spectator and speculator on a Lambeth Conference for Anglicans, which passed off more or less peacefully, even managing to avoid the consequences of various ecclesial manoeuvres in the American Episcopal Church (TEC) from overly distorting the agenda. But what is the connection between these two events? Quite simply, I want to suggest that some of the current crises in Anglican identity are partly rooted in some of the un-surfaced cultural and contextual assumptions that shape American life.

That said, this brief chapter is not intended to be a rant. It is, rather, an invitation to begin critically exploring the relationship between catholicity and enculturation, and sketch some of the dilemmas facing global Anglican polity. I should say at the outset that the choice of the word 'dilemmas' is itself deliberate: I do not say 'problems'. A problem is something that can be solved. Dilemmas are, however, arenas where issues and values can only be balanced. And I believe that part of the crisis facing Anglican polity at present is rooted in the inability to distinguish between problems and dilemmas. But I am ahead of myself already, so let me begin at the beginning.

One Event, Two People and Several Issues

With the inauguration of President Obama now many moons ago, it may seem a little strange to some observers looking back on the event that quite a bit of the focus was on Rick Warren, the pastor of Saddleback mega-church in southern California. Obama had chosen Warren to give the invocation on 20 January – conferring the kind of status on a pastor that would normally be reserved for the likes of Billy Graham. The other noteworthy person present at the inauguration was the Bishop of New Hampshire, Gene Robinson, who led the prayers. Robinson was elected bishop in 2003, and as a divorcee and gay man, has seen his elevation to the episcopacy become a focal point for the divisions in global Anglican polity. To some, he represents the ascendancy of imperialistic Episcopalian liberalism. To others, he is a prophetic forerunner – a champion for gay rights, who is challenging the innate homophobia of a church that is resisting both modernity and equality.

In choosing both Warren and Robinson to participate in the inauguration, Obama appeared to have selected two Christian leaders to represent the right and the left, and in so doing achieved some creditable political and religious balance. Here, perhaps, was the wisdom of Solomon in action? Yet I want to suggest that both Robinson and Warren have much more in common than might appear to be the case, and that this arguably highlights a problem in the relationship between catholicity and context. So let me say more, and begin with Warren.

It was Warren who hosted the first debate between Obama and McCain that kick-started the presidential race. Warren is a well-known exponent of conservative Christian values on all the cornerstone issues that currently unite and divide evangelicals: gay rights, abortion, and so forth. So selection of Warren to give the invocation is not without controversy. But what exactly was a black northern liberal doing inviting a white southern conservative to preach? Cue the predictable banshee cries and wailings of protest from the political left.

The choice of Warren, however, represented a more interesting conundrum in contemporary American life. Warren's books, such as *The Purpose-Driven Church*, have sold hundreds of millions.[1] The sentiments express that unique American recipe: the subtle and seductive fusion of religion and pragmatism; of manna and mammon. The ambiguity of this fission is printed on every dollar bill: in God we

---

[1]   Warren, *The Purpose-Driven Church*; Warren, The Purpose-Driven Life.

trust. So techniques in marketing and any kind of general organisational theory are imported into belief and practice, so that the potential of faith is maximised in its service of the consumer. Cue abundance: happiness and self-improvement is within the grasp of any faithful believer.[2]

In the USA, user-friendly forms of Christianity are a dime a dozen. The common DNA that unites them all is the promotion of religion as a panacea: something that will solve problems and improve the lives of individuals. It is a rather functional, pragmatic attitude to faith. And when it ceases to work, one simply discards and moves on. Barbara Ehrenreich suggests that the positive thinking has, amongst other things, powerfully infected religious belief and practice, turning demanding discipleship into forms of consumer-focused spirituality that meets individuals at their point of need.[3] So, there is bound to be something better in the spiritual market-place for the restless consumer. Something more 'me'; a faith that is even more effective and affective than the last. This is, after all, a faith-land where Jesus might be Lord, but the customer is actually king. (And, by the way, like any other customer, always right.)

However, the kind of Christianity espoused by Warren expresses both the problem and the opportunity that the Obama presidency faces. For with the collapse of confidence in capitalism, the dawning realisation that growth cannot be indefinitely expediential, and that not everyone can be a winner, comes the haunting sense that some deeper values may have to come to the fore in shaping the America of the next few decades.

To be frank, the pursuit of happiness and self-improvement, accompanied by a thick spiritual veneer, will not easily survive the ravages of a new Great Depression. Or for that matter, the new emerging world order. Something more substantial will be needed for the long road ahead. A collective vision for discipleship will be required, that is rooted in challenging American values as much as affirming them. Locating a vocation that will serve others, and not just be about sustaining one's self, will be a priority.

What, then, of Robinson's role in the inauguration? As the Bishop of New Hampshire, he is the first openly gay man to be called by an Anglican diocese

---

[2]   See for example Thomas Lynch and his critique of American culture, *The Undertaking*, p. 25.

[3]   Ehrenreich, *Smile or Die*.

to such a position. Despite the fact that Robinson was chosen by a two-thirds majority of the local electors, his elevation to the episcopate has caused a tsunami of international debate and disagreement, even threatening the unity and identity of the Anglican Communion. The resulting hullabaloo – even by Anglican standards – could be comfortably described as a hurricane of controversy. Indeed, and insofar as ecclesiastical tempests go, this particular one appears to be almost off the barometer scale.

Given that Robinson would be rendered culpable by some for creating the recent inclement ecclesiastical weather that has dogged so much of Anglican polity, even the title of his book seems open to the charge of hubris. Can it really be appropriate to infer that there is any calm place left in which to reflect on the nature of the gospel and the church, whilst in the midst of such heated exchanges on sexuality and biblical authority? Yet in his recent book, *In the Eye of the Storm*, we find a temperate, measured, lucid and composed writer – a rather touching irenic memoir, in fact, from a man who despite being at the centre of such controversy, and held responsible by many for the potential dismemberment of the Anglican Communion, is nonetheless keeping his cool.

Indeed, Robinson's book should be understood as a kind of quintessentially Anglican polemic: the very embodiment of fervent detachment – a delicate fission of biblical, personal, ethical, theological and reflective material. And the substance of the text ranges far and wide, covering a familiar litany of topics that are near and dear to the hearts of your average North American Episcopalian. Chapters concentrate on sexuality and justice; faith and life; diversity and exclusion; politics and inclusion; and end with communion and identity. This familiar terrain is, however, addressed in a manner that is simultaneously moderate and ardent, capturing something of the heart of Anglican polity (at least in style) – as well as neatly expressing its current dilemma (in substance). Here is a cradle Anglican expressing his mind and heart; baring his soul for the world to read.

However, the book cannot escape the production and reception of its underlying context. Anglicanism has never considered itself to be a sect or denomination originating in the sixteenth century. It considers itself to be both catholic and reformed, and with no special doctrines of its own. Yet there is something about the style of Anglicanism – its cadence and timbre – that gives it a distinctive feel. Whilst one can never generalise – there are, after all, several kinds of Anglican identity – there is nonetheless a unifying mood in the polity that rejoices in the tension between clarity and ambiguity, decisions and deferral, to say nothing of word and sacrament, or protestant and catholic.

Caught between extremes, critics of Anglican polity have often ruminated that Anglicanism cannot escape its Laodicean destiny. So neither too hot nor too cold – just warm. In other words, the classic *via media*: tepid – and proud. And because Anglicanism is born of England, just like its climate, the polity often struggles to cope with extremities. Anglicanism is mostly a temperate ecclesial polity: cloudy, with occasional sunny spells and the odd shower – but no extremes, please.

Temperature, then, is an important key to understanding the very context from which Robinson's book has emerged, as well as its content. For his work has materialised out of the new ecclesiastical climatology witnessed at the beginning of the twenty-first century, which just like the rest of the planet, now finds itself exposed to extremities. Normal and temperate weather configurations seem to have given way to immoderate and excessive patterns of behaviour that are driving a new agenda. The sense of 'furious religion' has returned. Cool, calm religion – that beloved export of Europe for so many centuries – is giving way to hot and sultry expressions of faith that despise moderation and temperateness. And Anglicans of all hues are caught up in the new extremes of spiritual weather. Ecclesiastical global warming has arrived.

So whilst *In the Eye of the Storm* offers us a telling *apologia* for calmness and centred-ness, in which Robinson acknowledges the weather around him, he inevitably abrogates any real responsibility for the conditions that have drawn so many into the subsequent hurricane of controversy. In many ways, he is probably right to be so coy. The turbulence that regularly erupts in Anglican polity has been around for many centuries, and has only recently found expression in the new debates on gender, politics, scripture and ecclesial order. Sexuality was never going to be any different; the storm merely points to the endemic weakness and strength embedded in Anglican diversity.

But what *In the Eye of the Storm* cannot help Anglicans with is how precisely to face and resolve the divisive dilemmas that seem to threaten the very future of the Communion. Some churches, of course, thrive on intensity and heat; it is a sign of vibrant life and feisty faith. But others who are of a more temperate hue find this disturbing: heated exchanges, anger and passions seem to dismay more than they console. Anglicanism, then, as a *via media* expression of faith, finds the soul of its polity profoundly troubled by excess. For as we noted earlier, it strains to embody what one distinguished Anglican has described as 'passionate coolness'.

'Passionate coolness' is a typically Anglican phrase: framing ecclesial identity within an apparent paradox. So I suppose one could say that what currently afflicts Anglicanism is not this or that issue – but the heat and intensity that often accompany the debates – because Anglicans are used to temperate, cool disputations. What Anglicans have in the sexuality debate is hot passions mixing with cool reserve: heated exchanges suddenly being expressed in a traditionally temperate climate. And when heat meets coolness, a storm can brew. Robinson is in there of course – and right at the centre too.

But this book is, as I say, a model of mild yet ardent temperate Anglican polity. And ultimately, that is the only grounded future where Anglicans will truly be able to face one another with their manifest differences. So perhaps this is where some of the hope lies for the Anglican Communion, and indeed for the wider world. For surely now, and in the immediate future, what societies need are robust models of breadth that can genuinely live with difference and diversity, and offer a passionately moderate polity that can act as a counter-balance to religious extremism and narrow forms of exclusion that vilify and divide.

Context and Catholicity

Given these opening remarks, I am aware of the risk of relegating a hurricane to the status of a storm in a teacup. Robinson's appointment is a serious matter for Anglican polity, to be sure. And confidence in the resilience of Anglicanism – as a robust and discrete culture that can ride out some aggressive and intemperate weathering – is only part of the reality that Anglicans face. There is no question that the danger of schism is serious. Wars, as wise folk know, can be started at any time of one's choosing; but the author cannot choose the time and manner of ending. So it is little wonder that the early church fathers, when faced with a choice of living with heresy or schism, always chose the former. Doctrine and practice can be corrected over time. But schisms are seldom mended; ecclesial fractures do not have a record of healing well.

That said, Anglicans could now look back at the most recent Lambeth Conference with some degree of satisfaction. In general, the verdict seems to be that for the most part, it passed off peaceably. Of course, much ink was spilled in the run-up to the Conference, writing off Anglicanism, attacking the leadership of the Archbishop of Canterbury or pointing to the gathering forces of conservatism in movements such as GAFCON (Global Anglican Futures conference) and FOCA (Fellowship of Confessing Anglicans). The media reporting prior to the conference was mostly gloomy and doom-laden: as helpful as a phalanx of Job's comforters staffing the telephones at your local branch of the Samaritans. Moreover, the last few decades have seen an unholy and viral trinity of individualism, impatience and intolerance unleashed. This has rapidly spread to very different quarters of the Anglican Communion, yet with unsurprisingly similar results. So now, each part of the worldwide church, whether liberal or conservative, white or black, can claim to be true and right, whilst expressing their individuality, irritation and annoyance with all those they disagree with.

I suspect the only antidote to this plague of rashness is an old Anglican remedy: the recovery and infusion of those qualities that are embedded in the gospels, and in deeper forms of ecclesial polity. Namely ones that are formed out of patience, forbearance, catholicity, moderation – and a genuine love for the reticulate blend of diversity and unity that forms so much of the richness for Anglican life. But in the woof and weave of the church, these virtues have been lost – or rather mislaid – in a miscibility of debates that are marked by increasing levels of tension and stress.

There is support for this kind of polity. For example, in Kenneth Locke's recent book we find a subtle and careful exploration of the ambiguities that help form Anglican identity.[4] Although he pays due and patient attention to some of the inherent weaknesses in this type of complex ecclesial formation, he is also clear about the depths and riches that make up Anglican life. Chapters cover authority, episcopacy and ecumenism – with some excellent comparative reflections drawing on Lutheran, Roman Catholic and Orthodox sources. The chapter on Anglican ecclesial authority is as illuminating as it is sobering. Locke recognises that rich

---

[4]   Locke, *The Church in Anglican Theology*.

and dense ecclesial communities are also complex; so it is not so easy to be simple and clear, as some may hope.[5]

So if Anglicans could settle for a little less clarity and simplicity, and embrace complexity and catholicity, would all be well? Yes and no. Part of the problem for Anglicans, at the moment, lies in our inability to discern the underlying issues that are causing tensions, and squabbling about the presenting issues. Or, put another way, dealing with symptoms, not causes. Sexuality is a classic example of the dilemma that Anglican polity faces at present, and I want to suggest that finding a new conciliation and peace in the Communion will rest with discovering and addressing some of the deeper cultural pulses that are causing similar kinds of problems for other denominations, institutions and societies.

There are some encouraging signs that some Anglican commentators and scholars have also perceived this, and Bill Sachs is one such.[6] True, many Anglicans could be forgiven for the almost audible inward groan that emanates at the mere mention of homosexuality and Anglicanism in the same sentence. Surely Anglicans have had quite enough of the issue? Worn out by the divisive debates and debacles, is it not time for the Anglican Communion to move on, and perhaps tackle something a little less contentious – such as mission and ministry, or justice and peace?

The answer to these questions is, of course, 'yes'. But that should take nothing away from Bill Sachs' remarkable, indeed peerless book, which surveys the terrain of one of the knottier problems to have arisen in Anglican polity for many-a-year. His thesis will repay careful reading, and is well worth the time one might invest to ponder how a crisis such as this assumed the proportions it did, and where any hope for the future of the church might lie.

There cannot be many Anglicans who don't hold an opinion on the subject in question. But as Sachs points out, eloquently, Anglicans across the globe, whether liberal or conservative, traditional or progressive, are often caught between their biblical, doctrinal, ecclesial and legalistic frameworks on the one hand, and their experiential, contextual and pastoral concerns on the other. Indeed, one of the great strengths of this book is the lucid articulation of emerging contextual theologies and the ways in which they compete with hitherto unarticulated but

---

[5]   See also Williams, *Anglican Identities*.
[6]   Sachs, *Homosexuality and the Crisis of Anglicanism*.

assumed notions of catholicity, homogeneity and more complex forms of global belonging. The local, indeed, is both one of the strengths of Anglican identity; but also a potential source of weakness when attempting to speak and act on a global scale. Sachs articulates this potentially problematic dynamic beautifully and clearly, and without recourse to party-based sniping. There is no siding with liberal or conservative slants. Sachs knows too well that the Anglican Communion and its somewhat patchwork polity is far more complex than it seems. Anglicans all agree on what the Bible says; we are just spending quite a bit of time – and acrimoniously, on occasions – figuring out what it means, and where, why and when to apply texts in the twenty-first century.

The first chapter sets the scene – the defining moments of the debates, as it were – which brought an issue that was bubbling below the skin of Anglican polity and identity boiling right to the surface. As Sachs suggests, even with regard to the elevation of Gene Robinson, and the proposed elevation of Jeffrey John to the episcopate, the ensuing divisions in the church were in fact already emerging. Tensions on sexuality existed long before 2003, and caused significant difficulties at the Lambeth Conference of 1998, and had already coloured and clouded the arch-episcopacy of George Carey.

Sachs, as a contextual theologian, then locates these difficulties and disagreements in the wider milieu of ecclesial polity. Tensions, for example, have always existed in the contention for the shaping of early Christian unity (chapter 2). Ideals and realities can also be conflictual, as are the concentrations of power (in the centre or on the periphery, and between local and catholic) in the formation of a global polity (chapters 3, 4 and 5). Sachs contends that the key to understanding the debate is the realisation that indigenous Anglicanism is both the foundation of its global polity, as well as its nemesis. Drawing on writers such as John Tomasi and Michael Sandel towards the end of his thesis, Sachs shows that the kind of activism which promotes rights – vindication through political processes – rather than seeking tangible social and communal harmony as a whole, and for the greater good of all, is bound to be deficient for a church, where there are higher goals to reach for.[7]

Sachs is in no doubt that there are difficult days ahead for the Anglican Communion. One way of resolving its future would be to plot a more assertive

---

[7]   Tomasi, *Liberalism beyond Justice*; Sandel, *Justice*; Sen, *The Idea of Justice*.

course; to chart a pathway, in effect, that was directive and hierarchical. This would have its champions, to be sure. Another way forward is to capitulate to despair, or simply to 'walk apart' – in effect, to cave in to endemic consumerist individualism. But there is another way, and Sachs carefully expounds this in his conclusion.

Taking respectful issue with Ephraim Radner and Philip Turner's recent *The Fate of Communion*, Sachs suggests that unity will need to continue to be progressed through careful listening and speaking, and recognition of the blend between interdependence, intra-dependence, independence and dependence. All Anglicans dwell within this framework, and have to work through the consequences of practising 'contextual reliance on the authority of Spirit without the balance of a wider collegiality'.[8] This is an issue for Sydney as much as it is for New Hampshire.

Sachs believes that the future of the Communion lies in recognition of multiple contexts that partially form ecclesial polity, even though these same realities may need challenging and addressing from time to time. Many Americans, for example, operate quite happily and unconsciously within a 'spiritual marketplace', leading to an individualist and consumerist mindset that picks a tradition or combination of traditions that suits lives at particular points in time. The result is that the local congregation tends to express and interpret the wider tradition for individuals, but at the expense of the broader and deeper adherence to a given denomination. Local congregational life, therefore, and for the purposes of constructing meaning, value and concepts of wider belonging and catholicity, is now far more dominant than it used to be.

That said, the 'Communion' of the future must entail a readiness to be in fellowship with one another, but without this necessarily meaning 'agreement' on all things, or ceding authority to one another. As Sachs points out, 'no position on homosexuality could embody the whole of (the) Anglican tradition'.[9] I am sure that this is right. However, the argument for the future of Anglican polity doesn't necessarily hinge on dissenting from this kind of view. It might rest, ironically, on accepting that some positions – amongst traditionalists, progressives, conservatives and liberals – whilst being faithful expressions of a localised contextual theology,

---

[8]   Sachs, *Homosexuality and the Crisis of Anglicanism*, p. 247.
[9]   Ibid., p. 249.

are nonetheless not easily able to fully commune within a body that is seeking to rediscover its catholicity.

I suspect, then, and following Sachs, that the roots of the current crises in Anglican polity lie not with sexuality (at least in the long term), but rather with some of the deeper cultural drivers that shape American life. These largely un-surfaced assumptions are exported the world over through Americanised versions of capitalism and democracy: the complete right to choose and self-determine; the intrinsic goodness of (almost unlimited) consumerism; the basic rightness of rights that lead to happiness and the pursuit of individual freedom and purpose, thereby subordinating a broader catholicity and sociality; and finally, that the ends justify the means.

Americans might be surprised at this short list. They may complain, with some justice, that these are by no means found and held exclusively on their continent, and they would be right to do so. Yet I think what is at issue here is this particular concentration of un-surfaced assumptions in American culture, which can be found in the market place, public sphere and in the media. Take, for example, the majority of American television programmes and series that concentrate on crime, justice and police work. Almost all of them uphold the rightness of the law; so justice is served. Yet many will also express something beyond this. Namely, that when justice is seen to fail or fall short, the righteous can take the law into their own hands. The law, in other words, is contingent, not absolute. Whilst this is clearly a generalisation, 'the ends justify the means' would serve as an adequate subtitle for many episodes for most American police, legal or crime dramas.

Small wonder, then, that whenever the American sense of liberal idealism in church polity is challenged by another power, Americans tend to react in a way that is true to their theological and cultural instincts. Are there not choices for all? Did this course of action not seem right to us at the time? Have we not done the right thing in moving forward now? Why then, should we be stopped? Local democracy becomes an apotheosis. It is the Boston Tea Party all over again. Don't argue and debate – it is time-consuming. Take control of your life: act now.

Were proof needed of this, I need only recall chairing a seminar some years ago in the US. We had taken as our topic the fall-out from the Gene Robinson affair, and were exploring Anglican patterns of mediation, and, in particular, the eirenic polity advocated by Richard Hooker. But this was too much for some. In the plenary that followed, one questioner exploded: 'We voted for this! What can be wrong with that? They voted for the creeds at Nicea. It's just the same!' Except it isn't. One group of voters in New Hampshire is not on a par with an ecumenical council that drew together the entire Christian world as it was then known.

Read like this, the cultural and contextual difficulties currently plaguing Anglican polity need some unmasking. Thus, Colin Podmore, in his discussion of American culture and ecclesial polity, explores how decisions are taken in the Church; the roles of synods, bishops and primates; how the Archbishop of Canterbury's ministry should develop; what being 'in communion' and 'out of communion' means; and how significant diocesan boundaries in an age of globalisation are.[10] Flowing from Podmore's study, we can see that sexuality is clearly an important issue here. But it is also an unnecessary distraction – exactly not the issue that the church and the wider Communion should be focusing on. Yet that Anglicans have become so hopelessly and helplessly distracted in recent years is hardly surprising, for it is also part of the wider cultural milieu and malaise. The play writer David Hare has characterised the last decade as a decade of distraction. Instead of looking at the issues and situations that truly need examination, many Christians have looked away and focused on other matters, allowing ourselves to be distracted by simple pursuits rather than wrestling with complexity.[11] Thus, when 2,948 people from 91 nations die in the Twin Towers of New York, the response is to invade Iraq – pursuing the wrong suspect for the crime. Afghanistan is also invaded. But most of the 9/11 hijackers, it turns out, are from Saudi Arabia.

In the church, with much angst and anxiety about declining church attendance, the response is interestingly not to reinforce the front line of mission (parish and established sector ministry), but rather to pour millions of pounds and resources into specious missiological schema that go under the nomenclature of 'fresh expressions' or 'emerging church'. Which, ironically, simply turn out to be ways of manoeuvring faithful Christians into lighter forms of spiritual organisation that do not carry heavy institutional responsibilities or broader-based ministerial burdens. The Christian consumer entering the new world of 'fresh expressions' or 'emerging church' can enjoy all the fruits of bespoke spiritual engagement and

---

[10]   Podmore, *Aspects of Anglican Identity*.
[11]   Hare, 'The Decade of Looking Away'.

stimulation, but with almost none of the tariffs incurred through belonging to an ordinary parish church.

As the oft-quoted saying goes, 'if you don't want to know the result, look away now'. Alas, many Christians do. Unwilling to do their sums and calculate the cost of weaning a new generation of Christian consumers on light, carefully targeted spirituality, the churches simply end up losing some of their brightest and best potential leaders to projects that are essentially a form of distraction. And who otherwise could bring much-needed energy and effort into helping shape the broader institution. Distraction is endemic: fed by consumerism, choice and the need to keep people engaged, fulfilled and happy, it is rife in the churches – to the left and right, amongst conservatives and liberals, traditionalists and progressives. It is a tough time to be an ordinary church member; but happy is the person who has found their cultural and contextual home in a new 'fresh expressions' or form of 'emerging church'.

This may seem harsh. Yet I want to return to the suggestion that a good deal of the presenting issues that seem to be de-stabilising Anglicans (and other denominations) at present are in fact symptomatic rather than underlying and causal. To be sure, many of the attempts to return polity to its truer or truest state are full of sincerely held beliefs and worthy goals. But the common denominator is the lack of deeper ecclesial comprehension here, resulting in a real failure to read the cultural and contextual forces that are shaping polity at deep and profound levels. The consequence of this is that the churches tend to miss the moment.

Christianity does indeed face dangers in the developed world. But they are not, I think, secularisation or industrialisation. Plenty of people will turn aside from such things to embrace faith and meaning if that is all society can offer. The real threat comes from both within and without. Within, it is the uncritical absorption of individualist, consumerist assumptions that corrode catholicity and bonds of belonging. This moves the church, effortlessly, from being an established institution or body that faithfully replicates and transmits trustworthy and historic values, to being a series of attenuated organisations that have more short-term and utilitarian goals, including competing with each other for numbers, truth and vindication.

The threat from without is also one of comprehension. Christianity is intrinsically 'foreign' in any context. Every believer is a citizen of somewhere, but also of Heaven. We are in the world, but not of it. Yet the foreign-ness of Christianity in the modern world has now begun to assume a new identity: alien. Whereas foreigners may speak other languages, learn yours and otherwise mingle, aliens are unwelcome, treated with suspicion and often repelled. Seen as invasive and intrusive, they are frozen out rather than welcomed in.

To some extent, 'fresh expressions' or 'emerging church' movements have tried to stem this tide. But all too often, and in so doing, many have sold the pass, culturally. By becoming too relevant they have lost the necessary otherness religion brings to society. Fearful of being alien, the foreigner has gone native. In the same way, liberals have sometimes been guilty of treading the same path. Many conservatives, on the other hand, have disengaged, and whilst succeeding in protecting their own identity, have only made an enclave for themselves, from which to make occasional and specious forays into the wider body politic. Each time this happens, the foreigners take one more step down the road to becoming aliens.

So, what's to be done? The risk of un-policed and uncritical enculturation has always been absorption – into one's self and into the society one is supposed to be transforming. And there is every sign at present that on issues of sexuality – secondary and symptomatic – the Anglican Communion, like all churches, needs to engage in two simple tasks. First, to figure out the constraints and opportunities afforded by balancing local contexts with catholicity. Second, to discern the potential for a higher vision of cultural transformation, that theology and mission might rightly seek.

Theodore Roszak, in *The Making of a Counter Culture*, suggests that the agenda before those who seek to transform society is not centred on organising, managing or repairing reality. It is, rather, about asking 'how shall we live?': 'The primary aim of counter-culture is to proclaim a new heaven and a new earth ... so marvellous, so wonderful, that the claims of technical expertise must of necessity withdraw to a subordinate and marginal status.'[12]

In a similar vein, T.S. Eliot's vision for a Christian culture is not one where right has triumphed over left, liberals have achieved ascendancy over conservatives or traditionalists and progressives have battled to a creditable stalemate. It is, rather, 'a society in which the natural end of man – virtue and well-being in community

---

[12]   Roszak, *The Making of a Counter Culture*, p. 122.

– is acknowledged for all, and the supernatural end – beatitude – for those who have the eyes to see it'.[13]

If Anglicans could find the grace and humility to conduct their debates with this kind of higher vision in mind, we might be able to see that the present difficulties and differences are also our opportunity. For if we can find a way forward to live with diversity, and yet in unity, we shall have held up to the world such an example of polity that the wider public sphere and body politic might itself seek the renewal of its mind and heart, as surely as Anglicans earnestly seek this for themselves.

Conclusion

The Anglican Communion, then, might take some comfort from the present problems it is experiencing. It may need to get beyond them too, and see that the presenting, besetting issues are not as serious as the stubborn and underlying cultural trends that have given them such force and identity.

The church, meanwhile, might take some comfort from the lips of Jesus. Like the mustard seed, the church can continue to be an untidy sprawling shrub. Like a vine, it can be knotted and gnarled. Neither plant is much to look at. But Jesus knew what he was doing when he compared his kingdom to these two plants. He was saying something quite profound about the nature of the church: it will be rambling, extensive and just a tad jumbled. And that's the point. Jesus seems to understand that it often isn't easy to find your place in neat and tidy systems. And maybe you'll feel alienated and displaced for awhile. But in a messy and slightly disorderly church, and in an unordered and rather rumpled institution, all may find a home.

At the same time, and to mix our metaphors for a moment, Jesus did not feed the storm. In one gospel, he apparently slept through the maelstrom, only stilling it when roused by his disciples. But calm it he did. So despite the current storms that bedevil the worldwide Anglican Communion, I predict that the outlook is ultimately calm, and the long-term forecast remains moderate. Indeed, this is the best hope for religion in the modern world. And I daresay we might discover that,

---

[13]   Eliot, *The Idea of a Christian Society,* p. 34.

when we look back in, say, a century, Bishop Robinson's role in the eye of this particular storm will have emerged as something more complex and ambiguous than many currently suppose.

The irony of the present debacle is that it reminds us of how significant current cultural and contextual bearings are on theological and ecclesial disputes. Americans are in love with choices. And this is the one American Anglicans now face. Whether, on the one hand, to go with a catholicity that will be experienced by many as constraining. Or, on the other hand, to capitulate to the endemic context of consumerism, which is sometimes at the expense of a broader catholicity. Or, put another way, the local against the global.

At this point Americans will doubtless remind themselves of their sacred duty – to uphold democracy, and not to give in to intimidating third parties; so no climb-downs. Yet the track record of American foreign policy does not paint such a neat picture. As many small nation states have found to their cost, in Central and South America, and in the Caribbean, democracy is fine – just so long as the right choice for Uncle Sam is made. That said, not all controversy, dis-ease, debate and difficulty is bad. Anglicanism is inherently 'open' and provisional. And as Bruce Reed's work reminds us, 'Biologically, (ecclesial) life is not maintenance or restoration of equilibrium, but is essentially the maintenance of dis-equilibrium, as the doctrine of open systems reveals. Reaching equilibrium means death and decay.'[14]

So to return to the inauguration with Warren and Robinson present, Obama is on stronger ground than many of his predecessors. His choice of these two ecclesial paragons, on one level, reaches out to both the right from the left, and implicitly calls for a pause in traditional liberal-conservative hostilities. It challenges the old cold war impasses of democrat versus republican, or traditionalist versus progressive. The old ways of trench-war debating will not suffice for the twenty-first century. Obama's campaign was framed on calling his country to higher and deeper principles. But what might these be rooted in?

Obama's strength lies not in the bewitching power of the new, but rather in the renewal of the old. His campaign, and much of what he stands for, is rooted in the original vision of the founding fathers of America. That freedom is an inalienable right – but only worth something if all can enjoy it. And that out of diversity comes

---

[14]   Reed, *The Dynamics of Change*, p. 56.

a genuine and collective strength. From the outset, America was birthed not in one dominant ideology, but rather a whole farrago of Christian expressions that forged a nation rooted in diversity, and still later was to become a more complex alloy of competing and complementary faiths.

So perhaps it now falls to Obama to inaugurate a new kind of presidency, in which religion plays a different role. This will undoubtedly be one that displaces the old hegemonies and rivalries that have characterised the country in the post-war era, and promises to establish new kinds of conversation that are generative and constructive for the common good. For a country that normally likes to keep religion and the state well apart, Obama's vision for the nation is already turning out to be one of profoundly deep Christian visualisation and realisation.

It is still far too early to say if President Obama will be ushering in a new age for American politics and religious rapprochement. Or for the culture that chose him. And Anglicans cannot yet know the true causes of their present difficulties. But in time, the malevolent forces that have brought such instability in to Anglican polity will be unmasked. And I suspect we shall see that sexuality and gender are mere symptoms of dis-ease, and not causes. Indeed, we may be surprised at the root and branch problem: perhaps it will be the assumptions we make about choice, individualism and the nature of institutions – all of which have eroded our sense of catholicity and moral responsibility for the parts of Christ's body we seldom see or know. We cannot tell. But what can be said with some certainty, is that the consumer age we have grown up with is now passing, as all ages must. In God we trust.

Chapter 11

Know Surrender: From Ulster to Windsor

One day, so the joke goes, the Archbishop of Canterbury is sitting alone on the beach, trying to enjoy a holiday and a retreat. It has been another hard year. He gazes out towards the horizon where the sun is still rising, and sighs. Presently, his eye catches something gleaming in the sand. He brushes away the grains, and pulls out a brass canister. Seeing an inscription, he spits on it and polishes it, but before he can read it, the canister explodes in a haze of blue smoke. The Archbishop rubs his eyes, and is surprised to find, standing before him, a large Genie. 'Your Grace', says the Genie, 'I will grant you one wish – whatever you want: just name it.' The Archbishop reaches inside his cassock pocket, and pulls out a map of the Middle East. With a crayon, he draws a large red circle around the whole area. 'I'd like you to bring peace to this region', he says. The Genie does not reply. He sits on the sand, and looks at the rising sun. He says nothing for 10 minutes. Then, turning again to the Archbishop, he says: 'I have never said this to anyone before, but what you ask is beyond me. It is too difficult. But if you have another wish, I will grant that.' The Archbishop pauses, and then reaches inside for another map. This is a map of the world, with 165 countries coloured in. 'This is the Anglican Communion', says the Archbishop, 'and all I ask is that you help all the many different parts to get on a little better.' The Genie sits back down on the sand again, and looks towards the sun. Again, for 10 minutes, he says nothing. Then he stands up, and turns to the Archbishop. 'Your Grace', he says, 'do you think I could have another look at that first map?'

Just for a moment, close your eyes. Not literally, obviously; the rest of the chapter could not be read if you did so. I mean metaphorically. And, for a moment, imagine a world – an ecclesial world, if you will – in which Peter Akinola embraces Gene Robinson warmly. The two smile as they do so: the greeting is warm, tender and reciprocal. Looking on is the Archbishop of Sydney and the Presiding bishop of the American Episcopal Church (TEC). Their eyes also meet, smiling. Other bishops witnessing this break into warm, gentle applause. There is peace, harmony and happiness.

You may now be rubbing your eyes, rather in disbelief. Yes, it was a dream. And I suppose, not the kind that will be to everyone's liking. But, as you know, our Anglican polity is laced with frustrations and tensions:

> The Church of England is the maddening institution it is because that is how the English like their religion – pragmatic, comfortable and unobtrusive. Small wonder that so many English writers have preferred the dramatic certainties of Catholicism. You simply couldn't write a novel like Graham Greene's *The Power and the Glory* about a Church built on the conviction that anything can be settled over a cup of tea ... There are other Churches in Christendom which take pride in their lack of ambiguity – in doctrine ... or in monolithic interpretation of the Gospel. Anglicanism in contrast is a synthesis, and a synthesis necessarily invites thesis and antithesis.[1]

How does the proverb go? 'The first casualty in war is truth.' So, Anglicans, ought to be doubly concerned when wars, rumours of wars, along with legitimised schisms and rifts start to surface within the mother church of the Anglican Communion – the Church of England. Standing as we are now, in the twenty-first century, it is still not difficult to forget some of the ugly scenes that took place at the Lambeth Conference at Canterbury during the summer of 1998. In contrast, 2008 was a rather peaceable affair, though not without its pain, emphasised largely by boycotts and noises off stage rather than anything that might take centre stage.

But back to 1998 for a moment. On matters of sexuality in particular, the talk was of irrational fears, of a new strident conservatism, of an old and dominant liberalism, of traditionalism, homophobia or homosexuality and of a split between North and South – reminiscent of the first Great Schism of over 1,000 years ago, between the East and West. It seems to be the usual story. In spite of the many good and excellent things that were going on at Lambeth, the public were nevertheless presented with a picture of a communion that was unravelling, unable to keep

---

[1]   Paxman, *The English*, p. 17.

itself together any more, agree on common services, ordination, consecration and its own future. Things are falling apart: the centre cannot hold.

At that Conference, it was Rowan Williams, the then Bishop of Monmouth, who won the dubious award – gifted by Andrew Brown, a Religious Affairs Correspondent who writes for a number of newspapers – of having 'the most interesting failure' of the Conference. Williams gave a keynote address on making moral decisions. It was a lecture of considerable subtlety and some substance, which, for all the effect it had, Brown noted that 'he might as well have delivered it in a motorway service station'. After the lecture, Brown states that Williams commented: 'Wittgenstein said that the most important thing a philosopher can say to another is "give yourself time". The question is whether we can, in some sense, bear to keep talking to each other.'[2]

From Ulster to Windsor

One of the chief virtues of living within a Communion is learning to be patient. Churches, each with their distinctive own intra-denominational familial identity, have to learn how to negotiate the differences they find within themselves. For some churches in recent history, the discovery of such differences – perhaps on matters of authority, praxis or interpretation – has been too much to bear: lines have been drawn in the sand, with the sand itself serving only as a metaphor for the subsequent atomisation. Yet typically, most mainstream Protestant denominations have sufficient breadth (of viewpoints and plurality) and depth (located in sources of authority and their interpretation, amongst other things) to be able to resist those assaults that threaten implosion. Where some new churches, faced with internal disagreement, have quickly experienced fragmentation, most historic denominations have been reflexive enough to experience little more than a process of elastication: they have been stretched, but they have not broken. This is perhaps inevitable, when one considers the global nature of most mainstream historic denominations. Their very expanse will have involved a process of stretching (missiological, moral, conversational, hermeneutical, etc.), and this in turn has led directly to their (often inchoate) sense of accommodation.

---

[2]   Brown, 'Press Watch', p. 12.

This is, of course, not to say that 'anything goes'. Even the broadest and most accommodating ecclesial traditions have their boundaries and limits. But the development of their global identity has involved them in a process of patient listening and learning, and of evolution and devolution. Speaking as an Anglican, therefore (and one who would locate himself in the broad 'centre' of the tradition), I hesitate to begin this brief chapter by confessing that I am continually surprised by the amount of passion and rhetoric that has been created by the issue of homosexuality. In three successive movements (in what must pass for, musicologically, both a tragic and comic opera), the Anglican Communion has threatened to unravel itself over arrangements in Canada, the USA and England. The historical minutiae of those events of the diocese of New Westminster, New Hampshire and Oxford have no need of reprise now, for they have each, in their own way, been responsible for the production of yet another Commission that attempts to deal with the (apparently) self-inflicted wounds that are said to afflict the Communion. And now that the *Windsor Report* has been published, it is interesting to note that one of its primary tasks has been to point towards the importance of listening to one another in that school of theology, which is the learning church.[3]

Broadly speaking, I consider the *Windsor Report* to be a fine piece of Anglican apologetics. Under the skilful chairing of Robert Eames, Archbishop of Armagh – a man who through his own painful experiences of the 'Ulster Problem' knows a thing or two about patience, peace processes and reconciliation – the Report manages to keep open the possibility of a future in which those people who profoundly disagree on some issues can nonetheless continue to regard themselves as being together and in Communion, even if the quality of that belonging is more strained than usual. In the process of its deliberations, the Commission, by any standards, set itself an ambitious question: what do we believe is the will of God for the Anglican Communion? In attempting to address the central issue, the members of the Commission have been well aware that:

> Since the 1970s controversies over issues of human sexuality have become
> increasingly divisive and destructive throughout Christendom. Within the
> Anglican Communion the intensity of debate on these issues at successive

---

[3]   Lambeth Commission on Communion, *Windsor Report*.

Lambeth Conferences has demonstrated the reality of these divisions ... Voices and declarations have portrayed a Communion in crisis. Those divisions have been obvious at several levels of Anglican life: between provinces, between dioceses and between individual Anglican clergy and laity. The popular identification of 'conservatives' and 'liberals', and 'the west' as opposed to 'the global south', has become an over-simplification – divisions of opinion have also become clear within provinces, dioceses and parishes. Various statements and decisions at different levels of leadership and membership of the Church have illustrated the depth of reaction. Among other Christian traditions, reactions to the problems within Anglicanism have underlined the serious concerns on these issues worldwide. Comparison has been made with the controversies on women's ordination years ago. But the current strengths of expression of divergent positions are much greater. Questions have been raised about the nature of authority in the Anglican Communion, the inter-relationship of the traditional Instruments of Unity, the ways in which Holy Scripture is interpreted by Anglicans, the priorities of the historic autonomy enshrined in Anglican provinces, and there are also issues of justice. Yet the Lambeth Commission has been aware that consideration within its mandate of any specific aspect of inter-Anglican relationships overlaps and relates to others and has a clear bearing on the sort of Anglican Communion which should enhance the life and worship of our diverse worldwide church family.[4]

Perhaps unusually for a Commission that deals with contested areas within ecclesiology, the *Windsor Report* gives particular prominence to the 'feelings', 'emotions' and 'passions' that the issue of sexuality raises. Even in the Foreword, words and phrases such as 'intensity', 'depth of feeling' and 'depth of conviction' pepper the pages. Eames notes that the 'harshness' and 'lack of charity' that has sometimes characterised the debate is 'new to Anglicanism'. Perhaps for this reason alone (although there are others), Eames is careful to note that: 'This Report is not a judgement. It is part of a process. It is part of a pilgrimage towards healing and reconciliation. The proposals which follow attempt to look forward rather than merely to recount how difficulties have arisen.'[5]

---

[4]   Ibid., Foreword.
[5]   Ibid., p. 3.

The process proposed by the *Windsor Report* is, of course, one predicated on a shared commitment to patience, listening and learning together. In order to maintain the bonds of affection that are vital to the life of the Communion, it will be necessary for each part of the body to act with restraint and courtesy. Thus, the Report affirms 'the importance of interdependence', whilst also acknowledging that Communion has been breached through particular initiatives, which are specifically identified and spoken of in terms of 'regret'. The Commission proposes to resolve the ensuing disputes through a period of calm and continued dialogue, with all parties urged 'to seek ways of reconciliation'.[6] The *Windsor Report* concludes on an upbeat-yet-sanguine note, calling for peace, patience, restraint and healing, earnestly setting forth a continued faith in a Communion, in which the participants choose to walk together for the sake of unity, and for its witness to the Gospel.

Can We Talk?

So to return to Wittgenstein's question, 'can we still talk to each other?' The earlier mention of Eames and Ulster is not accidental. Northern Ireland has seen some of the most bitter civil strife and violence over the last century, and much of it predicated on religious difference. Yet somehow, the province has come together, and the violence abated, and the possibility of deep and lasting peace established. The 'Balkanisation' of the province – dividing the places and peoples into smaller autonomous self-governing entities – has been avoided. There are many, of course, who would seek exactly that future with the Anglican Communion: third provinces, exclusions and so forth. In effect, an attempt to create an array of small 'safe' ecclesial homelands that no longer relate to neighbours. But the Communion, of course, is fiercely resistant to such Balkanisation. It knows in its soul that the sum is greater than the part; that the catholic whole is to be preferred to an assemblage of parts that are each sure of their own individual righteousness. Northern Ireland has taught us that peace with our neighbour (so yes, our enemy) is worth struggling for, and that independence from each other is a lesser vision.

---

[6]   Ibid., pp. 4–5.

So how might a fusion of political, emotional and ecclesial intelligence offer some kind of indicative pathway ahead for the Anglican Communion? Several things can be said. And in order to earth these brief ecclesial reflections more substantially, I am drawing upon the first-hand account of the peace-making process in Northern Ireland, written by Jonathan Powell. In *Great Hatred, Little Room* (the title of which is taken from W.B. Yeats' poem, 'Remorse for Intemperate Speech', 1931), Powell hints at several instructive, mediating, yet temporary paradigms that have implications for theology and ecclesiology. Here again, and for illustrative purposes our attention is drawn to current difficulties in Anglican polity.[7]

First, Powell notes how the uses of 'constructive ambiguity' can help establish conversation and rapport at the early stages of negotiation. In one sense, critics might say that this can mean two sides talking two slightly different languages. Speaking is taking place, but true listening is more limited than it may appear to be. Powell concedes that constructive ambiguity is fine for the beginning of a peace process, but not enough in the middle and end stages. Ambiguity has to be rejected in favour of clarity.

Second, Powell notes how consensus must be built from the centre. Again, this is vital to begin with. But you have to reconcile opposites. So for Anglicans, the Archbishop of Canterbury – or other instruments of unity – may be able to hold together competing convictions for some while. In effect, 'manage diversity'. But in the end, there is no substitute for the ultimacy of Peter Akinola shaking hands with Gene Robinson; or for Peter Jensen sitting down with Katherine Jefferts Schori. Whilst this may be hard to imagine, it is the kind of 'peace' that is anticipated in God's Kingdom; the end of rhetorical violence, and the ushering in of a community of blessing that transcends mere consensus.

Third, Powell's insights suggest that the fragmentation and 'Balkanisation' of polity be avoided at all costs, because it is difficult if not impossible to build consensus out of brokenness. In ecclesiological terms, if you have the choice between heresy and schism, choose heresy. You can correct the former; but it will always be difficult to ever heal the latter. This lays a particular burden on the identity and role for the so-called 'instruments of unity': the Archbishop of Canterbury, the Primates, the Anglican Consultative Council and the Lambeth

---

[7]   Powell, *Great Hatred, Little Room.*

Conference. The instruments will need to act lightly and precisely, lest they become part of the problem.

Fourth, these instruments of unity and peace may need to triangulate in times of crisis: it is not good hovering between passive–aggressive; liberal–conservative; traditional–progressive modes of behaviours. It will be necessary to get beyond these polarities; and for the instruments to become *facilitators of peace*, not mere persuaders for a temporary cessation in hostilities. The difference is crucial, clearly. But as Powell notes, bringing peace takes time, and necessarily involves setbacks. Underpinning this must be a resolute commitment to talking and listening – without which peace is impossible. And as the church is a community of peace, attentive listening to God, self and otherness is at the core of its very being.

Fifth, the exchange of peace is a central act of preparation and declaration in anticipation of receiving Christ in bread and wine. Communion is centred on companionship – literally, 'those we break bread with'. Because of this, compromise – literally to 'promise together' – is something rooted in the heart of the Eucharist as we pledge ourselves to one another and to God. In accepting the consequential company that our ecclesial belief and behaviour brings us, we commit to a form of unity that is predicated on peace and bound for unity. That form of Communion, of course, does not always mean agreement. Nor does it follow that there will never be anger and division. But because of God's economy of blessing, it remains the case that no 'height or depth' (cf., Romans 8) can separate us from the love of God that is found in Jesus Christ. And because of this – God's ultimate purpose for creation – we cannot be separated from one another.

But the last word in this section belongs to Powell, as he reflects on the long and arduous road to peace in Northern Ireland. His reflections are instructive for all those who seek peace and unity in any context, including those wracked by the pain of ecclesial conflict, where there can often seem to be no hope of peaceful resolution, let alone unity:

> The ambiguity that had been essential at the beginning [of the process] began to undermine the Agreement and discredit the government – the referee for its implementation. We then had to drive ambiguity out of the process ... and insist on deeds rather than words. This process of squeezing out the ambiguity and building trust was painful and it took

time, but a durable peace cannot rest on an ambiguous understanding ...

So if there is one lesson to be drawn from the Northern Ireland negotiations, it is that there is no reason to believe that efforts to find peace will fail just because they have failed before. You have to keep the wheels turning. The road to success in Northern Ireland was littered with failures. [But] there is every reason to think that the search for peace can succeed in other places where the process has encountered problems ... if people are prepared to talk.[8]

But, what kind of talk? According to Peter Kevern there is a reciprocal relationship between ecclesiology and practice in the Church of England.[9] Logical arguments are invoked in support of a given course of action; conversely, pragmatic positions adopted by the Church eventually find expression as ecclesiological arguments. The debate on women's ordination represents an anomalous instance of this process, because it has resulted in two parallel 'integrities'. Each integrity has separate beliefs about the wisdom of such ordinations, backed up in both cases by a range of internally coherent ecclesiological positions. Those of the opponents of women's ordination are on the whole, less widely noted, and less lucidly expressed.

Partly due to the fragile nature of the communion at present, and also to a rather odd enclave mentality, the practical beliefs of the two integrities are mutually exclusive. Of course, these ecclesiologies have far more in common than is immediately apparent. As I have argued before, Anglicanism is carried in a kind of kinship – a sort of familial morphology in which mutual recognition is often quickly discerned. There is initial evidence for this, in the fact that of those opposing the ordination of women, few have abandoned the Church of England, despite losing the debate. Oddly, both sides profess to share a structured way of thinking about the Church, a meta-ecclesiology, in which both wings and the centre recognise something of the other, even if they are so far not giving formal expression to it. This all sounds very serious on one level, yet it perhaps pays to recall James Gordon Melton's sociological treatment of churches in terms of

---

[8]   Ibid., pp. 315 and 322.
[9]   Kevern, 'Unity, Diversity and Trinity in the Rhetoric of the 1998 Lambeth Conference'.

'families'. For all the protestations of Forward in Faith, or proponents of Third Provinces, it is simply not very easy for your average Anglo-catholic to feel 'at home' in Roman Catholicism.[10]

Passion, Polity and Power

As we noted earlier, it was Jeremy Paxman who once quipped that the Church of England is the kind of body that believes that there was no issue that could not be eventually solved over a cup of tea in the Vicar's study. This waspish compliment directed towards Anglican polity serves to remind us that many regard its ecclesial praxis as being quintessentially peaceable and polite, in which matters never really get too out of hand. Often, congregational unity in the midst of disputes can only be secured by finding a middle, open way, in which the voices of moderation and tolerance occupy the central ground and enable a church to move forwards. In such situations, the cultivation of 'good manners' can be seen to be essential; civility quietly blossoms where arguments once threatened to lay waste. This is something that the *Windsor Report* understands, and it is interesting to note how much attention the Report gives to the virtues of patience and restraint, whilst also acknowledging the place of passions and emotions in the sexuality debate. Clearly, there is a tension between these apparent polarities, which is partly why the cultivation of 'mannered-ness' in ecclesial polity can be seen as being as essential as it is beguiling.

However, there are several important theological issues that surround this type of narration for a congregation, diocese, church or Communion, that tend to question its apparent wisdom. 'Good manners', for example, can be a form of quasi-pastoral *suppression* that does not allow true or strong feelings to emerge in the centre of an ecclesial community, and properly interrogate its 'settled' identity. This may rob the church of the opportunity to truly feel the pain of those who may already perceive themselves to be on the margins of the church, perhaps even disqualified, or who already feel silenced. 'Good manners' can also become a cipher for excluding the apparently undeserving, and perhaps labelling seemingly difficult insights as 'extreme voices'. The prophetic, the prescient and those who

---

[10]   Percy, *Power and the Church*, p. 163ff.

protest, can all be ignored by a church that makes a virtue out of overly valuing a peaceable grammar of exchange. Put another way, if the 'coolness' always triumphs over the 'passionate', then the church is effectively deaf in one ear.

Quite naturally therefore, there is the issue of anger itself, and of strong feelings – especially in relation to sexuality, on all sides of the debate – with which the *Windsor Report* is perhaps unusually concerned. In the body of Christ, how are these feelings received, articulated and generated? Quite apart from appropriate 'righteous anger' (e.g., on matters of justice), how does a mature church receive and respond to aggression within itself, and to strong feelings such as anger, dismay, passion, rage or enthusiasm? Rather like a good marital or parent–child relationship, learning to articulate and channel anger can be as important as learning to control it. It is often the case that in relationships where the expression of anger is denied its place, resentment festers and breeds, and true love is ultimately distorted. Strong feelings need to be acknowledged for relationships to flourish. If strong feelings on one or both sides have to be suppressed for the sake of a relationship, then it is rarely proper to speak of the relationship being mature or healthy. Indeed, some relationships that apparently present as being idyllic and peaceable (e.g., 'we never argue') can turn out to be pathologically problematic. Both parties, afraid of conflict and its consequences, deny their full truth to one another and themselves.

So in terms of ecclesial polity and pastoral praxis, the difficulty is this: the church is too used to defining all aggression as negative. Correspondingly, the church often fails to see the value of aggression or anger in the pursuit of just relations. Of course in retrospect we can acknowledge that freedoms for the oppressed have been won by aggressive behaviour, even when it has been militantly peaceful or pacifist: the Civil Rights movement in North America and the peaceful protests of Gandhi spring to mind. But all too often churches and society collude in a fiction, believing that an end to slavery, the emancipation of women and perhaps even the end of apartheid, could all have been achieved without the aggressive behaviour of militants. Typically, the church also fails to acknowledge the levels of inequality within itself. Many may still need to express or deploy aggressive behaviour in order for Kingdom values to be established.

Presently in the Church of England, the fear of conflict and aggression on issues of sexuality and gender makes it very difficult to air strong feelings; the neuralgic anxiety is that the manifestation of feelings leads to the loss of poise in ecclesial polity. And yet we live in a world and within a church that are shaped by human failings, and if we truly love these institutions then we will inevitably be angry about the ways they fall short. So what we Anglicans do with our strong feelings, and how we handle the aggression that moves for change, will depend on whether we can see them as a sign of life and growth, or whether we suppress them for fear they will rock the boat too hard.

In the Church, the desire to avoid conflict both in parochial matters and in relationships in the diocese can often be a recipe for atrophy. When situations arise which cannot be ignored, the scale of feelings aroused can surprise and disappoint those who believe that if we all try to love each other, we will all agree. To truly love is to take seriously the desire to deepen relationships and work against all that limits and devalues human worth. So discovering how to acknowledge and give voice to strong feelings – in ways that can enable radical working together for the growth of all – is a challenge that the Church needs to heed. In his ministry, Jesus consistently listened to the voices of the marginalised. Indeed, not only did he listen, but he assimilated such voices into his ministry, and often made the marginalised central, and placed those who were central on the periphery, thereby re-ordering society, forcing people to witness oppression and the response of the Kingdom of God to despair, anger and marginalisation.

The task for the Church, therefore, is to find ways that do not suppress or block out strong feelings of anger, or hurt and the aggression it arouses, but to help discern how to channel the energy they bring into the work of the gospel.[11] This means listening to the experiences that lead to aggression and anger, and seeing them as far as possible from the perspective of those with less power. It means humility on the part of those who hold power, and an acknowledgement of the fear of losing power and control. It means a new way of looking at power relationships that takes the gospel seriously in their equalising and levelling.

The *Windsor Report*, therefore, is to be commended for the attention it pays to experiences and feelings. In recognising their vital role in ecclesial polity, Eames and his colleagues on the Commission have understood that experiences and feelings need to be heard and received. The debate on sexuality (perhaps more so than that of gender?) is one that cannot be exclusively resolved by arid

---

[11]   See for example Groves, *The Anglican Communion and Homosexuality*.

academic disputations. But this in itself raises a question about how the process of deliberation is to be furthered.

Coda

In an essay for the *Church Times* some years ago, Peter Selby noted that part of the cost of belonging to a church is 'sacrificing a straight-forward confidence in our own purity'.[12] Communion is something that is necessarily shared, and correspondingly, we are all touched by one another's failures, and the necessary incompleteness of what constitutes church life. Selby's essay leans on the parable of the wheat and tares and presents a characteristically systematic and passionate plea for living together in tension, rather than trying to pre-empt the refining fire of God by building a pure church on this side of the *parousia*. As he noted, situating the church in that context, is not 'a plea for flaccid tolerance, let alone indifference on the matters of profound importance'.[13] It is, on the other hand, a plea to try to work together as much as possible for the widest common good.

Our friends in Ulster would know a thing or two about this. That there is hope in hybridity, rather than risk and pollution. That in giving ourselves to one another – sacrificially, and in a spirit of surrender – we do not lose our fight, but rather find ourselves, and something higher, that Jesus calls us to in his Kingdom. That in knowing surrender, we do not taste defeat; but rather, begin to sense something of the victory of the resurrection, that triumphs over differences and disagreements, and begins to bring us all together in a new hope for the world. This is the church, of course. A place and polity where we discover that in yielding to others, we do not lose our cause or the corner we have been fighting for. Rather, we gain more than we could have imagined. We find that in surrender, we are not defeated, but rather enriched by the new catholicity that emerges.

---

[12] Selby, 'The Parable of the Wheat and the Tares', p. 11.
[13] Ibid., p. 11.

Chapter 12

After Lambeth: Plotting the Future

An apocryphal tale from the vast annals of Anglican folklore tells of an occasion when someone wrote to the Archbishop of Canterbury to thank him for something he had said on the radio. It was an appreciative letter, and the correspondent kindly enclosed a cheque for £10 – made payable to 'the Church of England'. It caused some amusement at Lambeth Palace, for strange though this may seem, it could not be cashed. There is no organisation or bank account bearing that name. True, there is the Church of England Pensions Board, various divisions concerned with ministry and education, several dozen dioceses and of course the Church Commissioners – all of which refer to the Church of England. But no bank account bears the sole nomenclature. The cheque had to be returned with a note: 'thank you – but do you think you could be more specific?'

The problem is not as odd as it seems. It would be rather like me receiving a cheque for £10 made out to 'the Percy family'. Whilst grateful, I would be unable to cash it. To which branch of the family does the cheque refer? Aunts, uncles and cousins may claim an interest. To say nothing of the handful of readers of this final chapter who might share my surname, and are already experiencing a frisson of excitement at the prospect of an unexpected windfall.

It is perhaps no accident that when Jesus turned his metaphorically disposed mind to the subject of the church, he reached for a rather riveting analogy: 'I am the vine, you are the branches.' It is a suggestive, economic phrase, where one suspects that the use of the plural [branches] is quite deliberate. Even for an apparently homogenous organisation like the Church of England (let alone the Anglican Communion), 'branches' offers a better descriptive fit than most of the labels on offer. It suggests inter-dependence yet difference; unity and diversity; commonality yet independence; continuity and change; pruning, yet fruitfulness.

In other words, the analogy sets up a correlation between particularity and catholicity. This is, of course, a struggle that Anglicans are all too familiar with. There is a constant wrestling for the 'true' identity of Anglicanism; a struggle to reach a point where its soul ceases to be restless, and becomes more fully self-conscious. But in the meantime, the church finds itself easy prey to a variety of interest-led groups (from the theological left and right) that continually assert their freedoms over any uneasy consensus. The assumption made here is that any one branch is 'free' from the others.

Technically, this is correct. But the illusion of independence threatens to impoverish a profound catholic aspect of Anglicanism. The right to express and practise particularity is too often preferred to the self-imposed restraint that is hinted at by a deeper catholicity. Thus, one branch will exercise its assumed privilege of freedom – whether that is fiscal, political, theological or moral – over the others. The consequence of this is all too obvious. The branches attempt to define the vine.

Which is why issues of gender, sexuality and polity quickly become the primary foci that distinguish one branch from another, rather than secondary indicators of emphasis that are subjugated to an innate connectedness to the true vine. There seems to be little understanding that an unfettered claim to act freely can actually become anti-social, or even unethical. Great freedom comes with great responsibility.

Interestingly, bishops have a vital role here in presiding over diversity whilst maintaining unity. This is why the key to some of the current divisive Anglican dilemmas may lie in dioceses and provinces becoming more consciously expressive of their catholic identity, and celebrating their coherence amidst their diversity. A diocese is more than an arbitrary piece of territory. It is a part of a larger, living, organic whole. It is a branch of the vine. Therefore, exercising its freedom and expressing its particularity is less important than maintaining its connectedness. The trouble starts when any specific branch purports to speak and act for the whole, but without sufficient humility. Naturally, such restraint need not impose limits on diversity. It merely asks that the consequences of exercising one's freedom be more fully weighed.

As Anglican Primates continue to meet after the Lambeth Conference, there will be much to carry forward in contemplation and conversation. How to hold together in the midst of tense, even bitter diversity. How to be one, yet many. How to be faithfully catholic, yet authentically local. In all of this, an ethic of shared restraint – borne out of a deep catholicity – may have much to offer the Anglican Communion. Without this, Anglicans risk being painfully lost in the issues that beset the church – unable to see the wood for the trees. Or perhaps, as Jesus might have said, unable to see the vine for the branches.

It is partly for this reason that I continue to remain uneasy about the potential *use* of something like the proposed Anglican Covenant (as an arguably useful template for unity) rather than the actuality of the drafted text. Documents of this kind invariably contain the (potentially problematic) capacity to occlude their movement from textuality to instrumentality. And instruments, to be useful, require functions and authoritatively licensed users. So in one sense, I am not clear what the Covenant adds to the current instruments of unity within the worldwide Communion. One can see that it signals an intensification of the need to be in broad agreement on certain issues; to act with restraint, with provinces thinking more about the 'catholic' implications of their preferred local practice; and to strengthen the role of the Primates in the expression and delimitation of a common mind and shared practices.

Correspondingly, the question necessarily arises: who, or what bodies, will use the Covenant, and against what or whom, and how? Most of the dis-ease about the Covenant, one suspects, lies here – and not with the text itself. I think that the Communion will need to be reassured that the Covenant is not a specifically targeted text that is directed against apparent pain or problems (i.e., is neither palliative nor punitive), but is rather a document that arises naturally and organically out of our common life, and expresses our desire to clarify and deepen our bonds of affection. Put more sharply, it will serve the Communion better if it can be seen to express the shared wisdom that we seek, as well as being a celebration of our unity, diversity and collective witness to Jesus Christ and the gospel, rather than a text that is imposed unilaterally.

Closely linked to this observation, one might say that our Anglican ecclesiology is to be seen not only in terms of shared and agreed propositions, but also as a shared set of acquired skills and practices. We are formed not only by what we say, but by the manner and modes of our expression. In this regard, the censure of Bishop James Pike (over 40 years ago, in 1966) merits repetition:

When Episcopalians are questioned about the supposed orthodoxy or heterodoxy
of one of their number, their most likely response is to ask whether or not [this
person] wishes – sincerely and responsibly – to join them in a celebration of
God's being and goodness in the prayers and worship of the Prayer Book.
Assuming [this person's] integrity, they would not be likely to press the question
beyond that point.[1]

All of us in the Communion, I am sure, would accept the precedence
and priority that can be placed upon urgent matters in relation to identity
and decisiveness. However, our 'common' life and prayer together is also
an expression of our commitment to patience; and an understanding that the
relationship between practice and belief is a complex one within the Communion.
As Stephen Sykes (amongst others) has pointed out, it is inconceivable that
there has ever been complete agreement on the identity of Christianity. Part of
the genius of our faith lies in its contestability. Moreover, conflicts can only
really be made explicit and *managed* through processes of theological reflection
– but, I should add, not necessarily resolved.

So I would want to ask at this point: is it envisaged that something like the
Covenant helps us to manage and reflect upon our difficulties, or to resolve them?
The former produces clarity and charity, but not necessarily at the expense of
diversity. The latter, it seems to me, could be a rather ambitious enterprise for
any denomination to contemplate – but equally not impossible. Clearly, doctrinal
discussions do reach a point of *consensus* when they become decisions.

However, and without in any way wishing to undervalue consensus, I
would also add that there is something to be said for the Anglican virtue of un-
decidability. 'Un-decidability' is 'procrastination with purpose': the exercise of
extreme patience that enables polities to wrestle with high levels of seemingly
un-resolvable tension. Make a decision too early – even the right one – and you
may win the argument (note: may); but you will probably lose the people. In other
words, means may matter more than ends. This principle – indeed, virtue – is
something that the Covenant document or such like often fails to acknowledge. The
practice of patience over and against precision is what is at stake here; recognising
that a leap to the latter will leave many stranded and languishing in the former.

---

[1]   Bayne, *Theological Freedom and Responsibility*, p. 21.

This takes me back, neatly enough, to the questions around the use of the Covenant, rather than being concerned with the text itself. Indeed, I think a debate on the minutiae of the text, although clearly important, is only one half of the equation that needs to be considered. The fundamental question remains: namely how do we go about making decisions in relation to practice in such a way as to maintain the continuity of Christianity? Our 'problem', apparently, is that our identity partly resides in the celebration of breadth, and in a diversity of practice. And occasionally in a lack of clarity about how some local practices might impinge upon our collective catholic identity. I remain convinced, here, that we need to continue to carefully distinguish between essential practices (say in regard to doctrine, unity, etc.) and contextualised practices that are essentially secondary issues.

It seems to me that the promise and anticipation of the Covenant, in many ways, have already achieved some clarity in regard to the issues it seeks to address. There is more evidence – across the Communion – of patience, restraint and the practice of shared wisdom in the wake of the issues and circumstances that have prompted the Covenant document. This suggests that the very possibility of the Covenant (rather than its actuality) may have already achieved much. Whilst a few perceive the document as a threat, and a few perceive it to be inadequate, the majority have already come to see that its gradual formulation is an opportunity to rediscover consensus in the midst of diversity, and rediscover the discipline (and therefore some limits) of what is entailed in journeying together within the Anglican tradition.

However, this same observation also prompts me to urge the Primates (and other instruments of unity) towards the continued practice of patience, and to plea for pausing, reflection and space before committing ourselves to any kind of premature foreclosure. If the mere *possibility* of the Covenant has already helped us move to a place of deeper collective self-discipline and critical self-reflection, then there is a powerful argument for *prolonging* this period, where a greater degree of wisdom and charity has already been found, even amidst some considerable tensions. I am reminded of Wittgenstein's metaphor of the rope, where he draws our attention to how its strength depends on the tiny individual fibres that overlap and interlace. Our Communion – a rich tapestry of threads and colours – is, I believe, rediscovering its strength and identity through these testing times. So I would hope that the Covenant document, when it eventually and ultimately comes into being, would be able to find a more reassuring and celebratory rhetorical cadence than it has at present – one that focused less on the fear of unravelling, and more on the deeper reality of our becoming.

This is a more urgent task than it might at first appear. Because the discernment that is called for here is not simply one that picks its way through interpretative differences and then makes decisions. Such a strategy merely divides and conquers. The task is how to live with difference, rather than avoiding this. Our call is to a 'commonality' with diversity; unity with differences. And we affirm and witness to breadth because we sense that God is more than the sum of our parts; even though this makes for some difficult conversations amongst ourselves.

It is clearly no secret that the worldwide Anglican Communion contains tensions on how to read scripture. Everyone knows that Anglicans can agree on what the Bible says: but are on shakier ground when it comes to a common mind on meaning. On the surface, the manifest difficulties appear to be centred on issues such as sexuality, gender, the right use of the Bible and the appropriate interpretation of scripture. It is therefore possible to narrate the schismatic tendencies in Anglicanism with reference to authority, theology and ecclesial power. But on its own, as a thesis, this is clearly inadequate, as such tensions have existed within Anglicanism from the outset. There has not been a single century in which Anglicanism has not wrestled with its identity; it is by nature a polity that draws on a variety of competing theological traditions. Its very appeal lies in its own distinctive hybridity.

Another way of reading the current difficulties is to register that the polity itself is expressive of competing but covert cultural convictions. One might say, for example, that current Anglican difficulties begin with the American Revolution (or War of Independence), which caused American Anglicans to re-conceive their faith as Republicans rather than Royalists. The emergence of Samuel Seabury as the first American Anglican bishop (consecrated, incidentally, by Jacobite Scottish bishops rather than by the Archbishop of Canterbury) marks a seminal moment in the identity of Anglicanism. Although the gesture itself, at least on the surface, is not significant, it comes to represent the emergence of two competing streams of ecclesial polity within a single Communion.

The first is Royalist, bound to a culture that is aligned with hierarchy and obedience that is at least linked to divine right and ordering. But the second, which is Republican, is essentially democratic in orientation, and therefore about the rights of the people more than the princes and prelates. Moreover, there is a modification to the Royalist paradigm that needs to be factored in, for it is not an ancient quasi-feudal system, but rather that which emerged out of the seventeenth-century English Civil War, which had deposed outright notions of kingship, but had then restored kingly power, albeit checked by new forms of democratic and parliamentary power.

There is some sense in which a range of current Anglican difficulties can be read against these deep underground cultural streams that eventually cause the apparent seismic doctrinal shifts. The election of Gene Robinson (a genial, gay clergyman) as Bishop of New Hampshire is an expression of North American faith in the gift of democracy (from God) and the inalienable right to choose. A people who were chosen – liberated, as it were, from the yoke of colonial patrimony – are now called upon by God to continue exercising their God-given rights to choose. Thus, the will of a foreign power – or even the mild intervention of a friendly Archbishop of Canterbury – will be seen as an act of hostility and despotic feudalism.

These two streams of power, deeply embedded in their respective cultures (not unlike Churchill's notion of two nations divided by a common language) is all it takes to produce two kinds of very different theological grammar within the same Communion. And when such differences are mapped on to the worldwide Anglican Communion, and emerging post-colonial identity is taken account of within developing nations, which are suspicious of both the old ordering of kingly power and the apparent 'consumerism' of the democratic stream, the stage is set for some major divisions to emerge, which will disguise themselves in doctrinal and ecclesial difference.

Yeats' poem mourned that 'things fall apart – the centre cannot hold'. But the centre was always contested, not settled. So what is to be done? No one solution presents itself. Recognising that there are cultural factors in shaping and individuating churches is important. Valuing diversity alongside unity will be vital. And praying fervently with Jesus 'that we may all be one' will also be crucial – although we might perhaps mutter in the same breath: 'but thank God we are all different'.

Of course, much ink was spilled in the run-up to the 2008 Lambeth Conference, playing up these differences, as though they were manifestly signs of weakness and hopelessness. This accounts for the media-fest writing off Anglicanism, attacking the leadership of the Archbishop of Canterbury and pointing to the gathering forces of conservatism in movements such as GAFCON (Global Anglican Futures conference) and FOCA (Fellowship of Confessing Anglicans). The media reporting prior to the conference was mostly gloomy and doom-laden. Yet Anglicans hardly need the media to provide the dubious comforts of depressive consolation, for they are very good at squabbling amongst themselves. Mired in a culture of blaming and mutual castigation, Anglicans all but seem to have lost the knack of cultivating and practising the virtues of tolerance and patience amidst their differences and diversity.

The roots of this particular Anglican difficulty do not need spelling out. The election of Gene Robinson to the See of New Hampshire was, despite whatever personal merits he may have had, regarded by others as an example of North American individualism cloaked in the rhetoric of progression and justice. The trouble with such a decision is the lack of regard for a wider catholicity, and the attendant responsibility this carries. Furthermore, the Episcopal electors of New Hampshire should perhaps have paused to reflect that the (oft overlooked) cousins of individualism are impatience and intolerance.

So from the minute that Gene Robinson was consecrated, the unholy and viral trinity of individualism, impatience and intolerance was unleashed, and has rapidly spread to very different quarters of the Anglican Communion, yet with unsurprisingly similar results. So that now, each part of the worldwide church, whether liberal or conservative, white or black, can claim to be true and right, whilst expressing their individuality, irritation and annoyance with all those they disagree with.

But the only antidote to this plague of rashness remains a tried and tested Anglican remedy: the recovery and infusion of those qualities that are embedded in the gospels, and in deeper and denser forms of ecclesial polity. Namely ones that are formed out of patience, forbearance, catholicity, moderation – and a genuine love for the reticulate blend of diversity and unity that forms so much of the richness for Anglican life. But in the woof and weave of the church, these virtues have been lost – or rather mislaid – in a miscibility of debates that are marked by increasing levels of tension and stress.

Yet if this sounds like too much of a tangle for some, it is interesting to note that when Jesus reaches for metaphors that describe the Kingdom of God (and, by implication, the possibility and potential of churches), he often uses untidy images. 'I am the vine, you are the branches' comes to mind. No stately cedar tree of Lebanon here; or even an English oak. Jesus chooses a sprawling, knotted plant that requires patience and careful husbandry. And one that is hardly pretty to look at either. (But the fruit and what it produces, interestingly, is another matter for taste and looks.) In another short parable, he compares the Kingdom of Heaven to a mustard seed – one of the smallest seeds that can grow into 'the greatest of all shrubs and sprouts large branches' (Mark 4:30–32). The image is ironic, and possibly even satirical. One has every right to expect the Kingdom of God to be compared to the tallest and strongest of trees. But Jesus likens the church to something that sprouts up quite quickly from almost nothing, and then develops into an ungainly sprawling shrub that can barely hold up a bird's nest. Anglicans may need to learn to be a little more comfortable with their untidiness and incompleteness.

So there are no easy answers to the 'where next?' post-Lambeth question. Anglicanism is primarily a patient form of polity, because it gives time to issues, questions and dilemmas. And time and patience are rooted in charity and forbearance. We let the wheat grow with the tares; we do not separate the sheep from the goats. It will take more than one Lambeth Conference to work through the differences that currently appear to divide kith from kin, and to work out what they all mean. But in the meantime, all Anglicans need to heed one of the many calls that issued in the first Book of Common Prayer. Indeed, this is the last call before there can be any kind of Holy Communion:

> Ye that do truly and earnestly repent you of your sins, and are in love and charity
> with your neighbours, and intend to lead a new life, following the commandments
> of God, and walking from henceforth in his holy ways: Draw near with faith.

Coda

If the Lambeth Communion can be said to have passed off peacefully in 2008, the years since then (not many of them, granted), seem to have been a little less kind to the Communion. Debates on sexuality have returned to haunt the Instruments of Unity and the Provinces; and the Church of England has had some turbulent debates on women bishops. Moreover, there seems to be no sign of these difficulties disappearing. The fractious nature of the debates appears to be polarising as before, and the Communion under some strain and duress. Writing almost half a century ago, Stephen Bayne observed that

> the Church of England, alone among the churches of the Anglican Communion, has its unity given to it. That unity is given from the outside. It is given by the establishment of the church, by the formal identity of the church and the nation. The Church of England does not need to be held together by the voluntary loyalty of its members … [yet] this is not an unmixed blessing. But it has succeeded in giving to the Church of England – and in turn, to all the rest of the churches of our Communion – an extraordinary liberality of spirit and gentleness of mind, which tolerates wide differences of opinion and variations in theological outlook, within the working unity of the Catholic church of the land … this is one of the most precious gifts. And I rejoice to find it transplanted … to North America, to Japan, to Central Africa, to Brazil, to any other part of the world you can mention. It was given to the Church of England, because of its hopes and necessities as a national church, to discover a profound secret of unity – that the unity of the church does not consist of people thinking alike but in people acting together.[2]

There is nothing perhaps remarkable about such sentiments; except, perhaps, to note two profound changes in recent times. The first is that the Church of England is moving rapidly towards a culture where it is 'held together by the voluntary loyalty of its members'. And second, and linked to this, like-mindedness becomes a more important characteristic in such institutions, which paves the way for narrower and more sectarian modes of ecclesial existence.

---

[2]   Bayne, *Theological Freedom and Responsibility*, p. 181.

Whilst acknowledging this cultural shift, and its impact on the wider Communion, I nonetheless see no reason to despair. Our hope, after all, is not rooted in political compromise, but in the gospel. It is grounded in the virtues and character that all Christians are called to. Which is why, I suspect, we shall rediscover as a Communion something deeper in our calling to develop bonds of affection, and in the kind of story-swapping and listening that is encouraged through the ongoing Indaba process. The content of the stories and experiences exchanged and reflected upon in the Indaba process is, arguably not the issue for Anglicans.

Rather, the key question is can we listen to one another attentively, and patiently – mindful that this is God's time, God's church and God' future – and not ours to possess and shape to suit our own requirements and proclivities. Can we, as mature Communion, develop levels of intellectual and emotional composure – fashioning a deeper kind of ecclesial intelligence – that comprehends subtle relationships between content and mood, style and substance, the now and the not-yet? Can we, as a Communion, place our trust in God for each other, and commit to acting together for the sake of the gospel and God's Kingdom, even if we know we cannot be like-minded? I strongly suspect that the Anglican Communion will, through patience, forbearance, courage (and perhaps a little fear), rediscover its bonds and unity, even amidst its differences.

As we noted earlier, one of my predecessors at Cuddesdon used to describe Anglicanism as a matter of 'passionate coolness'. I am rather drawn to this stylistic interpretation of the Anglican mood, since it suggests an actual energy for temperate ecclesial climes. But it has a weakness too, which is that people can often dwell on the actual comfort that the accommodation and temperance bring. And temperance can be an over-rated virtue, if it is allowed to dictate moderation and exclude the passions. If it sets the tempo all the time, then the radical of excess, which drives religion, is inhibited.

One of the characteristics that marked out the early Christianity is that it understood faith to be an expression of passion and deeply held convictions. Faith, in terms of discipleship, is often not reasoned coolness. It is passion that spills over; the love that is stronger than death. Yet excessive, passionate faith is not the same as extreme faith. The former is intemperate and immodest; but it abounds in energy and love because it springs from the liberty of God. It is released as a kind of raw energy, precisely because it breaks the chains of inhibition, and springs forth from spiritual encounters that can border on ecstasy. But this is not, as I say, extremism. It is merely passion resulting from encounter, conversion, conviction, resurrection and transformation.

Yet our passion and energy as a Communion is also to be linked to our call to temperance and self-control – the kinds of virtues listed by Paul in Galatians. Yet temperance and self-control are not about control from without. The modelling of such virtue is rather the deep spiritual exercise of restraint for the sake of the self and the other. It is a spiritual discipline and a character that can only be exercised in proportion to the energy and passion that wells up from the same source. It is a steely and willed act of moderation or self-control that emerges out of passionate convictions, grace and love. That's why the list of the fruits of the Holy Spirit from Galatians is so important. Love, joy, peace, patience, kindness, self-control, humility, gentleness and faithfulness are all rooted in the passion of Christ – a putting to death of our desires, and seeing them reconfigured through the Holy Spirit into the heart of God. So excess and abundance are of God; extremism, however, is of the flesh.

In terms of Christian discipleship, these observations are important for several reasons. First, spiritual passion is not just about the expulsion of energy. It also has another meaning in religion which is concerned with the absorption of pain, sacrifice and suffering – like the passion of Christ. Here, passion is absolutely for the other; but it is passion that is almost entirely configured in its receptivity. Much like the passion of a parent or a lover, God's passion is sometimes spoken in eloquent silence; in sacrifice and in endurance. In solidarity and in suffering; in patience, kindness, self-control, humility and gentleness.

Second, it is perhaps important to remember that the example of the early church – those people that inspire us in our faith – is often to be found in the delicate combination of passion, practice and reason. One of the qualities I sometimes look for in ordinands is the inability to contain their passion – for the church, for Christ, and for others. I don't think there are many laurels or crowns being dished out in heaven for being slightly left-of-centre. Discipleship is not about being liberal, conservative or even somewhere in the middle. It is about knowing your place before God, and being passionate for the possibility of the kingdom.

Third, the temperance we Anglicans might seek should not be allowed to blunt the energy and enthusiasm that flows from living the gospel. To be sure, orderliness and calculation have their place. But if they are allowed to control and marginalise passion, then there is a great danger that temperance can become totalitarian. Religion in moderation is, arguably, a contradiction in terms. It should offend, cajole, probe and interrogate. More colloquially, one might say that a faith that does not get up your nose is hardly worth the candle.

Our call, then, is to consider the radical nature of commitment, and to call others to this radical discipleship. This is a faith that revels in the excessive, but is not extreme. It is passionate; and yet com-passionately held in such a way as to be persuasive rather than repellent. You may find this strange, but I happen to think that the good old Church of England, and indeed the wider Anglican Communion that Bayne says is born of the same ecclesial DNA, might just be on to something here. It is (always) far too easy to despair of the tepid nature of Anglican polity; and its interminable vacillations and argument. And yet, I find it strangely full of the fruits of God's Spirit – exactly the kinds of abundance and generosity listed by Paul in Galatians. Indeed, let me say a little more at this point.

As Christina Patterson has expressed it so powerfully and movingly (and here paraphrased from her article in 2009), I love the Church of England because it is patient.[3] It does not expect the world to change in an instant, or to be bludgeoned into belief, because it knows that certain things take centuries. I love it because it is kind. It is kind enough to welcome strangers, whatever their beliefs, and shake their hands, and offer them a coffee after church. I like the fact that it is neither envious (of more flamboyant, more attention-seeking and more successful-at-proselytising religions), nor boastful. I like the fact that it is not normally arrogant or rude. I like the fact that it does not insist on its own way, but is genuinely tolerant of other religious beliefs – and none. I like the fact that it does not rejoice in wrongdoing, but quietly presents an ethical framework of kindness. I like the fact that it believes in the values of the New Testament, and of St Paul's description of love, which I've just paraphrased, but also believes that it is more important to embody them than to quote them.

I like the fact that it doesn't speak like a child, think like a child or reason like a child. I like the fact that it is mature enough to value faithful doubt. I like the fact that it is mostly calm. I like the fact that it recognises that the religious impulse is here to stay, and that the more you try to crush it, the stronger it will become.

---

[3]   Patterson, 'Thank God for the Church of England'.

And that all human beings, irrespective of their beliefs, have yearnings for the transcendent. And I like the fact that although secured in scripture, tradition and reason, it is not afraid to seek and find God in our wider culture – in art, literature, nature and in society. Indeed, this is Faith, Hope and Charity.

As Paul says of the fruits of the Spirit, there are no laws against such things. So let us also celebrate this part of Christ's body – the Church of England – in to which God has been gracious enough to cultivate an abundance of fruit to savour. And let us therefore listen to one another attentively, and with graciousness. For 'the unity of the church does not consist of people thinking alike but in people acting together.'

Conclusion
The Nature of the Body and the Blessing of Leadership

In Stephen Pickard's recent *Seeking the Church*, he recognises that our understanding nature of the church will invariably shape our formation of that church, and its emerging identity. There are subtle temptations that the church must resist if it is to be true to what God is calling the church to be. Too much emphasis on the church being like or becoming like the kingdom risks an over-emphasis on idealism, and on flights of fancy.[1] Pickard – clearly appealing across the ecumenical and denominational penumbra – points out that 'nothing can be loved at speed', and that attending to the church in the here and now, including its complex contingencies and frustrating foibles, can lead us to a greater appreciation of how the church is created and built through the seemingly foolish things to the world, but which in God's hands are the seeds of wisdom.[2] Good things require incubation, gestation, savouring and stillness; 'slow church coming', argues Pickard, may be part of God's deeper and richer purposes.[3] Whatever our denomination may be, there is, perhaps, too much invested in frenetic missional activity. But equally, we must be actively attentive within the context of the slow, reflective church; it can sometimes be asleep, and needs a good prod.[4] In all of this, we must try and see the church not as 'our' project to make it work better; but as God's work, where we are invited to participate in active husbandry. The church is, in other words, more than an organisation to be managed and shaped by innovators, and driven by projects. It is God's body; and like all institutions, lives

---

[1]   Pickard, *Seeking the Church*, p. 212.
[2]   Ibid., p. 8.
[3]   Ibid., p. 216.
[4]   Ibid.

in the long shadow of its founder. In the case of the church, indeed, this is the long and eternal shadow of the Galilean.

One of the key insights threading its way through this volume is the recognition that the church is an institution rather than an organisation. This distinction is rooted in a classic sociological paradigm.[5] Philip Selznick argues that organisations exist for utilitarian purposes, and when they are fulfilled, the organisation may become expendable. Institutions, in contrast, are 'natural communities' with historic roots that are embedded in the fabric of society. They incorporate various groups that may contest each other, the institution, values and the like. Clearly, in Selznick's thinking, a church is an institution, requiring leadership, not mere management. So the church, when treated like an organisation, can only be managed. And such management will, inevitably, be somewhat deficient, since the church is an institution in which only certain types of management will be possible. Institutions, however, need leadership (which will include management): the kind of leading that has sufficient self-awareness to know what can and should be changed, and also what needs to be retained and safeguarded.

Our attention to the idea of the church as a complex body at this point is hardly accidental. Bodies contain systems and forms of organisations that require meticulous regulative management. Not all of these will be consciously apparent to the mind. But a body is clearly more than one single form of organisation. It contains naturally functioning parts that need no conscious instructions; it responds, reacts, grows and declines in relation to different circumstances and environments. It is something that can be trained and educated; yet is also in a constant state of complex formations, which may involve instinct, wisdom, memory and innate calculation. A body is a highly complex, yet single entity. Its identity, of course, is complex and contestable, yet obvious. It has to come to terms with the multiplicity of meanings that it inhabits, which vary across the range of discourses in which the body engages – medical, anthropological, sociological, spiritual and so forth. The body is one, yet capable of multiple interpretative possibilities.

Correspondingly, Paul's analogy of the church as the body of Christ allows us to reappraise the richness of the church as an institution (1 Corinthians 12:12–26). The human body is a 'natural symbol' by which people often order

---

[5]   Selznick, *Leadership in Administration*.

the systemic nature of their corporate life.[6] The human body is often an image of society; how a group views and values its own members will reflect upon notions of corporate and individual life. Therefore, to contemplate the church as a body is to invite reflection on the sensitivity of the church, its receptivity, its boundaries, barriers and definitions, all its complex processes of exchange, as well as its natural death and replenishment. It is 'osmotic' in character: giving and receiving nourishment, identity and love. The body is inescapably part of its environment, as well as separate and distinct. The body – with all its members – is incarnate in space and time.

Why, though, do these reflections matter in terms of leadership in Anglican churches, and, more generally, across the wider Communion? Indeed, for any denomination within the ecumenical penumbra? Arguably because the leadership of the church requires taking responsibility for such a highly complex organism, where obvious clarity of intention and attention cannot be taken for granted, and are not always apparent. The systems and micro-organisations within the institution/ body will maintain their foci in a dedicated (even myopic) manner, almost independent of any willed tactics or strategy that the body may consciously have articulated. Thus, the 'head' may well prioritise a range of tasks or opportunities. But the heart will still beat, and other micro-systems within the body will still carry on with their primary functions. This does not mean, of course, that the body is divided, or in any sense schizoid. It is simply the recognition that its complexity is part of its organic and mystical given-ness.

If the church is the body of Christ, then one of the tasks of leadership is to be attuned to the heartbeat of Christ. But at the same time, leadership also involves a very particular kind of attention to shape, sense and experience of that body: its interiority and exteriority; its skin and inner workings. So to contemplate the church as the body of Christ in this way is an invitation: to accept a complex identity that accepts both continuity and change. Indeed, leading such a body requires acceptance of both solidity and reflexivity. Here, the body of Christ is being used in its most positive way, namely to infer that God is *still* responsive within the world, and to its self. The human body therefore becomes that ultimate sign and symbol pointing to the myriad of ways in which individuals and societies begin to understand their ordered, connected and intricate existences. The human

---

6   Douglas, *Natural Symbols*; Hopewell, *Congregation*.

body can represent the sense of corporate life that in turn makes individual and social flourishing possible.

This kind of ecclesiology is, of course, closely related to recognisable forms of Christology, especially those that value the humanity of Christ and the church as an incarnation of the Spirit. Christology is relevant here, because the Church must always be about the business of answering the question posed in John's Gospel: 'Sir, we would like to see Jesus' (Jn 12:21). Christology is, in Barth's memorable phrase, 'the way of God into the far country'[7] and it therefore follows that the church is that body which bears us on our way, in essence becoming 'the form of Christ in the world' with Christ as its head.[8] Leading that body is what, with the Holy Spirit, carries and calls the church into its future, which is God's.

Yet in considering any kind of Anglican thinking about the shape and nature of the church – a complex institution that contains many different kinds of organisation – one must recognise the creative tensions that help to form its identity. So, and on the one hand, it is right and proper to describe the Church of England as primarily parochial. That is to say, there is a fair degree of autonomy at the local level which is absorbed with immediate concerns. This is not quite the same as congregationalism. A doctrine of parochialism recognises that the origins of the Church of England lie, often, in private and local patronage. The organisation, machinery and governance of a diocese is normally developed out of an aggregate of existing church communities. In other words, Church of England churches are somewhat akin to local voluntary associations, with contextual awareness and the interests of members at heart. Any theology of leadership must recognise that the primary focus of *value* for an ecclesial community will be its building, local fellowship and clergy, and not simply the supra-structure of a diocese or its bishop.

At the same time, the Church of England is also 'part of the one Holy, Catholic and Apostolic Church', and therefore accepts a kind of rightful authority, centralised powers and the governance of a diocese or bishop being complementary to and sometimes competitive with the local interests. Any kind of leadership that seeks transformation must recognise that different kinds of power are at work here. Local congregations have rights and interests, as much as the diocesan hierarchy may. A responsibly led economy of change will be a mixture between

---

7   Barth, *Church Dogmatics*, IV, 1, pp. 157ff.
8   Robinson, *The Human Face of God*.

local decisions, or even protests, and central strategies that are part of corporate or catholic organisation.

Leadership in this kind of body – whether Anglican or otherwise – must therefore recognise that strategies need to fit within the local and diocesan axes, which are the theologically legitimate parameters for forming the present and the future. Any proposed strategy for transformation must therefore be dialogical and consensual, respecting the tension between local needs and a broader catholicity. Where such respect is absent, change is often stifled. Where it exists, it may flourish, albeit in a characteristically gradualist fashion.

Indeed, the normal biblical conceptualisation for this praxis of leadership is also an old English word: 'husbandry'. This is both an art and a science, a kind of craft which manages birth, death, formation, decomposition, fallowness and fertility. All too often, the church is found to be a preservation society, pickling its past for the present: maintenance takes priority over ministry. Leadership, practised within this context, will recognise that the task of the church is to husband itself (in communion with the Spirit, and in relation to the world), such that the movement of the body of Christ is secured for each new generation of believers, and not overly weighed down with the past.

Leadership, however, is not simply there for its own sake. As the *Common Worship* Consecration service reminds us:

> *N*, remember always with thanksgiving that God has entrusted to your care Christ's beloved bride, his own flock, bought by the shedding of his blood on the cross. You are to govern Christ's people in truth, lead them out to proclaim the good news of the kingdom, and prepare them to stand before him when at last he comes in glory. You cannot bear the weight of this calling in your own strength, but only by the grace and power of God. Pray therefore that you may be conformed more and more to the image of God's Son, so that through the outpouring of the Holy Spirit your life and ministry may be made holy and acceptable to God. Pray earnestly for the gift of the Holy Spirit.[9]

To be sure, this is a demanding and weighty calling. Yet there is a comprehensive term for the powerful yet respectful interaction of God and the world, in which the

---

[9]   *Common Worship*, p. 63.

world is enhanced at every level, and which helps us frame this call to leadership. That same term might equally apply to the leader and the led; to the head and the body; to the episcope and the church. That term is 'blessing'.[10] Too often, the activity of blessing is seen as a formal act at the end of a liturgical act, or a spiritual address to something that is essentially static. Yet in being blessed, a person, object or situation is being affirmed by God in the way that is most appropriate to its nature and future. 'God rules creation by blessing', wrote the Jewish Rabbis in the first century. Blessing, constituted in leadership, is the bestowal of something *new*.

'Blessing' needs to be rescued from its magical and overly liturgical or performative associations. In reality, blessing is comprehensive praise and thanks that returns all reality to God. The activity of blessing is a process of mutual appreciation and delight, in which creation is fulfilled as coming from God yet belonging to God. The key to understanding it is to see blessing as *initiating* the bestowal *and* return of gifts. It is a form of relationality in which freedom and mutuality are celebrated, and responsibilities also discharged. Typically, therefore, a blessing is a form of commission: to bless others as we are blessed – to pass on the good news of the abundance of God. Blessing is the natural issue of God's generosity. It is within this economy that true leadership is located: the body affirmed, challenged, nourished and pushed – all for the blessing to itself, and for what it seeks to touch and transform.

The concept of blessing is vital for any theology of leadership. Because any review of church structures is normally prompted by some sense of crisis, or because of failure, or perhaps again because the 'organism' is withering in some places, and failing to flourish and bear fruit. It is Paul who writes about mature ecclesiology in the face of such constraints, in which the idea of blessing takes us forward:

> We rejoice in our hope of sharing the glory of God [i.e., we bless God for his blessings]. More than that, we rejoice in our present trials, knowing that suffering produces endurance, and endurance produces character, and character produces hope, and hope does not disappoint us, because God's love has been poured into our hearts through the Holy Spirit, which has been given to us. (Romans 5:2–5)

---

[10]   Hardy and Ford, *Jubilate*.

Paul is able to bless God in the midst of suffering, not because God is the cause of suffering, but because suffering, turned aright, can lead to blessing. The suffering church can be the place where hope is tested, faith matured, death and resurrection experienced and embraced and the abundance and new life of God celebrated afresh. All of which proceeds out of the church returning itself to God in thanks, recognising that when we ask for blessing, *we are asking for change*, not necessarily bland confirmation. It is here that the leader stands: as one able to creatively transform base and seemingly corrosive materials and situations into something with potential.

Similarly, one of the more familiar New Testament images of the church is that of the vine and the branches. For the vine to be a source of blessing, and for its fruit to flourish, it must be regularly and sometimes harshly pruned. The church, to be an agent of blessing here, is to be the source for new wine. (All too often, it produces a harvest of raisins.) The link between wine and vine serves to remind that the church is a Eucharistic community. Central to its life is the activity of thanksgiving, with a community gathered around the celebration of death and life. The seasons of the church also bear witness to this. The church is the transformed and transforming community; only as it dies with Christ can it be raised to live for others. It must continually live as the 'grain of wheat that falls and dies' (John 12:24) so that the harvest may come again. This, strangely, is the economy of blessing. Embracing death, change and life: not clinging to the past, but looking to the future, and embracing the *eschaton* of God. And here, the leader – with the weighty task of oversight – offers appropriate husbandry.

The advantage of beginning a theology of leadership from the perspective of blessing, and within the image of the body of Christ, is that it returns us to the idea of the church as a living organism. The church is an 'institution' (and natural symbol), containing many different forms of organisation; some of which are inward-facing and some of which face out. Moreover, the notion of leadership as blessing frees us to permit and affirm pluralism and particularity, yet also respecting unity of purpose, function and order; and it also anticipates change, as we reaffirm ourselves as clay in the hands of God. In the body, management and regulation is never for its own sake, but is there for all the 'members' of that body. In leading the Church of England, as a living organism, there is an understanding:

that its numerous organisational complexities cannot obscure its final task: which is to be a source of blessing to God, society and creation.

So where does this leave us? I end with three brief points by way of conclusion. And although I address these to Anglicans, I am profoundly aware that their currency carries across to many other denominations and churches. First, senior leaders in the church need to be capable of and enabled to address and hold the 'thick traffic' of ecclesial discourse and praxis that emerges in dioceses. This is a complex body that sends and receives many signals. As it receives and communicates, it needs a leadership of discernment and poise.

Second, leadership requires a genuinely deep appreciation of the actuality of the church – in all its depth and miscibility – to enable a culture of reflective and formational context in which training, education and development can flourish. The more deeply the church is understood, the more likely it is that the tasks and roles of leadership will emerge with clarity and acuity.

Third, we also sense that in the face of such institutional complexity, there is sometimes a danger that the mission to wider culture is lost. One of the pivotal roles that bishops have is to evangelise.[11] Our reflections suggest that the more complex and draining the problems encountered in the church are, the less free the leadership are to proclaim their faith. This in turn runs the risk of the body turning in on itself, and paying too much attention to our own inner workings.

To be sure, there is a time and place for a leadership of introspection and reflection: of managing, reordering and refining. But the body is also an agent of change for others. And our leaders are called to be catalysts for renewal: adapting the body to the environment it inhabits, in order to be the blessing for all that Christ intended his body to be. Undoubtedly, the Anglican Communion, and its many churches, provinces and dioceses, face tough and challenging times ahead. And for this, we shall need both poise and purpose. The poise is perhaps best encapsulated in the relatively recent retrieval of some older idiom: 'keep calm and carry on'. Fashionable though such catch-phrase sentiments are, they also have a remarkable ecclesial depth. They remind us to keep faith; that the church belongs to God; and that calmness carries virtue and character, enabling the church to continue through crisis after crisis. And in terms of purpose, we clearly cannot

---

[11]   For an illuminating discussion of how the church might engage with secular culture, see Norman, *Secularisation*, p. 103ff.

afford complacency – a degenerate form of calmness. So the purpose will need to come through seeing deeply, and acting wisely. Of not being prepared to merely ride the latest waves – be they cultural, spiritual or missional – and no matter how attractive such waves may look. We need leaders who can read the tides, and help us shape some medium- and longer-term polity that is rooted in thinking and wisdom. So we can inhabit a deep, thought-through proactive missiology, rather than something neuralgic and reactive.

Keeping calm, carrying on, reading tides and responding to change may not seem like much to some. Can the confidence, commitment and communion of Anglicanism really rest on such simple things? But sometimes as a church, we, as Anglicans, forget ourselves. We don't have to struggle to become the body of Christ. We are already that. Not perfect replicas, to be sure; but incomplete incarnations, certainly. Indeed, our salvation lies in our incompleteness, and a humble acceptance of that. We do not pursue outright success. But we do strive for faithfulness. And somewhere, deep in our ecclesial DNA, we know, perhaps, that our current vexed concerns with growth, decline, leadership, management, mission and maintenance will, in the end, all become illuminated in a richer, brighter light that puts our polity into a far truer perspective. A place and time where somehow, we will see, that in this frustrating, fruitful, faithful, fallible faith of ours, there is truth in the ambivalence, beauty in the infrastructure and wisdom in the making. And yes, always, God in the detail. All that is needed, then, is to continue our pilgrimage; to continue following Christ; to bear one another. To embody faith, hope and charity. To continue becoming the body of love and justice that Jesus Christ has called us to be.

Bibliography

Albrecht, P. *The Churches and Rapid Social Change*. London: SCM Press, 1961.

Astley, J., L. Francis and C. Crowder (eds). *Theological Perspectives on Christian Formation*. Grand Rapids, MI: Eerdmans, 1996.

Avis, P. *A Church Drawing Near*. London: Continuum, 2004.

Barth, K. *Against the Stream*. London: SCM, 1954.

Barth, K. *Church Dogmatics*. Edinburgh: T. & T. Clark, 1958.

Bayne, S. *An Anglican Turning Point*. Austin: Church Historical Society, 1964.

Bayne, S. *Theological Freedom and Responsibility*. New York: Seabury Press, 1967.

Bellah, R. *Habits of the Heart: Individualism and Commitment in American Life*. Berkeley and Los Angeles: University of California Press, 1985.

Blanning, T.C.W. *The Culture of Power and the Power of Culture: Old Regime Europe 1660–1789*. Oxford: Oxford University Press, 2003.

Bogdanor, V. *The Monarchy and the Constitution*. Oxford: Oxford University Press, 1995.

Bradley, I. *God Save the Queen*. London: DLT, 2002.

Brierley, P. *Act on the Facts*. London: Marc Europe, 1992.

Brown, A. 'Press Watch.' *Church Times*, August 3, 1998, 12.

Brown, C. *The Death of Christian Britain: Understanding Secularisation 1800–2000*. London: Routledge, 2000.

Browning, D.A. *Fundamental Practical Theology: Descriptive and Strategic Proposals*. Philadelphia: Westminster, 1991.

Clark, D. *Between Pulpit and Pew*. Cambridge: Cambridge University Press, 1982.

Collins, S. 'Spirituality and Youth.' In *Calling Time: Religion and Change at the Turn of the Millennium*, ed. M. Percy, 219–38. Sheffield: Sheffield Academic Press, 2000.

Common Worship. 'The Ordination and Consecration of Bishops.' London: Church House Publishing, 2007.

Cunningham, H. *Leisure in the Industrial Revolution*. Beckenham: Croom Helm, 1980.

Davie, G. *Religion in Britain since 1945: Believing without Belonging*. Oxford: Blackwell, 1994.

Davis, K. *Emancipation Still Comin': Exploration in Caribbean Emancipatory Theology*. Maryknoll, NY: Orbis, 1990.

Dawson, C. *Religion and the Modern State*. London: Sheed & Ward, 1936.

Dewey, J. *Democracy and Education: An Introduction to the Philosophy of Education*. New York: Free Press, 1966. Originally published in 1916.

Doe, N., and M. Hill. *English Canon Law: Essays in Honour of Eric Kemp*. Cardiff: University of Wales Press, 1998.

Douglas, M. *Natural Symbols*. London: Barrie & Jenkins, 1973.

Dykstra, R. (ed.). *Images of Pastoral Care: Classic Readings*. St Louis, MO: Chalice Press, 2005.

Ehrenreich, B. *Smile or Die: How Positive Thinking Fooled America and the World*. London: Granta, 2009.

Eliot, T.S. *The Idea of a Christian Society*. London: Faber, 1939.

Farley, E. 'Interpreting Situations.' In *Formation and Reflection: The Promise of Practical Theology*, eds L. Mudge and J. Poling, 59–73. Philadelphia: Fortress Press, 1987.

Ferris, R. *Renewal in Theological Education: Strategies for Change*. Wheaton, IL: Billy Graham Center, 1990.

Figgis, J. *Churches in the Modern State*. London: Longmans Green, 1913.

Foster, C., L. Dahill, L. Golemon and B. Tolentino (eds). *Educating Clergy: Teaching Practices and Pastoral Imagination*. San Francisco: Jossey-Bass, 2006.

Francis, L., and W. Kay. *Teenage Religion and Values*. Leominster, UK: Gracewing, 1995.

Freire, P. *The Pedagogy of the Oppressed*. London: Penguin, 1972.

Freire, P. *Pedagogy of the Heart*. New York: Continuum, 2006.

Giles, R. *Re-Pitching the Tent: Re-Ordering the Church Building for Worship and Mission*. Norwich: Canterbury Press, 1999.

Giles, R. *Always Open: Being an Anglican Today*. Boston: Cowley Publications, 2005.

Goldscheider, F., and C. Goldscheider. *Leaving Home before Marriage: Ethnicity, Familism and Generational Relationships*. Wisconsin: University of Wisconsin, 1993.

Graham, E. *Transforming Practice*. London: Mowbray, 1996.

Graham, E. 'Practical Theology as Transforming Practice.' In *The Blackwell Reader in Pastoral and Practical Theology*, eds S. Pattison and J. Woodward, 104–17. Oxford: Blackwell, 2000.

Greene, G. *The Power and the Glory*. London: Vintage, 2001. Originally published 1940.

Grierson, D. *Transforming a People of God*. Melbourne: Board of Christian Education, 1984.

Grigg, R. *Theology as a Way of Thinking*. Atlanta: Scholars Press, 1990.

Groome, T. *Christian Religious Education*. San Francisco: Harper & Row, 1980.

Groves, P. (ed.). *The Anglican Communion and Homosexuality: A Resource to Enable Listening and Dialogue*. London: SPCK, 2008.

Hall, J., and M. Neitz. *Culture: Sociological Perspectives*. New Jersey: Prentice Hall, 1993.

Hardy, D., and D. Ford. *Jubilate: Theology in Praise*. London: DLT, 1984.

Hardy, D. 'Theology through Philosophy.' In *The Modern Theologians: An Introduction to Christian Theology in the Twentieth Century*, ed. D.F. Ford, 113–39. Oxford: Blackwell, 1989.

Hare, D. 'The Decade of Looking Away.' *Guardian Magazine*, October 17, 2009, 5–7.

Hastings, A. 'The Case for Retaining Establishment.' In *Church, State and Religious Minorities*, ed. T. Modood, 33–45. London: Policy Studies Institute, 1997.

Hazell, R. (ed.). *Constitutional Futures: A History of the Next Ten Years*. Oxford: Oxford University Press, 1999.

Headlam, A.C. *Theological Education at the Universities*. Oxford: Oxford University Press, 1921.

Hervieu-Leger, D. *Religion as a Chain of Memory*. Cambridge: Polity, 2000.

Heywood, C. *A History of Childhood: Children and Childhood in the West from Medieval to Modern Times*. Cambridge: Polity, 2001.

Hodgson, P. *God's Wisdom: Toward a Theology of Education*. Louisville, KT: Westminster John Knox Press, 1999.

Holmes, U.T. *The Future Shape of Ministry: A Theological Projection*. New York: Seabury Press, 1971.

Holmes, U.T. *What Is Anglicanism?* Wilton, CT: Morehouse-Barlow, 1982.

Holy Bible: The New Revised Standard Version. Oxford: Oxford University Press, 1989.

hooks, b. *Teaching to Transgress: Education as the Practice of Freedom*. New York: Routledge, 1994.

Hopewell, J. *Congregation: Stories and Structures*. London: SCM, 1987.

Hull, J. *Mission-Shaped Church: A Theological Response*. London: SCM Press, 2006.

Inge, J. *A Christian Theology of Place*. Aldershot: Ashgate, 2003.

Kelly, T. *A History of Adult Education in Liverpool*. Liverpool: LUP, 1970.

Kett, J. *Rites of Passage: Adolescence in America, 1790 to the Present*. New York: Basic Books, 1977.

Kevern, P. 'Unity, Diversity and Trinity in the Rhetoric of the 1998 Lambeth Conference.' PhD diss., University of Birmingham, 1999.

Lambeth Commission on Communion. *Windsor Report*. London: Anglican Communion Office, 2004.

Laqueur, T. *Religion and Respectability: Sunday Schools and Working Class Culture*. New Haven, CT: Yale University Press, 1976.

Lears, J. *Fables of Abundance*. New York: Basic Books, 1994.

Lederach, J.-P. *The Moral Imagination*. Oxford: Oxford University Press, 2005.

Locke, K.A. *The Church in Anglican Theology: A Historical, Theological and Ecumenical Exploration*. London: Ashgate, 2009.

Long, R. *Theology in a New Key*. Philadelphia: Westminster, 1978.

Lynch, T. *The Undertaking: Life Studies from the Dismal Trade*. New York: Penguin, 1998.

March, A. *Islam and Liberal Citizenship: The Search for an Overlapping Consensus*. Oxford: Oxford University Press, 2009.

Markham, I., and M. Percy. *Why Liberal Churches Are Growing*. London: Continuum, 2005.

Martin, D. *On Secularization: Towards a Revised General Theory*. Aldershot: Ashgate, 2005.

MayBe; a community following in the way of Jesus for a better world now. 2012. http://www.maybe.org.uk (accessed 2010).

McGavran, D. *Understanding Church Growth*. Grand Rapids, MI: Eerdmans, 1970.

Mead, M. *Culture and Commitment: The New Relationships between the Generations in the 1970s*. New York: Doubleday, 1978.

Milbank, J. *The Word Made Strange*. Oxford: Blackwell, 1997.

Mission-Shaped Church. London: Church House Publishing, 2004.

Modood, T. 'Introduction: Establishment, Reform and Multiculturalism.' In *Church, State and Religious Minorities*, ed. T. Modood, 1–13. London: Policy Studies Institute, 1997.

New Jerusalem Bible. London: DLT, 1985.

Newlyn, L. (ed.). *The Cambridge Companion to Coleridge*. Cambridge: Cambridge University Press, 2002.

Nicholls, D. *Church and State in Britain since 1820*. London: Routledge, 1967.

Norman, E. *Secularisation*. London: Continuum, 2003.

O'Donovan, O. *The Desire of Nations: Rediscovering the Roots of Political Theology*. Cambridge: Cambridge University Press, 1996.

Orchard, H. *Hospital Chaplaincy: Modern, Dependable?* Sheffield: Sheffield Academic Press, 2000.

Parekh, B. 'When Religion Meets Politics.' In *Keeping the Faiths: The New Covenant between Religious Belief and Secular Power*, B. Parekh, 33–44. London: Demos, 1997.

Parks, S. *Big Questions, Worthy Dreams: Young Adults in Their Search for Meaning, Purpose and Faith*. San Francisco: Jossey-Bass, 2000.

Patterson, C. 'Thank God for the Church of England.' *Independent*, July 25, 2009, 12.

Pattison, S., and J. Woodward (eds). *The Blackwell Reader in Pastoral and Practical Theology*. Oxford: Blackwell, 2000.

Paxman, J. *The English: Portrait of a People*. London: Penguin, 1999.

Percy, M. *Power and the Church: Ecclesiology in an Age of Transition.* London: Cassell, 1998.

Percy, M. 'On Sacrificing Purity?' In *Theological Liberalism*, eds I. Markham and J. Jobling, 114–25. London: SPCK, 2000.

Percy, M. *Salt of the Earth: Religious Resilience in a Secular Age.* Sheffield: Sheffield Academic Press, 2001.

Percy, M. 'Mind the Gap: Generational Change and Its Implications.' In *Public Faith?*, ed. P. Avis, 106–22. London: SPCK, 2002.

Percy, M. *Engaging with Contemporary Culture: Christianity, Theology and the Concrete Church.* Burlington, VT: Ashgate, 2005.

Percy, M. *Clergy: The Origin of the Species.* London: T. & T. Clark, 2006.

Percy, M. *Shaping the Church.* London: Ashgate, 2010.

Percy, M. *The Ecclesial Canopy.* London: Ashgate, 2011.

Pickard, S. 'Church of the In-Between God: Recovering an Ecclesial Sense of Place Down-Under.' *Journal of Anglican Studies* 7 (2009): 35–54.

Pickard, S. *Seeking the Church.* London: SCM Press, 2012.

Pobee, J. (ed.). *Towards a Viable Theological Education: Ecumenical Imperative, Catalyst of Renewal.* Geneva: WCC, 1997.

Podmore, C. *Aspects of Anglican Identity.* London: Church House Publishing, 2005.

Poling, J., and D. Miller. *Foundations for a Practical Theology of Ministry.* Nashville: Abingdon Press, 1985.

Powell, J. *Great Hatred, Little Room: Making Peace in Northern Ireland.* London: Bodley Head, 2008.

Pritchard, J. *The Life and Work of a Priest.* London: SPCK, 2007.

Putnam, R. *Bowling Alone: The Collapse and Revival of American Community.* New York: Simon & Schuster, 2000.

Radner, E., and P. Turner. *The Fate of Communion: The Agony of Anglicanism and the Future of the Global Church.* Grand Rapids, MI: Eerdmans, 2006.

Rawls, J. *A Theory of Justice.* Cambridge, MA: Harvard University Press, 1971.

Rawls, J. *Political Liberalism.* New York: Columbia University Press, 1993.

Reed, B. *The Dynamics of Change: Process and Movement in Christian Churches.* London: DLT, 1978.

'Religions in European Union Law.' Proceedings of the Colloquium, Luxembourg/ Trier, November 21–22, 1996, Universita degli Studi di Milano: Guiffre Editore.

Riewoldt, O. *Brandscaping: Worlds of Experience in Retail Design.* London: Momenta Press and Basel: Birkauser, 2002.

Robin, J. *Elmdon: Continuity and Change.* Cambridge: Cambridge University Press, 1980.

Robinson, G. *In the Eye of the Storm.* London: SCM-Canterbury Press, 2008.

Robinson, J. *The Human Face of God.* London: SCM, 1973.

Rokeach, M. *Understanding Human Values: Individual and Societal.* New York: Free Press, 1979.

Roof, W.A. *Generation of Seekers: The Spiritual Journeys of the Baby Boom Generation.* San Francisco: Harper Collins, 1993.

Roof, W., and W. McKinney. *American Mainline Religion: Its Changing Shape and Form.* New Jersey: Rutgers University Press, 1987.

Roszak, T. *The Making of a Counter Culture.* London: Faber, 2000.

Runcie, R. *Church Observer*, March 1962, 11.

Russell, A. *The Clerical Profession.* London: SPCK, 1980.

Sachs, W.L. *Homosexuality and the Crisis of Anglicanism.* Cambridge: Cambridge University Press, 2009.

Sandel, M. *Justice.* London: Allen Lane, 2009.

Schillebeeckx, E. *Ministry: Leadership in the Community of Jesus Christ.* New York: Crossroads, 1985.

Schmiechen, P. *Saving Power: Theories of Atonement and Forms of the Church.* Grand Rapids, MI: Eerdmans, 2005.

Schon, D. *The Reflective Practitioner.* London: Ashgate, 1991.

Selby, P. 'The Parable of the Wheat and the Tares.' *Church Times*, December 17, 1999, 11.

Selznick, P. *Leadership in Administration: A Sociological Interpretation.* New York: Harper, 1957.

Sen, A. *The Idea of Justice.* London: Allen Lane, 2009.

Shanks, A. *Civil Religion Civil Society.* Oxford: Blackwell, 1995.

Shillington, V.G. 'Salt of the Earth?' *Expository Times*, 112 (2001): 120–22.

Stark, W. *The Sociology of Religion: A Study.* Volume 1. London: Routledge, 1966.

Stout, J. *Ethics after Babel*. Cambridge, MA: James Clarke, 1988.

Strathern, M. *Kinship at the Core: An Anthropology of Elmdon*. Cambridge: Cambridge University Press, 1981.

Streng, F., C. Lloyd and J. Allen. *Ways of Being Religious*. Englewood Cliffs, NJ: Prentice Hall, 1973.

Strinati, D. *Popular Culture: An Introduction to Theories*. New York: Routledge, 1995.

Taylor, C. *A Secular Age*. Cambridge, MA: Harvard-Belknap, 2007.

Thompson, E. (ed.). *Cultural Theory*. Boulder: Westview Press, 1990.

Tomasi, J. *Liberalism beyond Justice: Citizens, Societies and the Boundaries – a Political Theory*. Princeton, NJ: Princeton University Press, 2001.

Torry, M. (ed.). *The Parish: A Theological and Practical Exploration*. London: SCM-Canterbury Press, 2004.

Towler, R., and A. Coxon. *The Fate of the Anglican Clergy: A Sociological Study*. London: Macmillan, 1979.

Trumbull, H.C. *The Sunday-School: Its Origin, Mission, Methods, and Auxiliaries*. New York: John D. Wattles, 1893.

Volf, M., and D. Bass. *Practicing Theology: Beliefs and Practices in Christian Life*. Grand Rapids, MI: Eerdmans, 2000.

Walker, A. *Restoring the Kingdom*. London: Hodder & Stoughton, 1985.

Walker, A. *Telling the Story*. London: SPCK, 1996.

Warren, R. *The Purpose-Driven Church*. Grand Rapids, MI: Zondervan, 1995.

Warren, R. *The Purpose-Driven Life*. Grand Rapids, MI: Zondervan, 2002.

Wenger, E. *Communities of Practice: Learning, Meaning and Identity*. Cambridge: Cambridge University Press, 1998.

Weston, P. *Lesslie Newbigin: Missionary Theologian – a Reader*. New York: Eerdmans, 2006.

Williams, A., and J. Davidson. 'Catholic Conceptions of Faith: A Generational Analysis.' *Sociology of Religion* 57 (1996): 58–85.

Williams, R. *Anglican Identities*. London: DLT, 2004.

Winter, G. *The Suburban Captivity of the Churches*. New York: Doubleday, 1961.

Woodforde, J. *Diary of a Country Parson, 1758–1802*. Norwich: Canterbury Press, 1989.

Woodhead, L., and R. Catto (eds). *Religion and Change in Modern Britain.* London: Routledge, 2012.

Woodhead, L., and P. Heelas (eds). *The Spiritual Revolution.* Oxford: Blackwell, 2005.

Zaltman, G. *Processes and Phenomena of Social Change.* New York: Wiley, 1973.

Index